Contents

Section 10 The operating environment 303

Introduction

For the teacher

This book provides comprehensive coverage of AQA's Specification A for GCSE Information and Communication Technology. It has been structured to provide a framework for a typical two year scheme of work.

Year 10

Each section (apart from section 6) has six topics, and these can be covered over a period of six weeks. Section 6 is shorter, with only four topics, to allow for flexibility around the summer examination period.

At the end of each section there are one or two tutorials, designed to develop skills in the use of standard applications software (based on Microsoft products). Normally pupils will work through the skills pages over a period of six weeks in parallel with the theoretical topics.

A case study introduces each section, and is used to put the learning of the topics and skills in context. Differentiated practice questions round off each section.

Section		Number of topics	Skills development
Section 1	Getting to know your computer	6	Word processing Graphics
Section 2	Creating effective output	6	Desktop publishing Drawing
Winter break			
Section 3	Storing data	6	Spreadsheets Charts
Section 4	Networks and communications	6	Web design
Spring break			
Section 5	Managing data	6	Databases
Section 6	Keeping data safe	4	Mail merge

Year 11

Each of the four sections covers six topics. In parallel with these pupils will be working on their coursework assignments throughout the year. Guidance on tackling coursework is given in the last chapter of the book.

Section		Number of topics	Coursework
Section 7	Developing applications	6	
Section 8	Processing data	6	
Winter break			
Section 9	Control and simulation	6	
Section 10	The operating environment	6	
Spring break			
	Consolidation and revision		

Specification matching

You can download a specification matching matrix which shows where each of the elements of the specification can be located in the book. This can be found by going to *www.heinemann.co.uk/secondary*.

K Mary Reid, 2004

Getting to know your computer

Your computer

The computer you are using may look like this:

or like this:

or like this:

or like this:

Inside a computer

The computer you use is not a simple thing. It is made up of several hardware components linked together – a keyboard, a screen, a disk drive, a processor, etc.

You can see from the pictures on page 1 that sometimes all the hardware of a computer is packaged up in the same case. Sometimes the hardware components are provided in different cases which have to be linked together. You can often pick and choose which components to add.

Whatever your computer looks like, what you have is a complicated system made up of a number of hardware components.

INPUTS

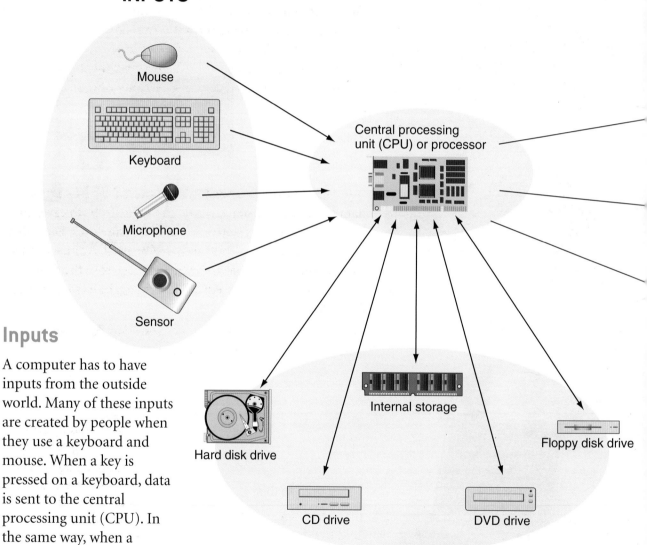

Mouse

Keyboard

Microphone

Sensor

Central processing unit (CPU) or processor

Internal storage

Hard disk drive

CD drive

DVD drive

Floppy disk drive

STORAGE

Inputs

A computer has to have inputs from the outside world. Many of these inputs are created by people when they use a keyboard and mouse. When a key is pressed on a keyboard, data is sent to the central processing unit (CPU). In the same way, when a button is pressed on a mouse or the ball rotates against a wheel inside, data is sent to the CPU.

What does it mean?

Hardware

Hardware refers to all the pieces of equipment that make up a computer.

Central processing unit

At the heart of any computer is the central processing unit (or CPU), which is often called the 'processor'. The CPU carries out the instructions in the programs. It also controls all the other hardware components. In many ways the CPU can be thought of as the brains of a computer. The CPU is normally stored on one silicon chip.

OUTPUTS

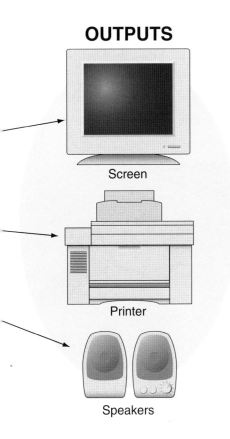

Screen

Printer

Speakers

Outputs

We would have no idea what a computer was doing if it did not create outputs. The most familiar output is to a screen of some kind. Outputs can also be sent to a printer. And most computers can also create sound outputs which are sent to speakers.

Data flows

Input data has to be transferred to the CPU and output data has to be transferred from the CPU. In both cases this is done by sending electronic signals along wires. Data also has to be stored, or 'saved', so it can be used again. In order for it to be stored it has to be transferred from the CPU to storage. And when it needs to be used again it is transferred from storage to the CPU.

The arrows in the diagram show how data flows between the components of the computer system.

Computer system

A computer system is the complete collection of components (hardware and communication links) making up a computer.

Storage

Storage is the computer's memory. Here the data is kept safely until it is needed. Some types of storage hold the data temporarily, whilst others hold it more permanently.

Input peripherals in the home, school and office

Keyboard

The standard keyboard (Fig 1.1) uses the QWERTY key layout, named after the top row of letters. This layout was originally developed for typewriters over a century ago. The arrangement of the keys was designed to prevent the levers from hitting each other and jamming the machine.

Office workers were familiar with this layout, so it was used on the first computer keyboards, even though the original reason no longer applied.

The standard keyboard includes a calculator-like numeric keypad. This has the same number of keys as those in the row above the letters, but you may find you can enter numbers much faster using the keypad.

The keyboard also has some control keys, such as Insert, Page Up and the arrow keys. You can use the arrow keys to control a pointer on the screen.

The keys labelled F1, F2, etc., are programmable function keys and have special uses in some programs.

Figure 1.1 *A standard keyboard*

Figure 1.2 *An ergonomic keyboard*

An ergonomically designed keyboard (Fig 1.2) uses a similar layout to the standard one, but is shaped to make it more comfortable to use.

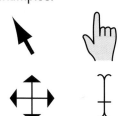
Mouse

A mouse fits neatly into your hand and is used to control a pointer on the screen. As the ball of the mouse is moved across a smooth surface the pointer appears to follow it.

The standard mouse has two buttons, which you can click or double-click. When you move the pointer over a button on the screen, clicking the mouse usually sends an instruction to the central processing unit to carry out an action. The action could be to display a menu, or to save a document.

A further button or fingertip wheel is sometimes added to carry out extra actions (Fig 1.3).

Fig 1.3 A mouse with a fingertip wheel

Tracker ball

A tracker ball is similar to a mouse but with the ball on the top (Fig 1.4). You rotate the ball directly, rather than moving it over a surface. Tracker balls are often built into portable computers as an alternative to a separate mouse, although they are being replaced by touchpads.

Touchpad

A touchpad does the same job as a mouse – it is used to control a pointer. But instead of moving a mouse across a surface, you can move your finger across the touchpad to give the same effect. Touchpads are often built into laptop computers (Fig 1.5) as they fit neatly into the space available. They usually have a couple of buttons as well, to match a mouse's buttons.

Figure 1.4 *A tracker ball*

Fig 1.5 *A touchpad on a laptop*

Joystick

If you play computer games then you may have used a joystick (Fig 1.6). It is another version of a mouse but is easier to use in action games. The stick itself can be rotated and tilted, corresponding to mouse movements. Buttons are placed on the stick or on the base.

Fig 1.6 *A joystick*

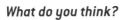

What do you think?

Suppose someone you know asked your advice about buying a new computer system to help him or her run a small business from home. What input peripherals should he or she buy?

Input peripherals for graphics and sound

All data in a computer is stored in a digital code. A digital code uses electronics to store each tiny bit of data, such as a letter of the alphabet, a spot of colour or a snippet of sound. All the letters in a document are stored in a document file, all the spots of colour in a picture are stored in an image file and all the snippets of sound in a piece of music are stored in a sound file.

The input peripherals shown on these pages create digital image and sound files.

Scanner

A scanner 'reads' paper documents and turns them into computer files (Fig 1.7). You can scan in a photo or a picture in a book, and the scanner will create an image file that you can then use in your work.

You can also scan in text. Special optical character recognition (OCR) software can recognise the letters and turn the text into a word-processor document.

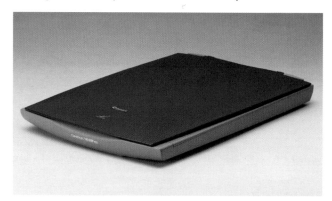

Fig 1.7 *A flat-bed scanner*

Graphics digitiser

You can use a mouse to create graphics, but if you want to produce some complex images, you will find it easier to use a graphics digitiser.

This is a flat surface that you place on the table. You can then move an electronic pen across the surface and the drawing you create appears on the screen. It can then be stored as an image file.

A graphics digitiser is also known as a graphics tablet or a digitising tablet.

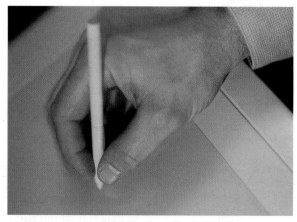

Fig 1.8 *A graphics tablet*

Digital camera

Digital cameras (Fig 1.9) do not use film. If you take a photo with a digital camera, it is stored in the camera as a computer image file in digital code. You can then transfer the file to a computer where you can add it to a document or website.

Fig 1.9 *A digital camera*

Digital video camera

Just as you can record still digital images with a digital camera, so you can take videos using a digital video camera (Fig 1.10).

Some digital cameras can take short videos as well as still images.

Fig 1.10 *A digital video camera*

Microphone

You can connect a microphone to a computer as an input peripheral (Fig 1.11). It has to be connected to a part of the computer called a sound card. The sound card samples the sound at regular intervals and stores the samples as a computer sound file.

What do you think?
Suppose you had plenty of money and could afford to buy the very best computer system for your own use at home. What would you choose?

Fig 1.11 *A microphone for a computer*

Specialised input peripherals

Touch-sensitive keyboard

A touch-sensitive keyboard (Fig 1.12) has a flat plastic surface. A printed overlay shows where the hotspots are. If you touch one of these it has the same effect as pressing a key.

The surface can be programmed so that different hotspots can be created. A new printed overlay can be used for each program. Touch-sensitive keyboards can be used by young children, or by people with disabilities, as the 'keys' can be made as large as necessary.

What do you think? Touch-sensitive keyboards can be seen in fast-food outlets, where the steam and oil could damage a normal keyboard. Can you think of other places where they could be used?

Fig 1.12 A touch-sensitive keyboard

Touch-sensitive screen

A touch-sensitive screen allows you to use a stylus or your finger to point to buttons and other spots on the screen. If an image of a keyboard is shown on the screen you can touch the keys to enter text.

You may have used the touch-sensitive screen of an interactive whiteboard in a classroom (Fig 1.13).

A touch-sensitive screen can also be seen on hand-held computers. You use a stylus to touch the screen (Fig 1.14).

Fig 1.13 An interactive whiteboard

Fig 1.14 A hand-held computer

Light pen

A light pen looks like a normal pen but it is connected to the computer (Fig 1.15). When you hold it close to the screen you can use it to make selections or to draw lines.

The light pen does not actually touch the screen, so it does not require a special screen. Light pens are not used as much today as they were in the past.

Fig 1.15 A light pen

Sensors

Some inputs come directly from other machines, with no human contact. For example, you could carry out a scientific experiment by plugging an electronic thermometer into a computer. You could then set it to record the temperature automatically at regular intervals.

Peripherals like this are known as sensors. A sensor is a piece of electronic equipment that can measure things in the world, such as temperature, humidity, light, sound. Sensors can also detect movement and pressure.

A sensor sends input data automatically to the CPU (Fig 1.16).

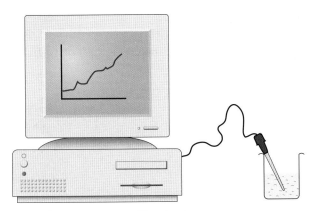

Fig 1.16 A temperature sensor (thermistor)

Other input peripherals

A number of other specialised input peripherals are described later in this book. They include:

◎ card readers, for magnetic stripe cards and for smart cards;
◎ bar-code scanners;
◎ optical mark readers; and
◎ magnetic-ink character readers.

Information systems

A computer on its own is a lifeless machine. To make it work it needs data. Data includes all the software programs that you use, all the keys that you press, all the documents that you create, all the image and sound files that you use.

A computer with the right data can produce all kinds of information for the people who use it. As soon as you switch on the computer on your table it becomes an information system for you.

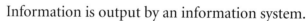

| Computer system | + | Data | = | Information system |

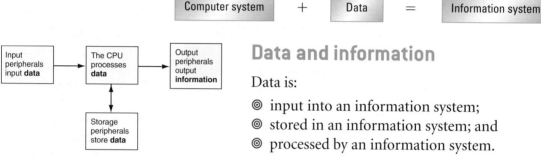

Fig 1.17 Data and information

Data and information

Data is:

◎ input into an information system;
◎ stored in an information system; and
◎ processed by an information system.

Information is output by an information system.

Think of it like this: the data on a music CD is organised across the surface of the disk. You can see it as silvery markings on the disk. If you look at the surface of the CD the markings make no sense at all to you. You can't tell what kind of music it is, or whether you will like it. But when you put the disk into a CD player, the data is input into a music system. This processes the data and turns it into musical information, which comes out as sound.

In the same way, data is input into an information system which processes it. It then produces useful information through an output peripheral like a screen.

More about data

All the data in a computer system is organised into files:

◎ A document that you create is one file.
◎ An image or sound is stored in one file.
◎ The software application that you use to create the document consists of many files.
◎ The operating system that you must have on your computer to make it work consists of many files. Some of these files are software programs. Some of the files simply hold numbers that are needed by the operating system.

More about information

Information is data that has been turned into something useful. The output peripherals of the information system present you with the information. An information system is very versatile, so information can be given to you in a number of ways:

◎ on screen;
◎ as a printed document; or
◎ as sound.

ICT and IT

ICT stands for 'information and communication technology'. IT stands for 'information technology'. In recent years the initials ICT have been used more commonly because they emphasise the important role of data communications and the Internet. But, in practice, they both mean much the same.

ICT includes the familiar desktop computers and a huge number of other machines and devices as well. Information systems are only a part of ICT. Some ICT systems don't actually give us information directly, but make other machines work for us.

ICT all around us

Every section of this book begins with a case study. Each case study demonstrates ways in which ICT has affected the lives of everyone in society. Today it is very difficult to imagine life without computers, just as it is difficult to imagine life without cars, trains and planes.

But we are not just affected by the desktop computers that we see in offices, in educational settings and in our homes. Almost all organisations use computer systems, although many of these are not obvious to us as we go about our daily lives.

We use all kinds of machines that are really input or output peripherals for computer systems, without realising that's what they are. Here are some examples of computer peripherals:

◎ Point-of-sale terminals (cash tills) in supermarkets.
◎ Train announcement screens at stations.
◎ Cash machines at banks.

Some ICT systems are hidden away inside other machines but are controlling them. Computer technology is used in cars, aircraft, washing machines, televisions, and in video, DVD and CD players.

On top of all that, we use a number of methods of communication which are dependent on ICT, such as mobile phones and digital televisions.

Give it a go

Think about all the things you have done since you woke up this morning. List all the activities that have been affected in some way by ICT. For example:

◎ Did you watch breakfast television on a digital set?
◎ Did you travel in a car that uses computer-controlled fuel injection?
◎ Did you use a mobile phone?
◎ Did you stop at a shop that uses cash tills that are connected to a computer system?
◎ Were you being observed by closed-circuit television cameras (CCTV)?
◎ Does your school keep information about you on a database?
◎ Have you been in a building that has an electronic security system?

Now look at the list you have written:

◎ Could you have done any of these activities if ICT had not been invented?
◎ If so, how would they have been different from doing them with ICT?

Applications software

When you are working on a computer you usually use a number of files of data:

◎ The applications software, such as Word or Paint.
◎ The documents you create.

Although you may get the impression that applications software like Word is a single program, in fact it consists of hundreds of programs and data files. We often refer to applications software like this as a software package.

Software

Software refers to the programs and other data files that are used on a computer.

The purpose of applications software

Applications software has been invented to help us to carry out useful tasks with our desktop and laptop computers. Here are some of the tasks that applications software can be used for:

◎ To create documents, such as letters, notices, leaflets and reports.
◎ To handle communications, such as access to the Internet and email.
◎ To present information to an audience, whether in printed or electronic form.
◎ To create and manipulate images.
◎ To carry out business, such as dealing with customer orders for a mail order company, sending out mobile phone bills, booking facilities in a health club or managing bank accounts.
◎ To manage finances.
◎ To design things, such as buildings and products.

Buying applications software

If you have a computer at home it probably arrived with some applications software. The software packages will normally be from the same software provider, such as Corel or Microsoft. Your school will also be equipped with applications software, which it will have bought from its ICT supplier.

Most large organisations also use well-known applications software, such as Microsoft Word or Corel Word Perfect. However some organisations find that the software on the market does not do what they want it to do. They can have software specially written for them by software engineers. This is a very expensive process so they will only do this if necessary.

Types of applications software

These are the main types of applications software used in offices, in schools and at home:

◎ *Word processing* – used for letters, reports, simple publications, mail merge, labels, presentation of information.

- *Spreadsheet* – used for statistical tables, graphs and charts, financial records, modelling.
- *Database management* – used for storing and working with data.
- *Desktop publishing* – used for publications that require complex layouts and a combination of text and graphics.
- *Drawing and painting* – used to create and manipulate images.
- *Web design* – used to create web pages.
- *Communications* – used to access and search the Internet, and to handle emails.

In the skills pages in this book you will learn to use some applications software. The instructions will be based on the Microsoft software packages, as follows:

- Microsoft Word – word processing.
- Microsoft Excel – spreadsheet.
- Microsoft Access – database management.
- Microsoft Publisher – desktop publishing.
- Microsoft Paint – painting.
- Microsoft Draw – drawing.
- Microsoft FrontPage – web design.

The book also refers to Microsoft Internet Explorer and Outlook Express which are used for communications.

Filenames

Every file that is saved on a computer system is given a name. The last three letters of the filename, after the dot, are known as the filename extension. (Occasionally, two or four letters are used instead.) The filename extension tells you – and, more importantly, tells the computer system – what type of file it is. Table 1.1 gives some clues to the meanings of some common filename extensions.

Table 1.1   Filename extensions

Filename extension	File type
.doc	Document created in Microsoft Word
.xls	Spreadsheet created in Microsoft Excel
.htm or .html	Web page written in the language HTML
.bmp	Bitmap image, produced by a painting package such as Microsoft Paint
.jpg	Photo image that has been compressed so that it uses less memory
.txt	Text file that uses only simple characters
.pub	Publication created in Microsoft Publisher
.exe	A program file, such as those used for applications software
.dll	A file containing data that is needed by applications software

Skills: word processing

Improving your word-processing skills

You will probably have used word processing software many times before, but you should learn some new tricks in these pages.

You will be word processing some notes about what you have been learning in this section. If you get into the habit of making notes like this, you will gradually build up a set of revision notes that will be useful at exam time.

Looking at the Word window

Open a new document in Word. The window looks something like Fig 1.18.

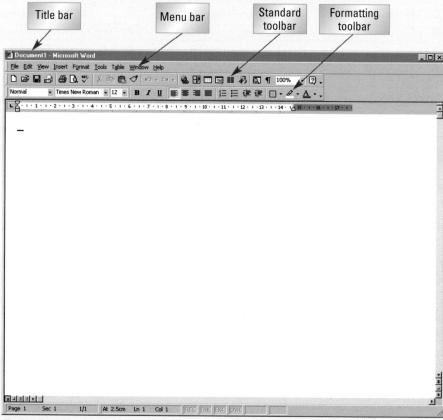

Fig 1.18 *The Microsoft Word window*

At the top of the window you can see the title bar. This shows the name of the document. The menu bar is immediately below the title bar. If you click on any one of the options a drop-down menu appears, with further options (Fig 1.19).

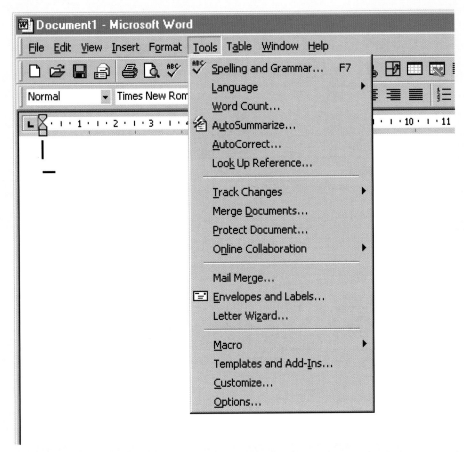

Fig 1.19 *One of the drop-down menus*

Below the menu bar you will see two or more toolbars. Pass the mouse over each button in turn; if you wait a few seconds a screen tip will appear to explain what each button does (Fig 1.20).

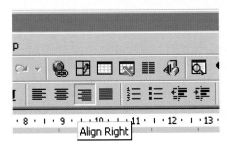

Fig 1.20 *A screen tip shows what the button does*

Each of the toolbars has a move handle at the left edge. You can click on this and drag and drop the toolbar into a new position:

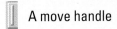 A move handle

If you drag the toolbar on to the page it turns into a floating toolbar which you can place wherever you like (Fig 1.21).

If you click on something on the screen and hold the mouse button down, you can sometimes move it to a new position. When you release the mouse button it stays in its new position. This is known as 'drag and drop'.

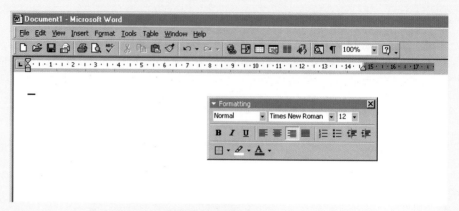

Fig 1.21 *The Formatting toolbar is now a floating toolbar*

You can then drag the toolbar back to its original position.

Entering text

Click on the page and then start entering your notes (Fig 1.22).

Save the document straightaway by clicking on the Save button in the Standard toolbar. Don't wait until you have done a lot of work before saving it. When you save a document in Word you give it a filename, and Word adds the filename extension .doc.

🖫 The Save button

When you save a file on a computer system you give it a filename, such as 'Input peripherals'. The software then adds a few extra letters, known as the filename extension, which identify the type of file it is. For example, Word saves documents with the filename extension .doc (see page 13).

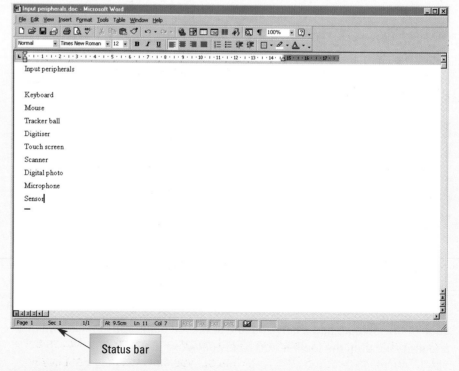

Fig 1.22 *Entering text*

The status bar at the bottom of the window gives some useful information, including the number of the page that you are looking at.

Editing text

You probably want to go back and make some additions to the text. Click in the spot where you want to add something and start keying in. A vertical cursor appears at the point where you want to insert text (Fig 1.23). The extra text is fitted in between the existing words (Fig 1.24).

Digitiser

Touch|screen

Scanner

Fig 1.23 *The cursor at the insertion point*

Digitiser

Touch sensitive |screen

Scanner

Fig 1.24 *The extra text inserted*

Instead of inserting text between existing words, you could also write on top of some text that you don't want. To do this you need to change to Overwrite mode.

On your keyboard press the **Insert** key once. You will see the letters **OVR** (for **OV**e**R**write) in the status bar (Fig 1.25).

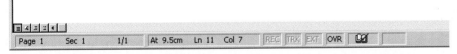

Fig 1.25 *Overwrite mode*

Now click where you want the new text to appear and start keying in (Figs 1.26 and 1.27).

Scanner

Digital|photo

Microphone

Fig 1.26 *The cursor at the overwrite point*

Scanner

Digital camera|

Microphone

Fig 1.27 *The overwritten text*

To change back to Insert mode, press the **Insert** key once more.

Changing the screen view

It is sometimes difficult to imagine exactly what the text will look like on the page. You are currently in Normal Layout but you can switch to Print Layout.

Select **View/Print Layout** (click on the View menu, then click on Print Layout – Fig 1.28).

This shows the page as a piece of paper.

Cursor

A cursor is the name for the marker that shows your position in the text. When you press a key the character appears at the cursor position. You can see cursors in Figs 1.26 and 1.27.

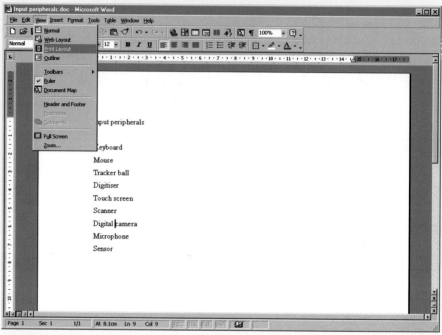

Fig 1.28 Print Layout

Highlighting text

You can select text that you want to change by highlighting it.

To highlight text, use the mouse to click at the beginning of the text. Then hold the mouse button down as you move the cursor across the text. When you release the mouse button the text will be highlighted. Highlighted text reverses the colours – that is, it switches black to white and white to black (Fig 1.29).

Input peripherals

Keyboard

Mouse

Tracker ball

Fig 1.29 Highlighted text

Changing the text style

The Formatting toolbar contains lots of useful buttons (Fig 1.30).

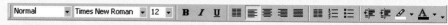

Fig 1.30 The Formatting toolbar

You can use one of these style buttons to change the style of any of the text:

B for **bold text**. You can use **bold** to emphasise words or phrases. It is normally used for headings.

I for *italic text*. You can use *italics* for emphasis as well, and it is sometimes used for quotations or for additional comments.

U for underlined text. You should be careful about using underline in printed documents. It is mainly used in handwritten scripts as a substitute for bold. Today, underlined text usually indicates a hyperlink, and you can use it in a web page or in a help file.

Start by highlighting the text that you want to change. Then click on one of the style buttons (Fig 1.31).

Input peripherals

Keyboard

Mouse

Tracker ball

Fig 1.31 *Bold text*

Character

A character is any letter, number or punctuation mark that you can use on a computer.

Changing the size of the text

The size of characters is measured in points (an old printing term) – 12 point is a common size for normal printed text.

To change the size, first highlight the text you want to change.

To the left of the Bold button you will see a small text box containing a number – probably 12. This is the point size of the characters you have highlighted. Click on the small arrow beside the number, then click on the size you want (Fig 1.32).

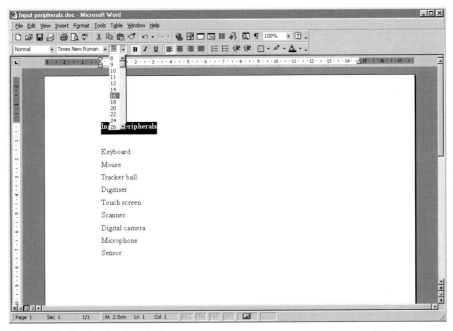

Fig 1.32 *Selecting the size of the text*

The text will now be larger or smaller (Fig 1.33).

Input peripherals

Keyboard

Mouse

Tracker ball

Fig 1.33 *Larger text*

Deleting text

You can delete characters in several ways. Try them all out, then use the method that suits you best.

Delete method 1

Click immediately *before* the characters that you want to delete. Press the key on the keyboard marked **Delete**. The character to the *right* of the cursor is deleted. Carry on until all the text you want to delete has gone.

Delete method 2

Click immediately *after* the characters that you want to delete. Press the **Back** key on the keyboard. This key is usually marked with a back arrow (←). The character to the *left* of the cursor is deleted. Carry on until all the text you want to delete has gone.

Delete method 3

Highlight the characters you want to delete. Press either the Delete key or the Back key.

Using the Standard toolbar

 **Clipboard**

The Clipboard is an area of internal memory where you can store text or images temporarily. If you want to see what is stored on the Clipboard, go to View/Toolbars and select Clipboard.

You can now use some of the buttons in the Standard toolbar (Fig 1.34). Pass your mouse over the buttons to see what each one does:

Fig 1.34 *The Standard toolbar*

✂ **Cut** – this deletes whatever is highlighted but stores it on the Clipboard.

Copy – this stores a copy of whatever is highlighted on the Clipboard.

Paste – this places on to the document a copy of the last item stored on the Clipboard.

Copying and pasting text

Sometimes you want to copy some of the text to another part of the document.

Start by highlighting the characters that you want to copy. Click on the Copy button as in Fig 1.35. This copies the highlighted text to the Clipboard.

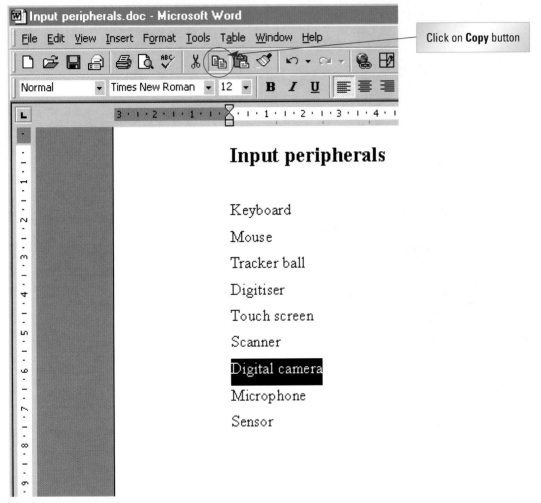

Fig 1.35 *Using the Copy button*

Click on the position where you want the copied text to appear. Then click on the Paste button.

The text will now be pasted to the new position as in Fig 1.36. Note that the words now appear twice.

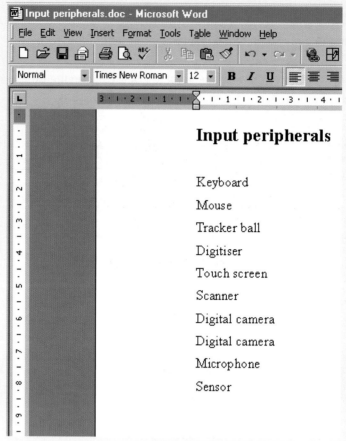

Fig 1.36 *The highlighted text has been copied to the new position*

In this example you can insert the word 'video' (as in Fig 1.37), and this means that you don't have to key in 'Digital camera' twice.

Input peripherals

Keyboard

Mouse

Tracker ball

Digitiser

Touch screen

Scanner

Digital camera

Digital video camera

Microphone

Sensor

Fig 1.37 *The revised text after copying, pasting and editing*

Moving text by cutting and pasting

If you want to move text you have to cut it first – which places it safely on the Clipboard – then paste it to its new position.

Once again, start by highlighting the text you want to move.

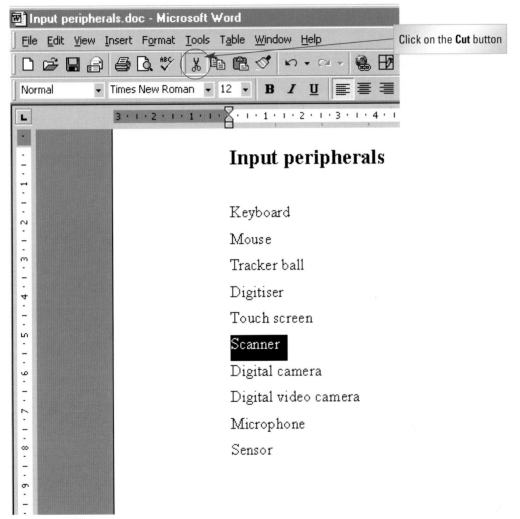

Fig 1.38 *Using the Cut button*

This time the text disappears. But it is safely stored on the Clipboard, even if you can't see the Clipboard. Now click on the position where you want the cut text to appear, and click on the Paste button (Fig 1.39).

Input peripherals

Keyboard

Mouse

Scanner

Tracker ball

Digitiser

Touch screen

Digital camera

Digital video camera

Microphone

Sensor

Fig 1.39 *The cut text has been pasted into a new position*

Moving text by dragging and dropping

You can also move text by dragging and dropping it. Highlight the text you want to move. Then click on the highlighted text and hold the mouse button down. Notice how the pointer changes.

Keep holding the mouse button down and move the pointer to the position where you want the text to go. The cursor is displayed as a broken line instead of a solid one. You can just see it before the word 'Microphone' in Fig 1.40.

Input peripherals

Keyboard

Mouse

Scanner

Digitiser

Tracker ball

Touch screen

Digital camera

Digital video camera

Microphone

Sensor

24

Fig 1.40 *Dragging the text to a new position*

When you release the mouse the text will appear in its new position (Fig 1.41).

Input peripherals

Keyboard

Mouse

Scanner

Tracker ball

Touch screen

Digital camera

Digital video camera

Digitiser

Microphone

Sensor

Fig 1.41 *The text has been dragged to the new position*

Undoing errors

If you make a mistake you can go back a step by clicking on the Undo button on the Standard toolbar:

↰   the Undo button

Using the spelling and grammar check

Everyone makes mistakes from time to time when keying in text. Sometimes you simply hit the wrong keys. Sometimes you can't remember how to spell a word. Sometimes you forget to put in some punctuation. The spelling and grammar check is a very useful way of making sure that these errors are corrected.

The best way to check your spelling and grammar is to set up Word so that it checks all your words and sentences as you key them in.

Select **Tools/Options**. The Options dialogue box will appear. The headings along the top of the Options dialogue box are known as tabs. Click on the tab labelled Spelling & Grammar and you will see the box in Fig 1.42.

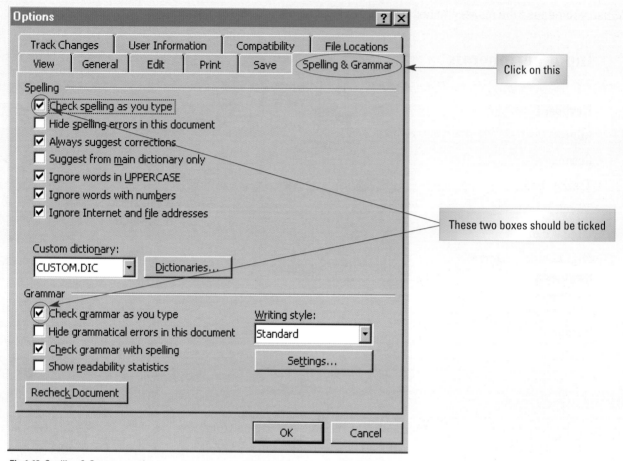

Fig 1.42 *Spelling & Grammar options*

What does it mean?

Dialogue box

A dialogue box is a window which asks you questions or allows you to make choices. Fig 1.42 is an example of a dialogue box.

Make sure that ticks are shown in the two boxes marked Check spelling as you type and Check grammar as you type. If the ticks are missing then click in the boxes. Click on OK.

Correcting a spelling error

Deliberately spell a word wrongly and you will see a wavy red line under the wrongly spelt word (Fig 1.43).

Input peripherals

Keyboard

Mouse

Scanner

Tracker ball

Touch screen

Digital camera

Digital video camera

Digitiser

Microphone

Sensor

Ergonomic keybord

Fig 1.43 *Wrong spelling is underlined in red*

Now right-click on the mis-spelled word and a menu will appear with some suggested corrections. If one of the words shown is the one you want, click on it (Fig 1.44).

 **Right-click**

If you click on the right-hand button on your mouse a menu will pop up on the screen alongside.

Input peripherals

Keyboard
Mouse
Scanner
Tracker ball
Touch screen
Digital camera
Digital video camer
Digitiser
Microphone
Sensor
Ergonomic keybord

| keyboard |
| keyword |
| keyboards |
| |
| Ignore All |
| Add |
| |
| AutoCorrect ▶ |
| Language ▶ |
| ✓ᵃᵇᶜ Spelling... |

Fig 1.44 *Corrections suggested in right click menu*

Correcting a grammatical error

Word will pick out all kinds of grammatical errors and indicate them with a green wavy underline. It will tell you if you do not begin a sentence with a capital letter, if you mix up singulars and plurals, or if you use the wrong verb.

If you right-click, once again corrections will be suggested (Figs 1.45 and 1.46).

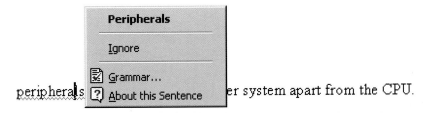

peripherals   er system apart from the CPU.

Fig 1.45 *A grammar error – sentence does not begin with a capital*

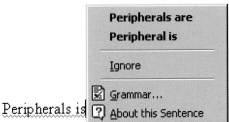

Peripherals is   system apart from the CPU.

Fig 1.46 *Another grammar error – plural noun with singular verb*

Using help

If you need any help when using Word you can call on the Office Assistant to help you (Fig 1.47).

Fig 1.47 *The Office Assistant*

If you can't see the Office Assistant on screen, click on the Help button in the Standard toolbar:

? the Help button

When you click on the Office Assistant, it will try to work out what you want to know and give you a list of possible topics (Fig 1.48). If none of these is relevant then you can enter a question in the search box and click on Search.

Fig 1.48 *The Office Assistant's list of topics*

Page setup

You can change the size, layout and margins of a page.
Select **File/Page Setup**. The Page Setup dialogue box will appear as in Fig 1.49. There are four tabs – Margins, Paper Size, Paper Source and Layout – along the top of the dialogue box.

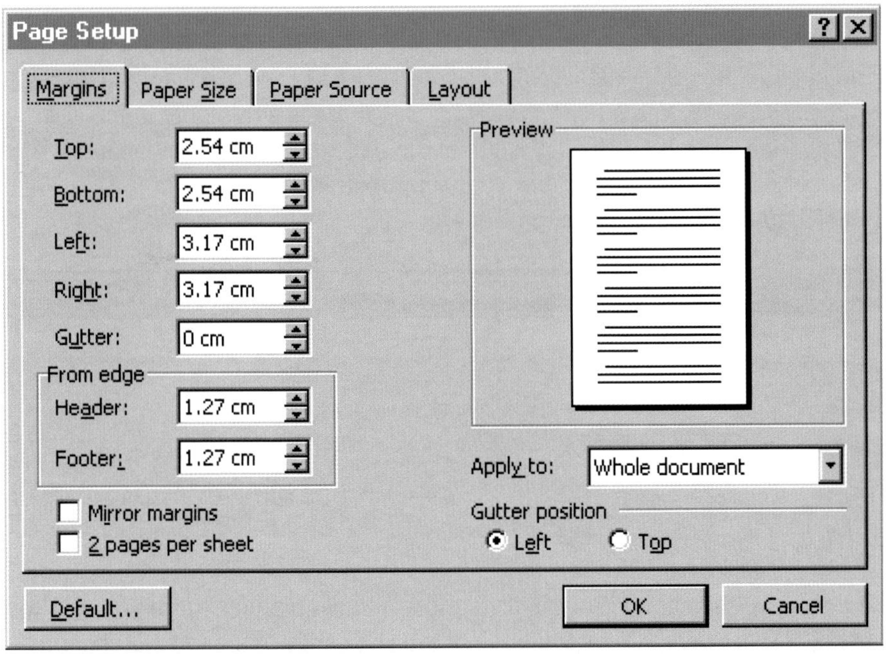

Fig 1.49 *The Page Setup dialogue box*

Changing the orientation of the page

You can arrange a document so that the text runs across the length of the paper (landscape) or across its width (portrait). This is the orientation of the paper.

In the Page Setup dialogue box, click on the Paper Size tab. In the Orientation section click on Landscape, then click on OK (Fig 1.50).

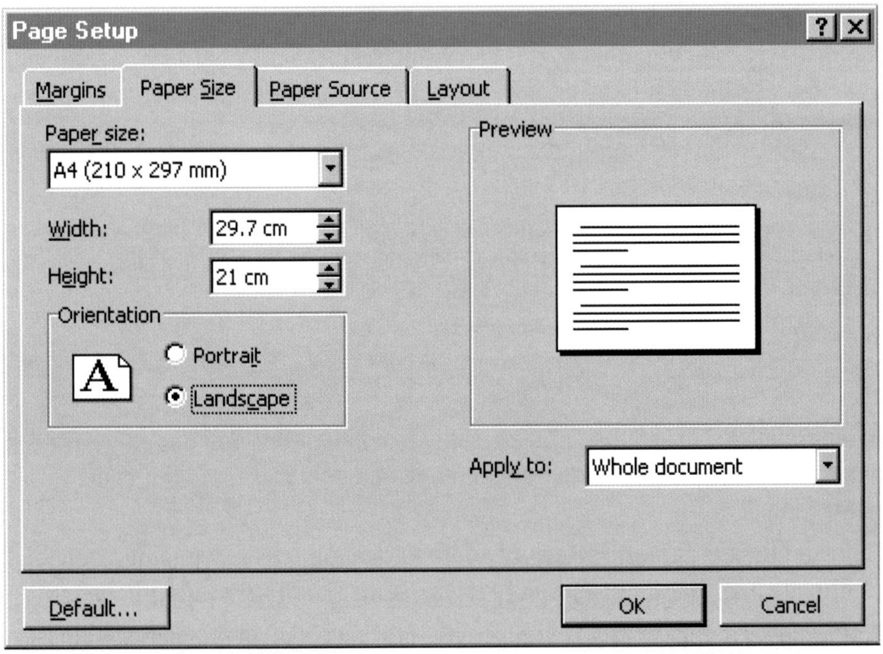

Fig 1.50 *Changing the orientation of the page*

Changing the margins of a page

First change the orientation back to portrait, as it is easier to view the whole width of the page. In the main Word window, there is a ruler just below the toolbars (Fig 1.51). It shows the width of the page, usually measured in centimetres. (You can switch between centimetres and inches in **Tools/Options**, by clicking on the General tab.)

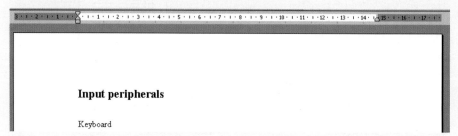

Fig 1.51 *The ruler at the top of the page*

The white section on the ruler shows the area on the page where you can key in text. The grey areas on either side of the ruler show the widths of the left and right page margins. The margins on the page are always kept blank.

The page also has top and bottom margins, which can be seen in the ruler placed vertically on the left of the screen.

You can change the margins in the Page Setup dialogue box. Under the Margins tab (see Fig 1.50) you can change the size of the Top, Bottom, Left and Right margins. Change these and see the effect on the layout of the page and on the appearance of the rulers.

Line spacing

When you are keying in and get to the end of a line, Word automatically puts the next words on the next line. If you want to start a new paragraph then you should press the Enter key on the keyboard. This places a gap between the two paragraphs (Fig 1.52).

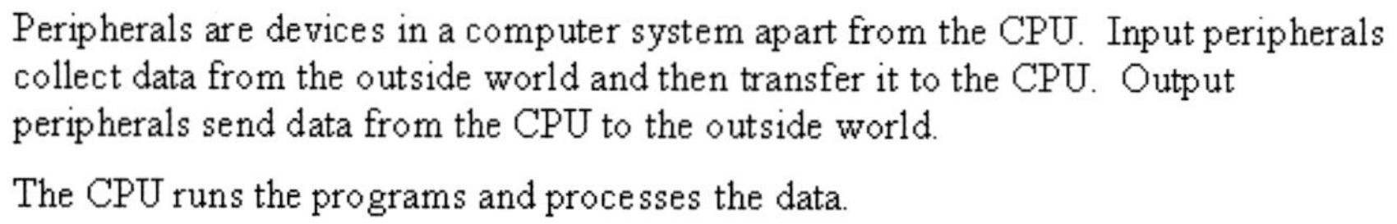

Peripherals are devices in a computer system apart from the CPU. Input peripherals collect data from the outside world and then transfer it to the CPU. Output peripherals send data from the CPU to the outside world.

The CPU runs the programs and processes the data.

Fig 1.52 *The gap between the two paragraphs was created by pressing the Enter key*

In a normal paragraph the lines are fairly close together. You can increase the line spacing – that is, the gap between one line and another in the same paragraph.

Highlight the paragraph where you want to change the line spacing, then right-click and select **Paragraph** (you can select **Format/Paragraph** instead).

You will now see the Paragraph dialogue box (Fig 1.53). In the Line spacing box select **Double**, then click on OK.

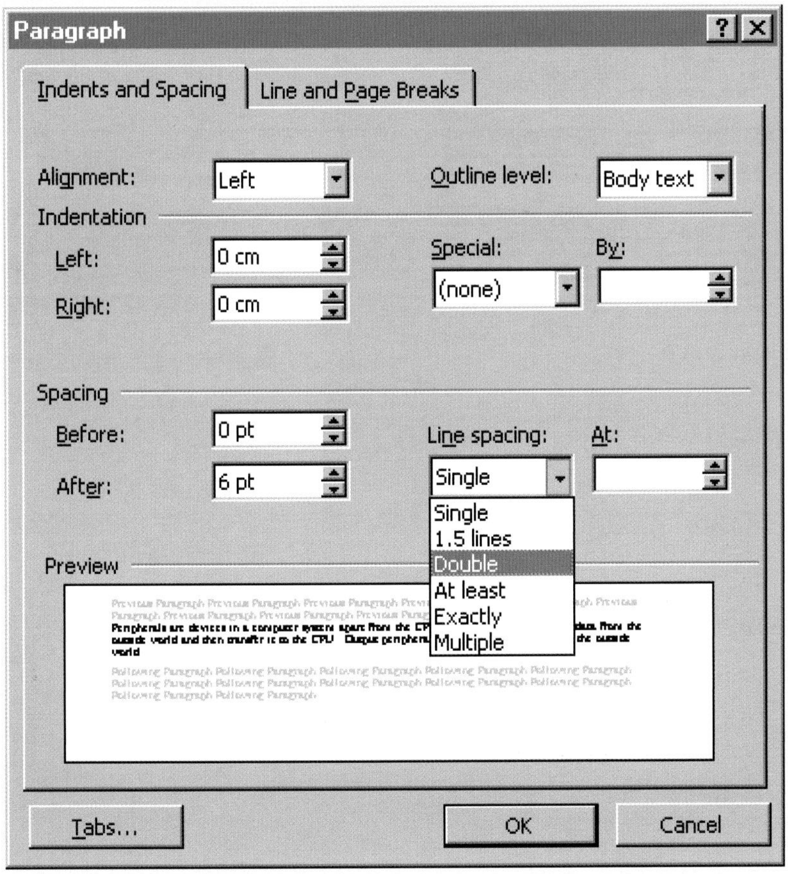

Fig 1.53 *The Paragraph dialogue box*

The paragraph will now be in double line spacing (Fig 1.54).

Peripherals are devices in a computer system apart from the CPU. Input peripherals

collect data from the outside world and then transfer it to the CPU. Output

peripherals send data from the CPU to the outside world.

Fig 1.54 *Double line spacing*

Aligning text

Text can be aligned – that is, lined up – in relation to the margins on the page.
Alignment is sometimes referred to as justification. You will find the alignment
buttons in the Formatting toolbar (see Figs 1.55 – 1.58).

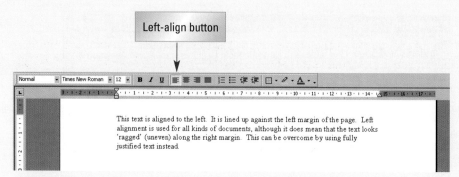

Fig 1.55 *Left-aligned text*

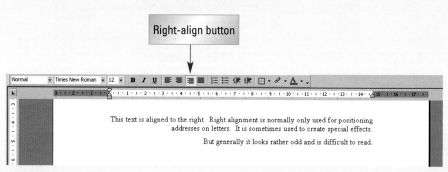

Fig 1.56 *Right-aligned text*

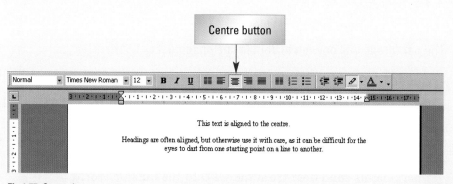

Fig 1.57 *Centred text*

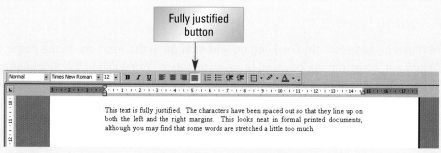

Fig 1.58 *Fully justified text*

Tabulation

The key to the left of **Q** on the keyboard is known as the tabulation, or tab, key. When you press it the text is shifted along the line by a fixed amount (Fig 1.59).

        If you press the tab key on the keyboard, as I did at the beginning of this sentence, the cursor moves a short distance to the right.

        If you press the tab key more than once, the cursor makes a number of jumps.

| You can | use tabs | in the same line | to space out words |
| And then | use them | on the next line | to keep them in columns |

Fig 1.59 *Use of tabulation*

Skills: graphics

Graphics

The term 'graphics' covers all kinds of images stored in digital form. It includes photos that have been scanned in or downloaded from a digital camera, or images 'painted' or 'drawn' using graphical software. Clip Art is used to describe pre-drawn images that you can use freely in your documents.

Graphical images are created in two basic formats – bitmap or vector:

- A **bitmap** image is made up of thousands of tiny cells of colour known as pixels. If you zoom in on a bitmap image you can see clearly that it is made up of lots of individual square dots (Fig 1.60).

Figure 1.60 *Enlarged bitmap image showing the individual pixels*

An applications software package for creating bitmaps is often known as a painting application. It offers many different pens and brush shapes that can be used for drawing images.

- A **vector** image consists of one or more separate objects, such as lines, circles and other shapes. You can work on each object individually without disturbing the others. For example, you can draw a rectangle and then move it around, enlarge or reduce it in size, fill it with a colour, or delete it, without affecting the other objects on the page.

When a vector image is saved, what is actually stored is information about the properties of each of the objects, such as shape, position or colour. So a more complex image with lots of objects will require more information than a simpler image.

An applications software package for creating vector images is often known as a drawing application.

Photographs

Photographs can be stored as bitmaps. They can be edited in painting software, but specialist photo-editing packages are usually used for this purpose.

High-quality photographs consist of a great many pixels and take up a lot of storage memory. The amount of memory needed can be reduced by using special compression techniques.

Creating bitmapped graphics

You can create simple bitmapped images using Microsoft Paint. You may be able to use more sophisticated software, such as Adobe PaintShop, but you can achieve a great deal using Microsoft Paint.

Paint has two floating toolbars, the Tool box and the Color box (Fig 1.61 – notice the American spelling 'color' here). If you cannot see them both on screen then go to *View* and click on *Tool box* or *Color box*.

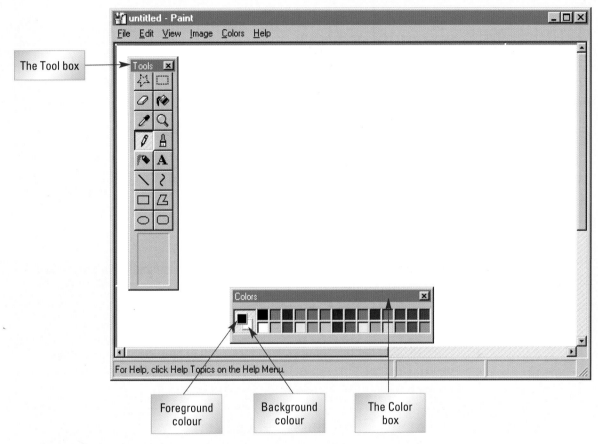

Fig 1.61 *The Microsoft Paint window*

Microsoft Paint does not have a Standard toolbar, so you will need to right-click with your mouse to use most of the functions like Copy and Paste.

Choosing colours

The two squares of colour at the left side of the Color box show the foreground and background colours.

Click on any colour in the Color box to make it the foreground colour. Right-click on a colour to make it the background colour.

Using the Rectangle tool

Click on the Rectangle tool in the Tool box (Fig 1.62). Hold the mouse button down anywhere on the page, then drag the pointer to draw out a rectangle. The outline of the rectangle will be drawn in the foreground colour.

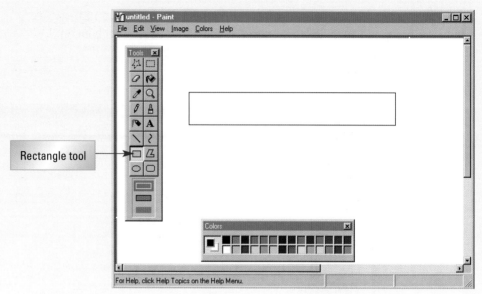

Fig 1.62 A rectangle drawn using the Rectangle tool

Drawing a square

To draw a perfect square, hold down the Shift key on the keyboard while using the Rectangle tool.

Undoing errors

You can undo the last thing you did by selecting **Edit/Undo**. Repeat this to undo up to three previous actions. Try it out by undoing the last rectangle you created.

Using the Filled Rectangle option

Click on the Filled Rectangle option at the bottom of the Tool box (Fig 1.63). You can now draw a rectangle with the outline in the foreground colour and filled with the background colour. Choose the colours you want to use.

In this example the foreground colour is black and is used for the outline of the shape. The background colour is grey and is used to fill the shape.

Save your image before you go any further. The filename will have the filename extension .bmp (for bitmap).

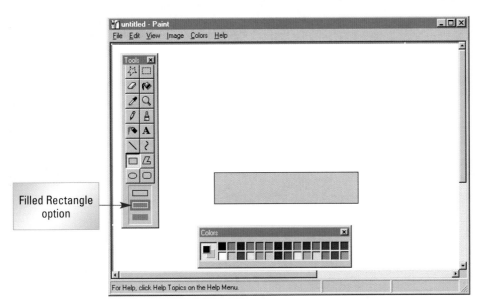

Fig 1.63 *Drawing a filled rectangle*

Using the Rounded Rectangle tool

The Rounded Rectangle tool is very similar to the Rectangle tool, but the corners of the shapes are neatly curved (Fig 1.64).

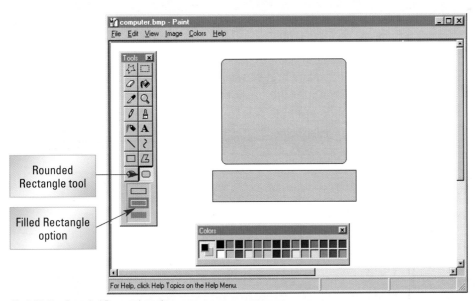

Fig 1.64 *The Rounded Rectangle tool*

Using the ellipse tool

The Ellipse tool works in much the same way as the Rectangle tool, but produces oval and circle shapes (Fig 1.65).

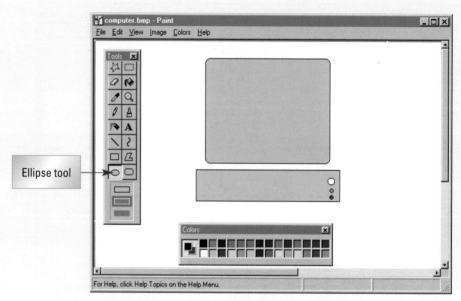

Fig 1.65 *Using the ellipse tool*

Drawing a circle

To draw a perfect circle, hold down the Shift key on the keyboard while using the Ellipse tool. The circular buttons and lights on the front of the computer system in Fig 1.65 were drawn using the Ellipse tool.

Moving parts of the image

You can move a part of the image to another position. It will leave an empty space which will be filled with the current background colour.

Click on the Selection tool in the Tool box (Fig 1.66). Draw a rectangle to select the area of the image that you want to move. Make sure that the background colour matches the background of the selected area. Click inside the selected area, then drag the selection to its new position, as in Fig 1.67.

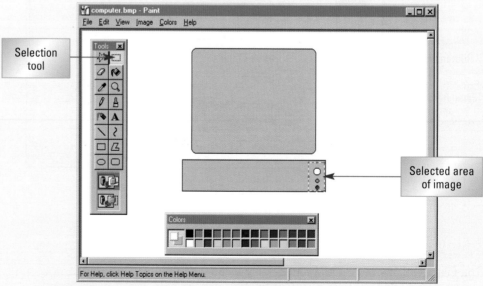

Fig 1.66 *An area of the image selected using the Selection tool*

Cutting parts of the image

To cut part of an image, first select an area with the Selection tool. Right-click on the selected area, then select **Cut**. The empty space will be filled with the current background colour.

Copying and pasting parts of the image

Select an area of the image with the Selection tool. Then right-click inside the area and select **Copy**. Right-click again anywhere on the page and select **Paste**. A copy of the selected area will be placed on the page. Click inside it and drag it to its new position (Fig 1.67).

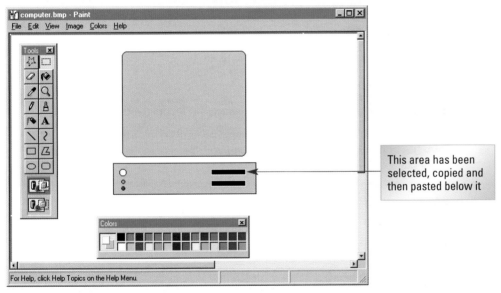

This area has been selected, copied and then pasted below it

Fig 1.67 Copying and pasting a part of the image

Using the Straight Line tool

Click on the Line tool. Then select the line width you want from the bottom of the Tool box (Fig 1.68). Click on the page and draw a line in any direction. The line will be drawn in the foreground colour.

You can draw a perfectly horizontal or vertical line by holding down the Shift key at the same time.

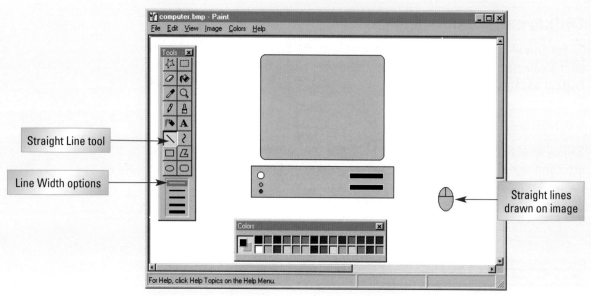

Straight Line tool

Line Width options

Straight lines drawn on image

Fig 1.68 The Straight Line tool

Using the brush tool

The Brush tool draws freehand lines using the foreground colour.

Click on the Brush tool in the Tool box. Then select the brush shape you want from the bottom of the Tool box and use your mouse to draw a line or shape (Fig 1.69).

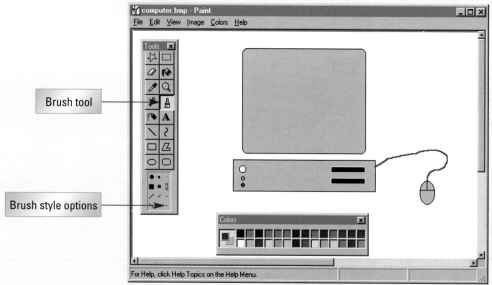

Brush tool

Brush style options

Fig 1.69 The Brush tool

Using the Text tool

The Text tool lets you add text to the image. The text will be written in a text box. The text will be in the foreground colour, and the background of the text box itself will be in the background colour, so make sure that you have chosen the right colours in the Color box.

Click on the Text tool in the Tool box. Click on the image with the pointer, then drag out a box to hold the text. This is a text frame.

The Text toolbar appears on the screen – this lets you choose the style and size of the text (Fig 1.70). Choose a small text size, say 10, then click inside the text frame and start keying in.

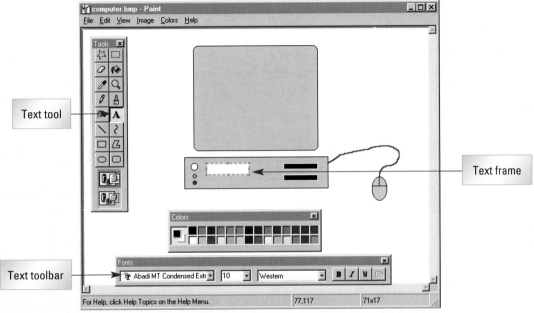

Fig 1.70 *Using the text tool*

You can change the size of the text frame by dragging on the corners and edges.

When you click on another tool in the Tool box the text is fixed in place and you won't be able to change it. If you make an error then use **Edit/Undo**.

Completing the image

We can finish our picture of a computer by adding an image of a real screen. Start by drawing a round-edged rectangle filled with black (Fig 1.71). Make sure you save the image before you go any further.

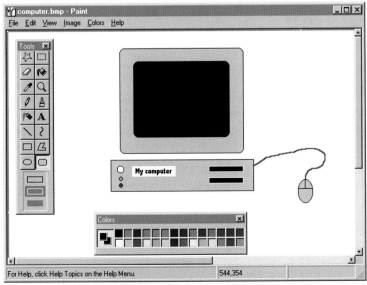

41

Fig 1.71 *Blank screen ready for a screen shot*

Taking a screen shot

Open a file or software application that you would like to display. This could be a Word document or your favourite website.

Press the key on the keyboard marked Print Screen. This is on the top row of keys, towards the right-hand side. Print Screen copies the complete screen to the Clipboard.

Switch to Paint and select **File/New** to create a new blank image. Now right-click on the page and select **Paste** (Fig 1.72). Save the image before you do anything else.

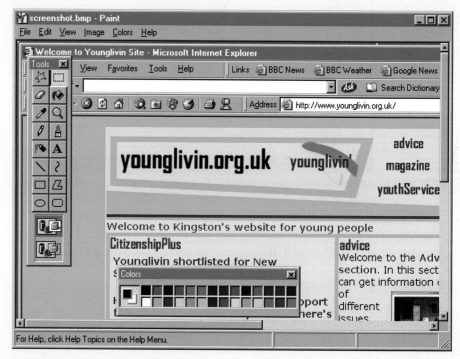

Fig 1.72 *The screen shot pasted into Paint*

Scaling an image

The screen shot image is too large so we need to scale it. We do that by stretching the image. You may think that stretching an image would make it larger but, in computer terms, 'stretching' covers both enlarging and reducing the size of an image.

Right-click on the image and select **Stretch/Skew**. The Stretch and Skew dialogue box will appear (Fig 1.73). Change the value for the Horizontal scale to 20%. This will reduce the width of the image to one-fifth (20%) of its original width. Now change the Vertical scale to 20% as well.

To keep the proportions of the image correct, you should always enter the same value for the Horizontal and Vertical scales.

Now save the scaled-down image (Fig 1.74).

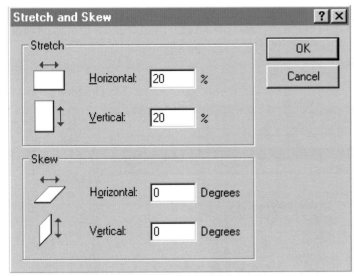

Fig 1.73 *The Stretch and Skew dialogue box.*

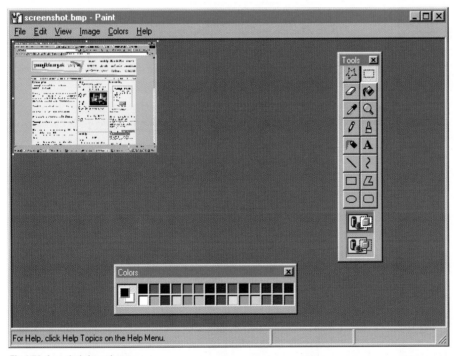

Fig 1.74 *A scaled-down image*

Importing an image

Select **File/Open** and open the image of a computer that you created earlier. You are now going to import the screen shot image and place it on the computer image.

Right-click on the page and select **Paste From**. Find and select the screen shot image. It will be pasted somewhere on the image.

Click inside the screen shot image and drag it to the correct place on the image of the computer.

The screen shot image may not be exactly the right size. Move the pointer to the bottom right corner of the screen shot image. The Diagonal Resize pointer will appear and you can drag this to adjust the size of the image:

↖ the Diagonal Resize pointer

Once you click on another tool in the Tool box the screen shot image merges with the computer image and you will not be able to make any more changes.

Save the completed image of a computer (Fig 1.75).

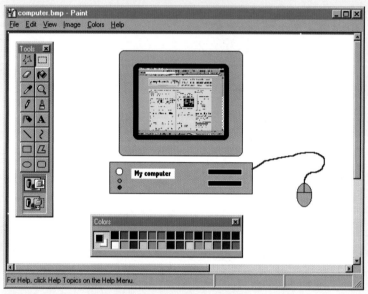

Fig 1.75 *The completed image*

Adding an image to a Word document

First, use the Selection tool in the Tool box to select the area that you want to use (Fig 1.76).

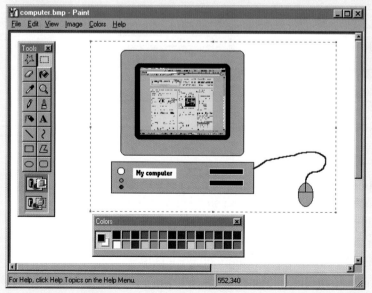

Fig 1.76 *The selected area*

Right-click and select **Copy** to copy the selected area to the Clipboard.

You can now add the image to a Word document. Open the 'Input peripherals' document. Click on the document at the position where you want to insert the image. Click on the Paste button (Fig 1.77).

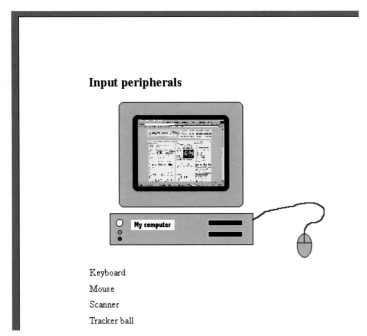

Input peripherals

Keyboard
Mouse
Scanner
Tracker ball

Fig 1.77 An image added to a document

questions

Foundation

1 Some of these are hardware and some are software. Which is which?
- ◎ Hard disk drive
- ◎ Mouse
- ◎ Desktop publishing package
- ◎ Word processing package
- ◎ CD-ROM disk

2 Here is a list of computer devices.
- ◎ Keyboard
- ◎ Screen
- ◎ Printer
- ◎ Sensor
- ◎ Microphone
- ◎ Speaker

  a Which are input devices and which are output devices?
  b Name one other input device that is not given in the list.

3 Some computer systems do not have a mouse attached. Which of these devices could be used instead to control the pointer?
  A A scanner.
  B A touchpad.
  C A sensor.
  D A screen.

4 For each of the following, give the name of a device in a computer system that
  a reads a paper document and turns it into a computer file
  b lets you touch buttons on a screen
  c measures temperature, light or sound
  d takes photographs without using film.

5 Which of these best describes the central processing unit (CPU) of a computer?
  A The CPU holds all the data that is put into a computer.
  B The CPU carries out all the instructions in a program.
  C The CPU is another name for the hard disk drive.
  D The CPU is a special program.

6 Which of these could you NOT do using applications software?
  A Write a letter.
  B Create a website.
  C Take a photograph.
  D Store names and addresses.

7 A school newsletter is sent to parents every month. The school secretary prepares this using a word processing package.
  a Give one piece of information that should appear on each newsletter.
  b Give four features of a word processing package that could be used to improve the presentation of the newsletter.
  c Choose one of the features and explain how it could be used to improve the newsletter.

Higher

8 Here are two types of keyboard. For each, give one reason why it might be a better choice than a standard QWERTY keyboard.
  a An ergonomic keyboard.
  b A touch-sensitive keyboard.

9 A document is saved with the filename *report.doc*, where doc is the file name extension. Explain why computer files use file name extensions.

10 Some people still want to have nothing to do with computers. Describe how computer systems affect the lives of everyone in our society, even if they never use a desktop computer.

Creating effective output

Case study: ICT at Kingsmond Community School

ICT is a very popular subject at Kingsmond Community School. It is chosen by a large number of pupils at GCSE, and many go on to study it at AS level or take a vocational course in Year 12.

The ICT suite has several rooms that are used by pupils. Two of the rooms are used by Years 7 to 11, and two smaller rooms are set aside for sixth-form studies.

Recently the school has installed some new computer equipment.

There is also an office which is used by the teachers and the computer technician. The servers for the computer networks are kept in the office.

The staff have to make sure that the ICT suite is safe for all the users.

Open day is coming up and the school wants everything to look good for the visitors. They also want to prepare notices and leaflets to give visitors information.

Output peripherals in the home, school and office

CRT Monitor

The traditional computer screen looks very much like a television. In fact, like a television, it uses a cathode ray tube (CRT) to project beams of electrons from the back on to the front screen.

The majority of us still use CRT monitors on desktop computers. They take up quite a lot of space, and are heavy to carry, but they are cheaper than the alternatives.

Fig 2.1 A CRT monitor

LCD flat-panel screen

Flat-panel screens are used on all portable computers (Fig 2.2). Larger ones can be used with desktop computer systems (Fig 2.3).

The screen on a traditional CRT monitor is slightly curved, and this can distort the image. A flat-panel screen overcomes this by using a liquid crystal display (LCD), which fires up tiny liquid crystals on the surface of the screen.

Fig 2.2 A notebook computer

Fig 2.3 A flat-panel LCD screen

Ink-jet printer

An ink-jet printer squeezes tiny bubbles of ink on to the paper to form the characters and images. It can print on a variety of papers, including glossy photo paper. The images can be of a very good quality.

The ink is stored in ink cartridges and these have to be replaced from time to time. Four colours are used – black, cyan (a greenish-blue colour), magenta (a reddish-blue colour) and yellow (Fig 2.4). These can be combined to give any colour at all.

Fig 2.4 The four print colours

Ink-jet printers are cheap to buy and are popular in the home (Fig 2.5). They are quite slow, compared with laser printers. Their cartridges do not last very long, so they can work out quite expensive if they are used heavily.

Fig 2.5 An ink-jet printer

Laser printer

Laser printers use the same technology as photocopiers. A laser is an intense narrow beam of light. The laser inside a printer places an electrostatic charge on a drum to match the image. Toner powder is attracted to the charged areas on the drum, and the image is printed when the paper is pressed against the drum and briefly heated.

Most laser printers use a single black toner cartridge. When the toner runs out you need to replace the toner cartridge with a new one.

Before you use paper in a laser printer you should always check that it is suitable. Some papers can damage the printer.

Laser printers are more expensive to buy than ink-jet printers. But they are faster, so can be used in a busy office or school. Although the toners cost more than ink-jet cartridges, they last much longer. In many offices, colour printing is not required, so a normal laser printer is the best option (Fig 2.6).

Fig 2.6 A laser printer

Colour laser printer

Colour laser printers use the same colours as ink-jet printers, but the paper has to be charged and printed four times, once for each colour.

Colour laser printers are much more expensive than black and white laser printers, and they need four toner cartridges instead of one. They do give the best quality of printing, so are used when very high quality output is needed (Fig 2.7).

Fig 2.7 A colour laser printer

Dot-matrix printer

A dot-matrix printer uses tiny pins which press against an ink ribbon and print dots on the paper. Anything printed by a dot-matrix printer looks decidedly dotty, and is not considered good quality. A dot-matrix printer would not be used for an important document, such as a letter to a customer.

You will have seen the output from a dot-matrix printer on a shop receipt (Fig 2.8). Full-size dot-matrix printers were used in offices before laser printers came along, and they are still to be found in some places of work.

Multi-part stationery is paper that comes in several sheets so that, when something is printed on the top sheet, a copy also appears on the sheets below. You may have seen multi-part stationery used for credit card slips in shops. A dot-matrix printer is the only type of printer that works with multi-part sheets (Fig 2.9).

Fig 2.8 A shop receipt

Fig 2.9 A dot-matrix printer

Specialised output peripherals

Speakers

All desktop computers have a small speaker, which produces the pings and other sounds that you hear. The quality of the sound is not good, so extra stereo speakers can be added.

Speakers are very popular on home computers. Audio CDs can be played on the CD player on a computer system, and the music and sound effects for games can sound very realistic. The quality of the sound will depend on how good the speakers are (Fig 2.10).

Fig 2.10 A computer system with two external speakers

Extra speakers are often not installed in an office, as the sound could disturb other workers.

Fig 2.11 Computer headphones

Headphones

You can also listen to the sounds on a computer through headphones. This makes sure that no one else can be annoyed by the sound.

Multimedia projector

One of the problems with a computer screen is that it cannot be viewed at the same time by a large audience. This can be overcome by projecting what is shown on the screen on to a large surface.

Fig 2.12 A multimedia projector

A multimedia projector (Fig 2.12) projects the screen output from a computer on to a wall panel. Multimedia projectors are used in schools and colleges for teaching. In business they are used to give illustrated talks, known as presentations.

Plasma screen

A plasma screen (Fig 2.13) is a large flat computer screen that is used for displays and presentations. The surface consists of lots of tiny gas cells which glow with colour.

Fig 2.13 A plasma screen being using for a presentation

Plotter

A plotter is a special kind of printer that is used for maps, architectural drawings and engineering designs.

A pen is gripped in a holder above the paper and moves across the paper to draw lines and curves. Pens with different-coloured inks can be used. The plotter will draw all the lines with one colour then use another pen to draw the next colour.

There are two types of plotter. The most common type is the drum plotter (Fig 2.14). The paper passes over a cylinder, known as a drum. The drum can move the paper backwards and forwards whilst the pen is drawing lines. The pen moves from side to side above the paper. Complex curves can be drawn by combining pen movement with the moving paper.

The paper for a flat-bed plotter (Fig 2.15) is placed flat on a table and does not move. The pens are moved around, drawing on the paper. Flat-bed plotters can work with very large sheets of paper but take up a lot of room.

Fig 2.14 A drum plotter

Fig 2.15 A multi-colour flat-bed plotter.

Motors

A computer controls the electric motors that move the pens and paper in a drum plotter. The computer controls the speed at which the motors run, it can also reverse the direction of the motor.

Computers can also be used to control all sorts of machines. You might not be able to see the computer itself, and the machines it controls may not look anything like the usual computer peripherals. But the computer is sending output to the motors which make the machines work.

Computer-controlled motors are used in many kinds of vehicles, in the machinery used in factories (Fig 2.16) and also in robots.

Fig 2.16 An automated production plant

Switches

Computers can also control simple on-off switches (Fig 2.17). For example, in the heating system in a large building, the heaters and fans may be switched on and off according to the temperature in the rooms. Data about the temperature would be sent from a sensor to the computer and the output to the switches would be generated automatically.

Fig 2.17 A computer-controlled heating system in a greenhouse

What do you think?

Have you seen any of these specialised output peripherals? If so, state what they were used for. Can you suggest some new uses for any of them?

Presenting information

What does it mean?

Hard copy

Hard copy refers to any documents printed from a computer.

If you want to give some information to a number of people, there are a number of methods for doing it. Some methods give the information as hard copy, some give it on screen, some use both hard copy and screen, and some use neither.

Writing a report

You can write all the information in a formal report. This will be set out with headings and subheadings, and the information will be given in concise paragraphs. Start by making a first attempt at the report, known as a draft. You should then check it carefully, and maybe get someone else to read it, before producing the final version.

Use this method if you have to give quite a lot of complicated information. It is a good method if you want to make sure that your readers have full and detailed information they can keep and refer to when they need it.

Reports are often used within a business or organisation. An employee may be asked to write a report to describe how things are working at present, or to propose some changes in the future.

You can use word processing software to create a report (Fig 2.18).

Fig 2.18 A report

Producing a leaflet

You can set out the key points of information in a leaflet. Leaflets can be made with any size of paper (Fig 2.19). From a sheet of A4 paper or card you can have a single-sided, double-sided, two-fold or three-fold leaflet. A leaflet can be made eye-catching by the use of colour and images.

Fig 2.19 Leaflets

Use this method if you want to give some straightforward information. Make sure that all the important information is clearly stated, such as contact details, dates and times, etc.

It is a good idea to produce a leaflet if you want to make sure that people can keep the information to hand without taking up too much space.

Leaflets are often used to give information to the general public about an event or a service that is offered.

You can use desktop publishing software to create a leaflet (Fig 2.20). Simple leaflets can be created with word processing software instead.

Fig 2.20 *A three-fold leaflet*

Designing a notice

You can only give a small amount of information in a notice which will be pinned to a noticeboard. You will have to use a large font size so it can be read from a distance. If you need to print several copies of the notice, print one out first, pin it on a noticeboard and check that it can be read easily.

Notices can be made with any size of paper or card. Coloured card does help to draw attention to the notice. You can also add images, but be very careful as they can be distracting. One strong image is much better then several smaller ones.

Use this method if you want to give some very simple, but important, information.

Notices are often used in organisations to give people instructions, to remind them about things they should be doing, or to advertise a meeting.

You can use desktop publishing software to create a notice (Fig 2.21). Simple notices can be created with word processing software instead.

Activities

For one week, collect all the leaflets that are delivered to your home. Then share them with other pupils and discuss these questions:

- Which leaflets are printed on A4 paper?
- Which leaflets are printed on other sizes of paper? Can you tell what size paper was used?
- Which leaflets are single-sided, double-sided, two-fold or three-fold?
- Which leaflets use colour and images? Do you think they use them effectively?

Fig 2.21 *A warning notice*

More ways of presenting information

Giving a talk

You can invite people to a meeting and tell them all the information. You should make some notes before the meeting on what you want to say to make sure that you remember everything.

The problem with this is that your listeners may not remember what you have told them. You can't be sure that they have understood what you have said correctly. They may take notes, but you can't be sure that the notes are accurate (Fig 2.22).

Fig 2.22 Some talks can be boring!

Use this method if you have to give some information urgently and do not have time to prepare anything else.

Making a presentation

A talk can be very dry and boring. You can keep people's interest much better if you illustrate a talk with images and texts shown on a large screen. This is known as a presentation.

The material that will appear can be prepared on a computer and then projected on to a screen using a multimedia projector. The material is arranged into individual 'pages' called slides.

On the slides you can include a summary of what you want to say to your audience. There should only be a few lines on each slide, so you can hold their attention and talk about the points before moving on to the next slide.

You can include all kinds of images on presentation slides – photographs, charts, graphs, cartoons, maps, etc. (Fig 2.23). You can also add sound effects or short movies.

Some speakers like to print out the slides on to paper to give to their audience. People can then write extra notes on the handouts and keep them to remind them of the presentation.

Fig 2.23 Images used in presentation slides

Use this method if you want to talk directly to people and to ensure that they listen and take in what you say.

Presentations are often used in organisations when someone wants to get support for an important proposal. They are also used at conferences and large meetings, and for training people.

You can use presentation software to create the slides for a presentation (Fig 2.24).

Fig 2.24 *Giving a presentation*

Creating web pages

Web pages present information to a very wide audience. They are useful if it is impossible to get people all in one place for a presentation, or if the information is needed by a large number of people. People can visit a web page whenever they like and they can keep returning to visit extra pages. Web pages can also be changed easily, so they can be kept up to date when new information appears.

Most web pages are stored on the Web, which is open to anyone who has a suitable connection to the Internet.

It is also possible to hold web pages on a private network within an organisation, known as an intranet. (Note that the Internet has an 'e' in the middle and is spelt with a capital 'I', whereas intranet has an 'a' in the middle.) Web pages on an intranet can only be viewed within the organisation and cannot be seen by anyone surfing the Internet.

Use this method if you want to give some information to a restricted audience.

Web pages are often used to provide information to the general public (Fig 2.25). They can also be used on an intranet to provide employees with the information they need to have in order to do their jobs.

You can use web-authoring software to create web pages.

World Wide Web

The World Wide Web – also called WWW or the Web – is one of the most important parts of the Internet. It is the vast collection of public web pages that anyone can visit. Web pages are linked to each other.

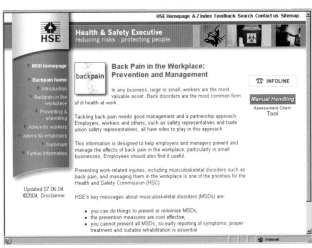

Fig 2.25 *A Health and Safety at Work web page*

Health and Safety for computer users

Computer users can develop some physical health problems as a direct result of their work, but you can avoid them yourself if you take care.

Repetitive strain injury (RSI)

Repetitive strain injury gives you pain in the arm, wrist or hand. It is caused by making the same movements over and over again. You could develop RSI if you spend long periods of time keying in data or playing games on a computer.

Shoulder and back pain

You can develop pain in the shoulders or back if you sit at a computer without proper back support.

Eye strain

Computers do not damage the eyes but they can give you headaches and sore eyes. Eye strain is caused by using a computer for a long time without a break, so you can avoid eye strain by taking regular breaks from using a computer. You may also find that you get eye strain if the screen is too bright.

Tripping

A lot of cables are used in computer systems. They should be tucked away behind desks so that you don't catch a foot in them. It is very easy to trip on a cable lying across a room, and you should never allow this to happen.

Electrical shock

It is very important that power cables are placed safely so that you cannot pull on them or damage them by accident.

Keep liquids well away from electrical equipment.

Stress

A lot of people suffer from stress. Stress makes you feel tired and irritable and can lead to more serious anxiety and depression. Stress is caused when you are under pressure to achieve a lot of tasks and you do not feel completely in control. Most people find that a certain amount of stress actually helps them to finish their work, but too much can make you ill.

It is very easy to get absorbed in a task on a computer and to forget about other things that should be done. When you take a break from using a computer, check the time and think about what else you have to do.

Don't let computers damage your health

Here are some suggestions to help you keep healthy and safe:

Look after yourself

◎ When working on a computer, take a short break every hour.
◎ Whilst you are using a computer try not to sit in exactly the same position for long periods.
◎ Adjust the brightness control on your computer screen so that it does not glare. Try to match the screen display to the brightness of the room.

Keep yourself safe

◎ Make sure that all the cables run along a wall or behind furniture.
◎ Give yourself plenty of room. You should be able to use the mouse mat without risking knocking things over.
◎ Don't place drinks close to any electrical equipment.

Sit comfortably at a computer

◎ Use a proper adjustable computer chair if at all possible (Fig 2.26). Make sure that it supports your back. The best chairs can be raised and lowered, and you can change the angle that the back makes with the seat. Some also let you tilt the seat. This is called an ergonomic chair.
◎ If your feet are not touching the ground then use a footrest (see Fig 2.27). This does not have to be anything special – you can use a pile of old books or telephone directories.
◎ Tilt the screen and adjust the height of your chair so that you are looking slightly down at the screen.
◎ Angle your keyboard so it is not flat on the table.
◎ Try using a wrist support with your keyboard.
◎ Check whether your forearms are horizontal, as that is the most comfortable position.

Fig 2.26 *A fully adjustable computer chair*

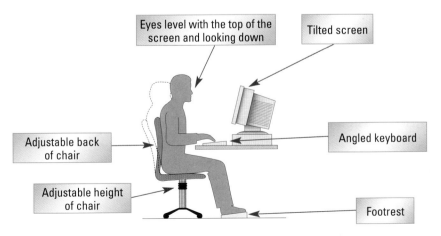

Eyes level with the top of the screen and looking down

Tilted screen

Adjustable back of chair

Angled keyboard

Adjustable height of chair

Footrest

Fig 2.27 *The correct position when using a computer*

What do you think?

Are you left-handed? What changes could you make to the furniture and computer equipment to suit you?

Are you very short, or very tall? What if you were using a wheelchair?

A healthy environment

Temperature

You will not be able to work well if you are too hot or too cold. The ideal temperature is around 21°C.

To keep yourself comfortable, try not to sit too close to radiators or doors. Check the settings on the heating or air-conditioning system.

Computer equipment also will not work properly if it is too hot or too cold. Computers can overheat if the sun shines on them through a window on a summer's day. They should not be placed close to a window. If the sun is hot, you should also be able to draw blinds and maybe switch on a fan.

Noise

Background noise can disturb you if you are trying to work on a computer.

Check that all the peripherals are reasonably quiet. Disk drives and printers can make annoying sounds. There is a fan inside the computer unit which keeps the CPU cool, but this can be noisy.

In a computer room at a school or in an office, carpets can help to muffle the sounds in the room.

Lighting

The lighting in a room must be suitable. In the past a certain type of low-frequency fluorescent strip lighting used to interfere with the screen and cause flickering for computer users. This must no longer be used in rooms that have computers.

Radiation

Some years ago, people were worried about the level of electromagnetic radiation that was given off by computer monitors. International recommendations were adopted in the UK and in many other countries, which forced the manufacturers to produce monitors that came well within the safety limits. It is now impossible to buy a screen in the UK that emits radiation above the safe level.

What do you think?

Have a good look at the room where you use a computer. This could be at home or at school. Is it a healthy environment for computer users?

Health and safety regulations

People at work are protected by a number of government regulations. These have been drawn up to keep employees safe and healthy and to prevent injury.

The regulations do not apply to students and school pupils at their colleges and schools, because they only cover people when they are employed by someone. Teachers are employees, so the regulations do cover them.

All employers have to make sure that they obey these regulations.

There are health and safety regulations that cover temperature, lighting, noise and electrical safety. These apply to everyone at work, whether or not they use a computer.

Health and Safety (Display Screen Equipment) Regulations

There are some regulations that particularly apply to computer users.

The Display Screen Equipment Regulations apply to employees who regularly use a 'workstation' that includes any kind of display screen. Under the regulations employers have to:

◎ **Assess workstations and reduce risks.** This means that they must look at the complete workstation, including all the furniture. They have to take into account any special needs of individual staff.

◎ **Make sure that workstations meet minimum standards.** The regulations list the standards that have to be met by keyboards, desks, chairs, lighting as well as screens.

◎ **Plan work so there are breaks or changes in activities.** The employer must plan these breaks with employees. Short, frequent breaks are better than longer, less frequent ones.

◎ **Arrange eye tests (if requested), and provide spectacles if special ones are needed.**

◎ **Provide health and safety training and information.**

What do you think?

What would happen if the Health and Safety Regulations applied to pupils and students? Would your school or college be OK?

What does it mean? **Display screen**

A display screen is any kind of screen that is used with electronic equipment. It includes the computer output peripherals that you have looked at, such as CRT monitors, LCD and plasma screens, as well as cash terminals in shops and on mobile phones.

Skills: desktop publishing

Desktop publishing software was originally designed for newspapers and magazines. Before the software was available, editors would assemble stories provided by journalists and literally cut and paste the stories on to a board. They would then add photographs, illustrations, headings and lines.

Desktop publishing works in the same way, but in electronic format. Individual contributors can send their word-processed stories to the editor's system, who can then import them into the page layout. Stories, headings and images can be easily edited and moved around to fit the space.

Once a publication is ready it can either be printed or be sent, still in electronic form, to a specialist printing company.

 **Publication**

A publication is a document created in desktop publishing software.

Case study

Kingsmond Community School is planning an open day for prospective pupils and their parents. The ICT department wants everyone to come along to see their new equipment. It needs a number of publications, such as notices and leaflets.

In these activities you can either create publications for the imaginary Kingsmond Community School or for your own school.

The first publication will be a simple notice welcoming visitors to the ICT Department.

Microsoft Publisher

 **Wizard**

A wizard is a small program that helps you to create something, such as a document or a web page. It asks you a series of questions, then creates it for you.

Small businesses and home computer users want to produce professional-looking documents but cannot afford to use professional designers or editors. Publisher is a desktop publishing package that has been created especially for them. It includes hundreds of ready-designed publications that you can use straightaway or adapt for your own needs.

Wizards in Publisher

When you launch Publisher the first screen you see is the Catalog (Fig 2.28) (note the American spelling of 'catalogue')

You can return to the catalogue at any time by selecting **File/New**.

The left-hand column shows the different categories of wizard. The right side shows the individual wizards within each category.

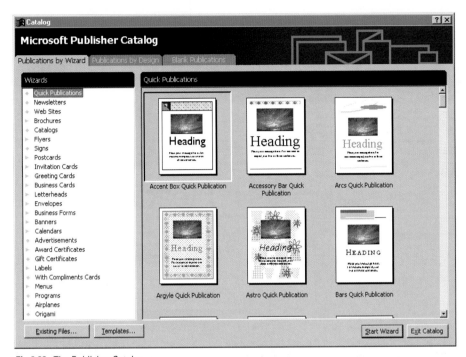

Fig 2.28 *The Publisher Catalog*

Using a Quick Publication wizard

Click on one of the wizards in the Quick Publications category, then click on the Start Wizard button. In this example, we will be using the Accent Box Quick Publication.

If this is the first time you have used Publisher you may see the dialogue box shown in Fig 2.29. You will come back to the personal information later, so just click on the close button.

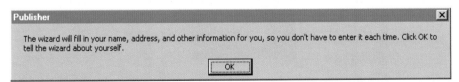

Fig 2.29 *Publisher wants to collect your personal information*

The publication appears on the screen. But the wizard is not finished yet. It can help you to customise the publication so that it looks just as you want (Fig 2.30).

Click on the Next button.

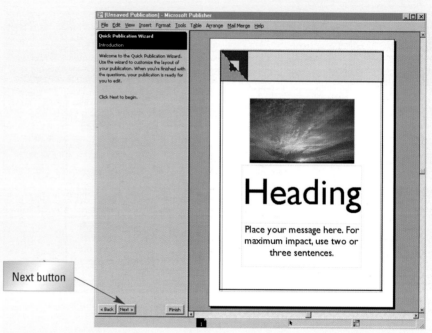

Next button

Fig 2.30 *The publication is ready for you to customise it*

The wizard now gives you a choice of colour schemes. Click on different ones to see the effect they have (Fig 2.31). Choose a colour scheme. In the example the Tropics colour scheme is chosen.

Click on Next.

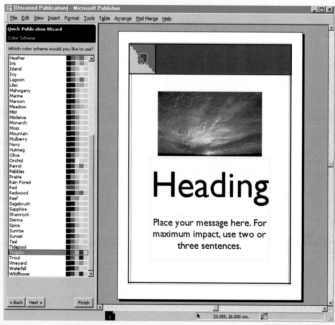

Fig 2.31 *Colour schemes*

The wizard next offers you a choice of layouts. Again, try them out to see what each does, then make your choice. In Fig 2.32 the layout with the large picture in the middle was chosen.

Click on Next.

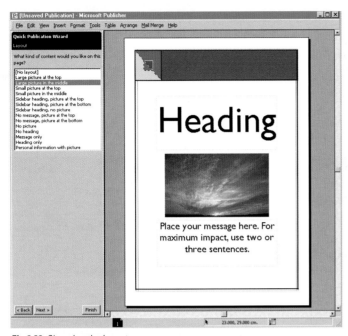

Fig 2.32 *Choosing the layout*

You are next asked which set of personal information you want to use. You are going to store information about your own school, or about Kingsmond Community School.

Click on Update (Fig 2.33).

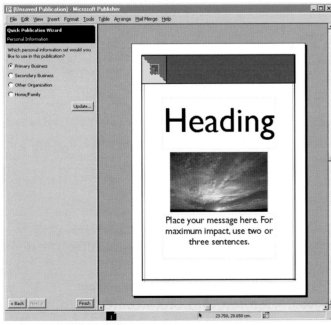

Fig 2.33 *Click on Update to enter personal information*

In the Personal Information dialogue box (Fig 2.34), you can fill in the information that you want Publisher to save. Several different publications can use these details. You can leave any box blank.

In the top box, there are four sets of personal information (see Fig 2.34). You are preparing publications for use at a school, so select **Primary** (that is, most important) **Business**. Enter the details of your own school, or of Kingsmond Community School, as shown in Fig 2.34. You can go back and add other personal information later.

Click on Update.

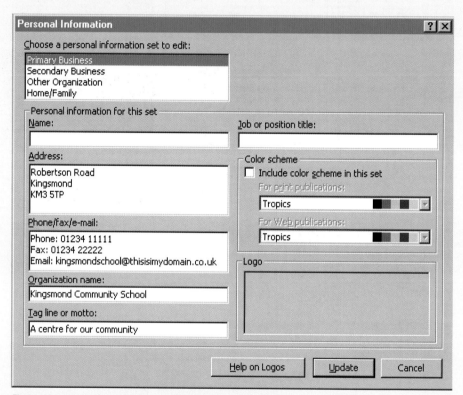

Fig 2.34 Personal information saved in Publisher

Back in the Quick Publication wizard, click on Finish.

Before you do anything else, save your publication. All Publisher files are given the filename extension .pub.

Looking at the Publisher window

You should now be in the main Publisher window (see Fig 2.35). You can now make any changes that you want to your publication, but the wizard remains on hand to help you:

◎ The **Standard toolbar** is similar to the Standard toolbar in Word.
◎ The **Formatting toolbar** changes depending on what you are working on.
◎ The **Objects toolbar** is something like the Tool box in Paint. It contains buttons that let you add different kinds of objects, such as lines, text or images, to your publication.

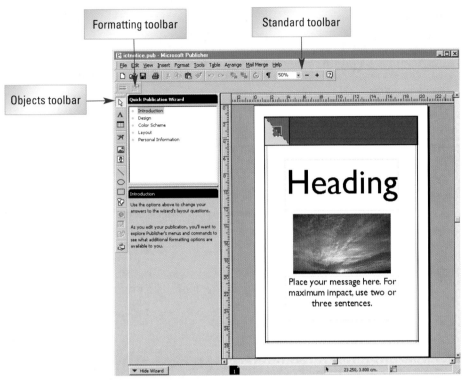

Fig 2.35 *The Publisher window*

Zooming

You can zoom in to see details of the document more clearly. You can zoom out to see the overall effect. Click on the Zoom buttons in the Standard toolbar:

+ the Zoom In button   **—** the Zoom Out button

Objects

Each item on the page is known as an object:

⊙ Click on the heading – this is a text object (Fig 2.36).
⊙ Click on the picture – this is a picture object.
⊙ You may also find shape objects, such as lines, rectangles, ovals and other shapes.

Click on each of the objects on your page. How many objects have you got?

Each time you click on an object, handles appear around it.

You will also notice a grey line around some objects – this is known as a frame. The frame holds the object and shows where it begins and ends. With some objects you can only see the frame when you click on it. The frame does not show up when the page is printed.

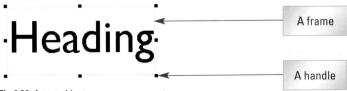

A frame

A handle

Fig 2.36 *A text object*

Margins

Fig 2.37 *Margins*

On the publication you will notice blue and pink dotted lines near the edges. These are margins, and they are not printed.

Making changes to the publication

You can click on each of the options in the Quick Publication wizard to go back and change any of the choices you made before.

Changing the text

Click somewhere in the middle of the heading. This is a text object. Several things happen (Fig 2.38):

- The text is highlighted.
- Handles appear around the text frame.
- The Formatting toolbar changes and now looks like the one in Word.

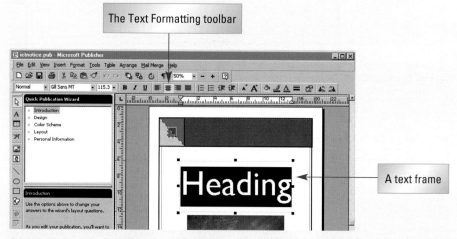

Fig 2.38 *A text frame and the Text Formatting toolbar*

Key in your own heading. The text automatically changes size to fit the space (Fig 2.39).

Now click on the other text object and key in some text.

Fig 2.39 *Suitable text has been added*

Changing the image

The picture of a sunset is not quite what you want. Click once on the picture object and you will see the picture frame, with handles, and the Picture Formatting toolbar (Fig 2.40).

The Picture Formatting toolbar

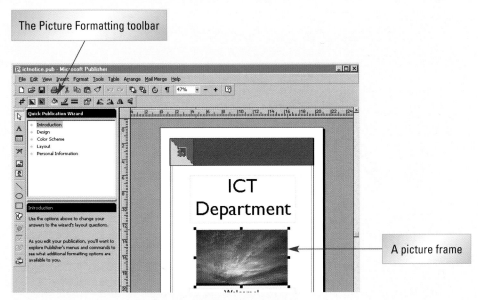

A picture frame

Fig 2.40 *A picture frame and the Picture Formatting toolbar*

To change the image you should double-click on the picture. This takes you to the Insert Clip Art dialogue box (Fig 2.41).

All Categories button

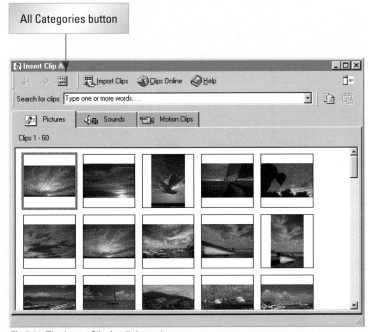

Fig 2.41 *The Insert Clip Art dialogue box*

If you cannot see an image that you want to use, key in a descriptive word in the Search for Clips box, and press **Enter**.

 *What does it mean?* **Clip Art**

Clip Art images are ready-drawn graphics that you can use in your own work. Many software applications provide you with many Clip Art images to get you started.

If this is not successful, click on the All Categories button and browse.

When you have found a suitable image, click on it. A small tool box will appear (Fig 2.42). Click on the Insert Clip button, which is the top one.

Fig 2.42 Inserting a clip

Close the Insert Clip Art dialogue box and you will see your chosen picture inserted in the publication (Fig 2.43).

Fig 2.43 *The publication with a suitable image*

Moving objects

You can move any of the objects to a new position. Move the pointer over an object until the Mover pointer appears. This looks like a removal van:

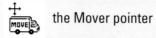 the Mover pointer

Click on the object and then drag it to a new position.

Adding personal information

You can add some of the information about the school that you stored under personal information.

In the Quick Publication wizard, select **Personal Information** (Fig 2.44). In the Personal Information section, Primary Business should be selected.

Click on Insert Component, then click on Organization Name.

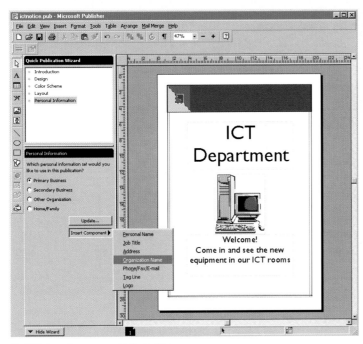

Fig 2.44 *Inserting personal information*

The name of the school appears in a text frame in the middle of the page. Move it to its correct position (Fig 2.45).

Your publication is now ready to be printed.

Fig 2.45 *The finished publication*

Using another wizard

Make sure you save a publication before you start a new one.

Select **File/New**. The Publisher catalogue appears again.

Choose from the list of wizards. The wizard will take you through a series of questions, as before.

Some of the wizards automatically insert the information from the personal information.

Some documents have more than one page. You can switch between the pages by clicking on the page numbers at the bottom of the window (Fig 2.46).

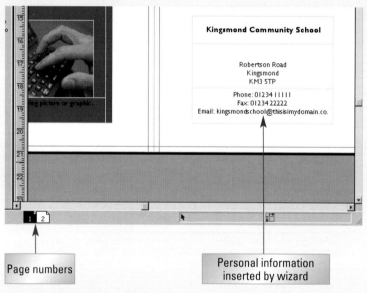

Kingsmond Community School

Robertson Road
Kingsmond
KM3 5TP

Phone: 01234 11111
Fax: 01234 22222
Email: kingsmondschool@thisismydomain.co.

Page numbers

Personal information inserted by wizard

Fig 2.46 *Working with another wizard*

Case study

In the ICT rooms at Kingsmond Community School there should be some notices reminding pupils about health and safety. These should be in place before the open day.

For this activity you will start a publication from scratch and not use the Publisher wizards.

Starting a publication from scratch

Although the wizards are very helpful, there are times when you will want to start with a blank page and create your own publication.

Select **File/New**. In the Publication catalogue, click on the Blank Publications tab (Fig 2.47).

Click on Full Page, then click on Create.

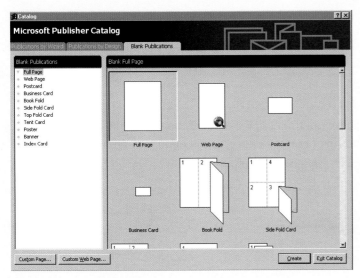

Fig 2.47 *Selecting a blank publication*

The Quick Publication wizard appears, but you are going to ignore that and strike out on your own. You can hide the wizard by clicking on Hide Wizard (Fig 2.48).

Fig 2.48 *The Hide Wizard button*

Changing the orientation of the page

Select **File/Page Setup**. You can now choose to have the page in landscape orientation.

You will be using the Objects toolbar to create new objects on the page (Fig 2.49).

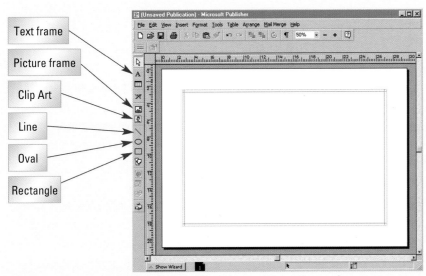

Fig 2.49 *Objects that can be inserted on a page*

Changing the margins on the page

The blue and pink dotted lines mark the margins of the page. You should not place any objects in the margin areas between the margin lines and the edges of the page.

You can change the margins. Select **Arrange/Layout Guides** (Fig 2.50).

Some printers cannot print right to the edge of the paper, so you should always keep a margin of at least 1 cm on each edge.

In this example the margins are changed to 1.5 cm on the left, right, top and bottom of the page.

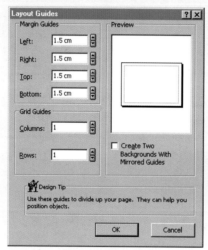

Fig 2.50 *Changing the page margins*

Inserting a text object

Save your publication before you go any further.

You are now going to insert a heading on the page. Click on the Text Frame button in the Objects toolbar. Click on the page, at the position where you want the heading to start. Then hold the mouse button down and drag out a rectangle – this is the text frame. You can change its size later if necessary.

You will see the cursor blinking inside the frame, waiting for you to start keying in some text (Fig 2.51).

Before you do this you should select a suitable size of text from the Formatting toolbar. Start by changing the font size to 28. Again, you can change this later if you like.

Now key in the text for the heading.

You can change the appearance of the heading by highlighting the text in the usual way. You can click on the Bold, Italics or Underline buttons, or change the size, just as you do in a word processor.

In general, do not underline a heading – there are much better ways of drawing attention to it.

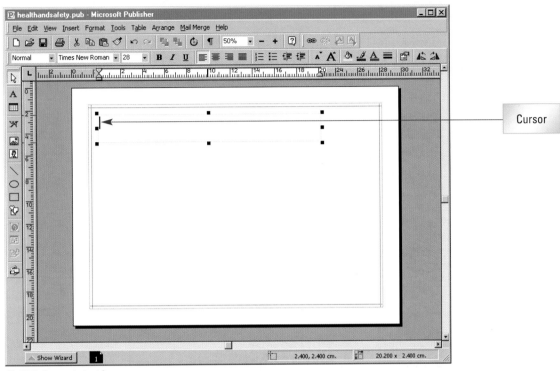

Fig 2.51 *An empty text frame*

You can also align the text within the text frame. Align the text to the centre.
The frame may still not be in the centre of the page, so move the text frame
(Fig 2.52).

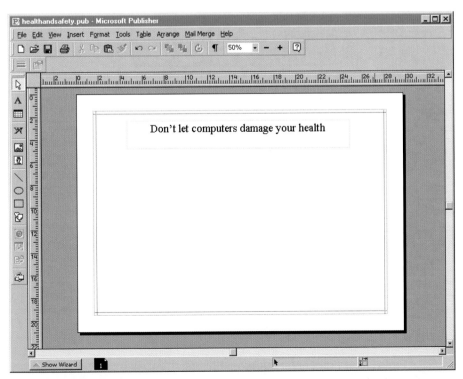

Fig 2.52 *The heading taking shape*

Learning about font types

The heading text will probably be displayed in the font type called Times New Roman. You will have a large number of font types to choose from. To see the list of font types available on your computer, click on the small down arrow to the right of the Font box.

The drop-down list gives the names of the font types and shows what each looks like. The list on your system may be different from the one shown in Fig 2.53.

How do you choose which font type to use?

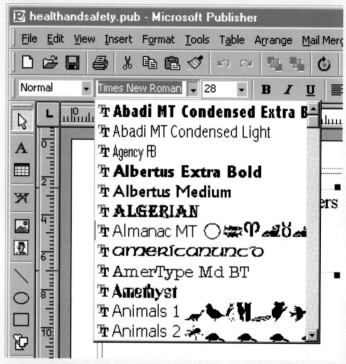

Fig 2.53 *The list of font types*

There are three main kinds of font type:

○ *Serif* fonts (Fig 2.54) have extra marks (serifs) at the ends of the strokes. These imitate the chisel marks left when letters are carved into stone. The most widely used serif font is Times Roman – so called because it was used by the *Times* newspaper and imitated the lettering used in ancient Rome. Serif fonts are used in newspapers because they are easy to read.

> Using Times New Roman
> Using Bookman Old Style
> Using Century School Book
> Using Calisto
> **Using Poster Bodoni**

Fig 2.54 *Serif font types*

Serif fonts look traditional. Readers often feel they can trust text printed in a serif font.

- **Sans serif** fonts (Figs 2.55) lack the extra marks and appear much plainer. But you will find a greater variety of shapes amongst sans serif fonts.

Using Arial
Using Verdana
Using Futura
Using Graphite Light

Fig 2.55 *Sans serif font types*

Sans serif fonts look modern and friendly.

- **Cursive** fonts (Fig 2.56) imitate handwriting, although some of them are based on handwriting styles from over a century ago. They are not very easy to read, especially in a small size.

Using Bradley Hand
Using Lucida Calligraphy
Using Signet Roundhand
Using Viner Hand

Fig 2.56 *Cursive font types*

Cursive fonts look warm and informal, but they should be used with care. They are best used for headings, or for mock signatures.

Give it a go

Have a look at books, notices, posters and other publications to see whether they use serif, sans serif or cursive font types.

Which font types look best?

Choosing a font type

Fonts convey a hidden message to the reader, so choose the ones that give the right impression.

Choose no more than two different font types in a publication – one for headings and the other for the text. You can use different sizes of each font within one publication.

In Fig 2.57 a sans serif font type called HandelGothic is used for the heading.

Highlight the text then select a font type. Experiment a bit until you are pleased with the result. Some font types look better in a heading if bold is used; others look worse.

When you change font types you will find that the text may get wider or narrower. You may decide to change the size of your chosen font. And you may have to change the size of the text frame to fit the heading in one line.

Don't let computers damage your health

Fig 2.57 *Choice of font for heading*

Resizing a text frame

You can stretch or resize a text frame. Click on it, then move the pointer over one of the handles. A resize pointer will appear:

 a resize pointer

Drag on the handle to resize the frame.

Choosing a colour scheme

You can use colours for text and for decorations, such as lines, on your publication. But only do this if you have a colour printer, of course.

It is very easy to use too many colours on a page. You should also use colours that go well together. Publisher lets you choose a colour scheme for your publication. This is a small set of colours that will work together. You used a colour scheme before with the Quick Publication wizard.

Select **Format/Colour Scheme** and make your choice (Fig 2.58).

Alternatively, you can click on Show Wizard at the bottom of the window, then click on Color Scheme. Hide the wizard again, when you have made your choice.

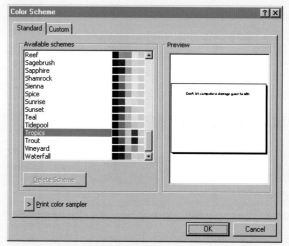

Fig 2.58 Choosing a colour scheme

Font Color button

Scheme colors

More Color Schemes...

More Colors...

Fill Effects...

Fig 2.59 The Font Color button and drop-down menu

Choosing colours for text

Highlight the text, then click on the Font Color button in the Formatting toolbar (Fig 2.59). The colours in your colour scheme will be shown, so select one of these.

You will probably be printing on white paper, so use dark colours from the colour scheme for the text. Light colours cannot be read easily (Fig 2.60).

The only exception to this might be if you want to place light text on a dark background.

Fig 2.60 *Coloured text*

Importing text

Desktop publishing software is very good at importing text and images that have been developed in other software applications.

When you inserted Clip Art in the first publication you were importing the image. You can also import a Word document into your publication.

First, create a new text frame as before.

Select **Insert/Text File**, then find the Word document that you want to import. The text of the file will appear in the frame (Fig 2.61).

Make sure that the Word file you import does not have too much text to fit on the page.

Importing

When you import text or images you add them to your document, even though they have been prepared in a completely different software application.

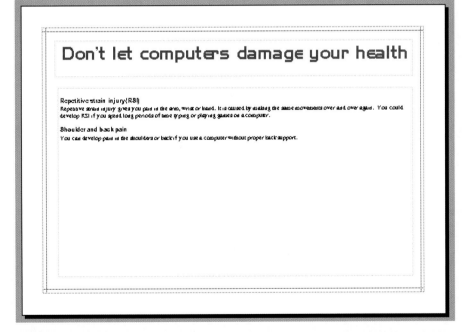

Fig 2.61 *Imported text*

Formatting the imported text

On a notice you will want to use a larger font size than on a normal document. Highlight the text and increase the font size.

If you make the font size too large so that it does not all fit inside the frame, you will notice the **Text in Overflow** symbol (Fig 2.62). This means that some of the text is hidden. To see all the text you must either make the text frame larger or the text size smaller.

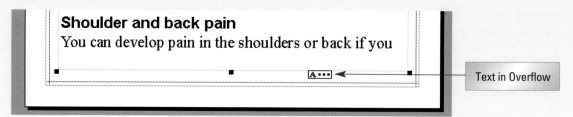

Shoulder and back pain
You can develop pain in the shoulders or back if you

Text in Overflow

Fig 2.62 Text overflow

You can also change the font type. In Fig 2.63, a serif font type called Lucida Bright is used for the text.

If you want to use a colour for some of the text, choose one from your colour scheme.

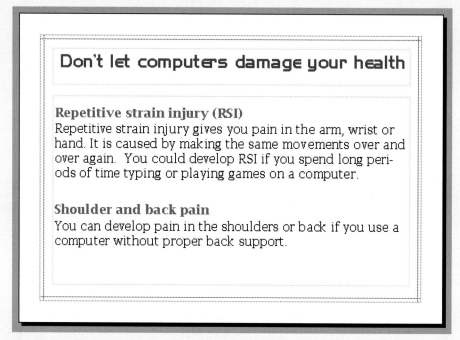

Don't let computers damage your health

Repetitive strain injury (RSI)
Repetitive strain injury gives you pain in the arm, wrist or hand. It is caused by making the same movements over and over again. You could develop RSI if you spend long periods of time typing or playing games on a computer.

Shoulder and back pain
You can develop pain in the shoulders or back if you use a computer without proper back support.

Fig 2.63 Formatted text

Importing Clip Art

You will probably want to add some Clip Art to your notice. It is a mistake to try to add too many images – just choose one or two that draw attention to what you write in the publication.

Click on the Clip Art button on the Objects toolbar. Then click on the page and drag out the picture frame to hold the image.

In the Insert Clip Art dialogue box find a suitable image and insert it as before. Close the Insert Clip Art dialogue box, and you will see the image on the page (Fig 2.64).

You can move the image around to the best position. If you move it over the text frame the characters will shift to get out of the way of the image. This is known as text wrap.

Don't let computers damage your health

Repetitive strain injury (RSI)
Repetitive strain injury gives you pain in the arm, wrist or hand. It is caused by making the same movements over and over again. You could develop RSI if you spend long periods of time typing or playing games on a computer.

Shoulder and back pain
You can develop pain in the shoulders or back if you use a computer without proper back support.

Fig 2.64 *An imported image with text wrapped around it*

Resizing images

You can resize the image by clicking on it then dragging on the picture frame handles.

Be careful about resizing images. If you drag on one of the handles along the sides of the picture frame you will stretch (or squash) the picture in that direction only (Fig 2.65). If you want to keep the picture in proportion choose one of the corner handles.

Fig 2.65 *Images that have been resized in one direction only*

Reflecting an image

You may think that a Clip Art image is the wrong way round. Click on the image to see the Formatting toolbar. You can use the Flip buttons to reflect the image horizontally or vertically (Fig 2.66).

 the Flip Horizontal and Flip Vertical buttons

Fig 2.66 *Using the Flip Horizontal button*

Importing other images

You can import any other image files you have, such as photos or pictures that you have created.

Click on the Picture Frame button in the Objects toolbar, then drag out a frame on the page. Select **Insert/Picture/From file**, and then find the image you want.

Adding a border

You can add a plain or decorative border to a document.

Click on the Rectangle tool in the Objects toolbar, and then use it to draw a rectangle that fits exactly on top of the pink margin.

When you click on the rectangle the Formatting toolbar appears. Click on the Line/Border Style button, then select **More Styles** (Fig 2.67).

Fig 2.67 *The Line/Border Style drop-down menu*

The Border Style dialogue box appears (Fig 2.68). Note the two tabs at the top – Line Border and BorderArt.

In the Line Border tab, you can select the thickness and colour of the line.

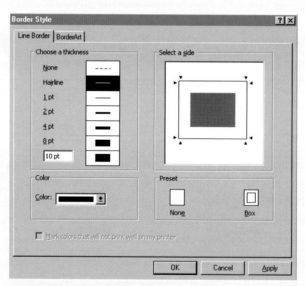

Fig 2.68 *The Border Style dialogue box*

Click on the BorderArt tab to see what it has to offer (Fig 2.69). A border should draw attention to the contents of the document, but it should not be distracting. It is better to choose a simple border, rather than a fussy one.

Choose a border, then choose a colour from your colour scheme.

It may be difficult to see the border properly because of the pink and blue margin lines. You can hide these. Select **View/Hide Boundaries and Guides**. You can make them visible again by selecting View/Show Boundaries and Guides.

Finally, adjust the position and size of all the objects until you are happy with the publication (Fig 2.70).

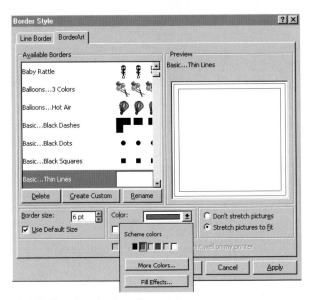

Fig 2.69 *Choosing a border style*

Fig 2.70 *The finished notice*

Skills: drawing

Creating vector graphics

Graphical images are created in two basic formats – bitmap or vector. You used Paint to create bitmap images. In this section you will be creating vector images.

Often the term 'drawing' is used for vector images, whereas 'painting' is used for bitmap images. So if you come across some software with the word 'draw' in its name, it probably lets you create vector images.

Using Microsoft Draw

You can use Microsoft Draw to create vector images. Draw is an unusual piece of software, because you will not find it if you search in the Programs list on your computer. Instead it exists inside other software.

You can find Microsoft Draw in Word and Publisher. You can also use its features in other Microsoft software.

In this activity you will be using Draw within Word, but all the instructions will work just as well in Publisher.

Case study

Visitors to the open day at Kingsmond Community School want to find their way around. You have been asked to draw a plan of the ICT Suite. There are four ICT rooms and an office.

You can, of course, draw a plan of the ICT Suite at your own school instead.

Creating a drawing with Draw in Word

Launch Microsoft Word. Give it a heading then save the document immediately. In Fig 2.71, the page has been set to landscape in **File/Page Setup** by selecting the Page Size tab.

Click on the page where you want the drawing to go. Select **Insert/Picture/New Drawing** (Fig 2.71).

Fig 2.71 *Inserting a new drawing*

Several things now happen.

- A drawing frame appears on the page.
- The Drawing toolbar appears at the bottom of the screen.
- The Autoshapes floating toolbar appears on the screen – don't worry if you can't see this.
- Extra buttons appear in the Standard and Formatting toolbars.
- If you click on the menus at the top of the screen, you will see new options.

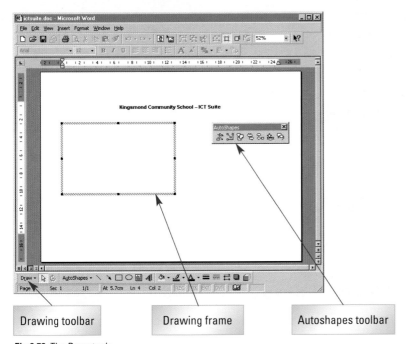

Drawing toolbar   Drawing frame   Autoshapes toolbar

Fig 2.72 *The Draw tools*

In fact, you have started using a new software application, called Draw. Inside the drawing frame you are using Draw; outside the drawing frame you are using Word.

You can change the size of the drawing frame by dragging on one of its handles. Notice that the drawing frame has a thick striped border. This will not be shown when the drawing is printed.

Drawing a rectangle

The Drawing toolbar contains several useful tools.

Click on the Rectangle tool button (Fig 2.73). Draw a rectangle inside the drawing frame. This is the plan for one of the rooms.

The rectangle is an object, just like the objects you used in Publisher.

Move the pointer around the rectangle and you will notice that the pointer changes.

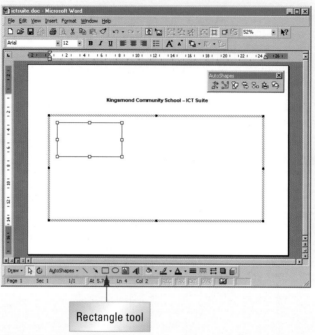

Rectangle tool

Fig 2.73 *Drawing a rectangle*

✛ the Move pointer

↕

↔ the Resize pointers – these are seen when the pointer is over one of
⤡ the handles

⤢

When you see the Move pointer you can drag the rectangle to a new position.

When you see one of the Resize pointers you can change the size of the rectangle. You can keep the proportions of a rectangle if you hold the Shift key down as you drag the corner handle.

Drawing a straight line

Click on the **Line** tool button in the Drawing toolbar:

Use it to draw the door into the room.

╲ the Line tool button

You can draw a line that is exactly horizontal, vertical or at 45 degrees by holding down the Shift key as you draw.

Understanding objects in a vector drawing

You now have two objects in the drawing – a rectangle and a straight line. You can click on each in turn. You can move each object and you can resize each object without affecting the other one.

Click anywhere **inside** the drawing frame but **outside** the rectangle. The handles on the objects now disappear. You can click on an object again to select it and to see the handles.

Remember that you could not do this with a bitmap image in Paint.

Keep saving your document at regular intervals.

Deleting objects

You can delete an object at any time. Click on the object, then press the Delete key on your keyboard.

Returning to the Word document

Click anywhere outside the drawing frame. The drawing frame disappears and the drawing of a rectangle is now part of the Word document (Fig 2.74). You now have the normal Word toolbars back again.

But the drawing frame is still there – it is just hidden.

Click once in the area where the drawing frame is hidden and you will see the frame (Fig 2.75). This time it has a solid edge and handles.

You can use the handles to resize the drawing itself. This will resize the complete drawing and all the objects in it (Fig 2.76).

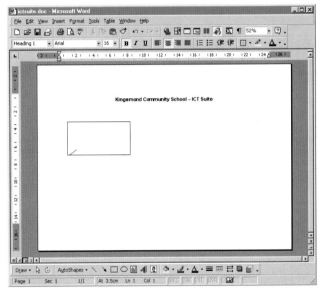

Fig 2.74 *The drawing in the Word document*

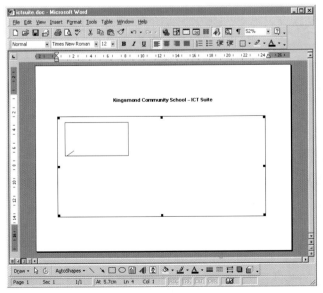

Fig 2.75 *Click to see the frame and handles*

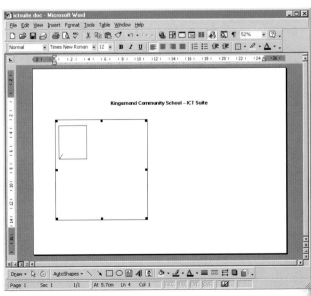

Fig 2.76 *Resizing the complete drawing*

Correcting errors

If you make a mistake at any time, you can click on the Undo button.

Returning to Draw

You can return to Draw and add to your drawing at any time.

Double-click inside the area where the drawing frame is hidden. You will be back again in Draw.

Add further rooms and doors to the plan of the ICT suite (Fig 2.77).

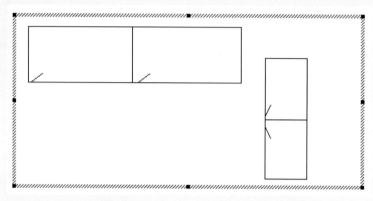

Fig 2.77 *Working on the drawing*

Drawing a square

Fig 2.78 *A perfect square*

If you want to draw a perfect square (Fig 2.78), hold down the Shift key whilst you use the Rectangle tool.

Drawing ovals and circles

You can draw an oval with the Oval tool in the Drawing toolbar. If you want to draw a perfect circle, hold down the Shift key as you draw (Fig 2.79).

Fig 2.79 *An oval and a perfect circle*

Placing an object in front of others

Draw an object in front of another object, like the rectangle in Fig 2.80.

The object behind it cannot be seen. Think of each object as a separate piece of paper that is moved around and placed on top of other pieces of paper.

You can send an object to the back – this has the effect of placing it behind the other objects. This changes the order in which the objects are placed on the drawing.

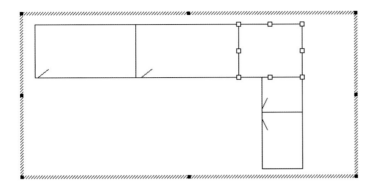

Fig 2.80 *One object in front of another*

Click on the object that you want to send to the back. In the Drawing toolbar, click on Draw, then Order, then Send to Back (Fig 2.81).

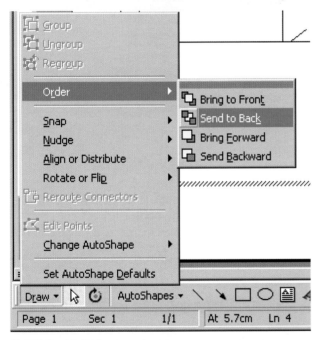

Fig 2.81 *Send to Back command*

The object is now behind the other objects (Fig 2.82).

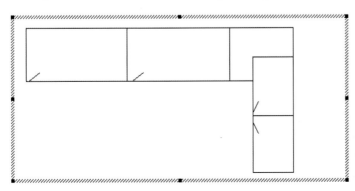

87

Fig 2.82 *Placing an object behind others*

Changing the thickness of lines

You can change the thickness of a line. Click on the line, then click on the Line Style button in the Drawing toolbar (Fig 2.83). Select the thickness you want.

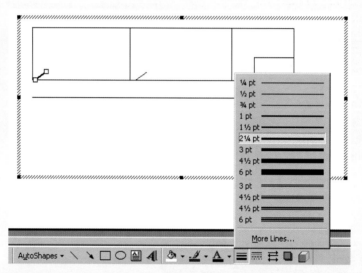

Fig 2.83 *Choosing the thickness of a line*

Changing the colour of lines

You can change the colour of a line. Click on the line. Find the Line Color button in the Drawing toolbar. It shows a colour beneath a brush:

the Line Color button

If you click on this button it will change the colour of your line to the colour shown on the button.

If you want another colour, click on the arrow beside the button, then make your choice of colour.

You can also use the Line Color button to change the colour of the lines around a shape, such as a rectangle (Fig 2.84).

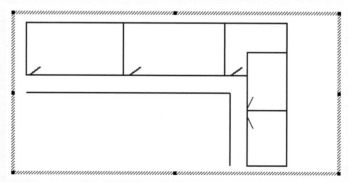

Fig 2.84 *Lines are now thicker and in colour*

Filling an object with colour

You can fill a closed shape, like a rectangle, with a colour.

In the plan you can use colours to identify the rooms. For example, the rooms used by Years 7–11 could be filled with one colour, and the rooms used by Years 12 and 13 could be in another colour.

Click on a rectangle, then click on the Fill Color button in the Drawing toolbar:

the Fill Color button

This will fill the rectangle with the colour shown on the Fill Color button. To choose another colour, click on the arrow to the right of the button (Fig 2.85).

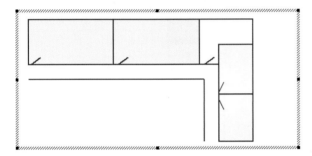

Fig 2.85 *Some rectangles have been filled with colour*

Filling an object with a texture or pattern

The odd-shaped room in the corner is an office. You can fill it with a pattern to indicate that it will not be open to visitors on open day.

Click on the object, then click on the arrow beside the Fill Color button. Then click on Fill Effects (Fig 2.86).

There are four tabs at the top of the Fill Effects dialogue box. Click on the Pattern tab.

Click on the pattern you want. Then select the colours for the pattern in the Foreground and Background boxes (Fig 2.87).

You can use a texture instead of a pattern. In the Fill Effects dialogue box, click on the Texture tab and choose the texture you want.

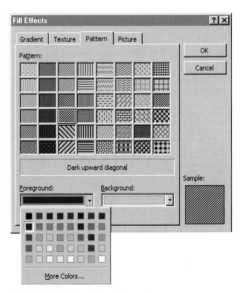

Fig 2.86 *Choosing a fill pattern*

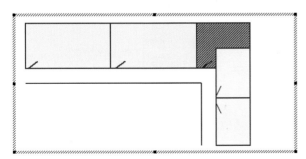

Fig 2.87 *A fill pattern*

Adding arrows

You can add an arrow to your drawing by clicking on the Arrow tool button in the Drawing toolbar:

↘ the Arrow tool button

You can change the appearance of an arrow. Click on the arrow, then click on the Arrow Style button in the Drawing toolbar:

⇄ the Arrow Style button

Choose the style from the options shown.

Use the Line Style button to change the thickness of an arrow (Fig 2.88).

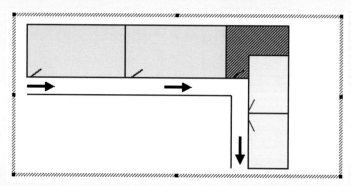

Fig 2.88 *Arrows added to the drawing*

Using Autoshapes

You can show the layout of the furniture in a room by adding extra lines, rectangles and autoshapes.

Autoshapes are useful line drawings that you can add to your drawing. They can easily be resized. You can select an Autoshape by either using the button in the Drawing toolbar, or by using the Autoshape floating toolbar, if you can see it.

Click on the Autoshape button in the Drawing toolbar, and you will see a choice of categories – lines, connectors, etc. (Fig 2.89). You are going to use a simple shape to represent a chair. You can look through all the Autoshapes to find one that is suitable. In the Flowchart category there is a half circle which will do the trick.

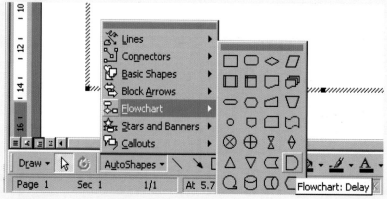

Fig 2.89 *Choosing an Autoshape*

Click on the Flowchart category and select the shape, which is called Flowchart:Delay.

Click on the drawing and the shape appears. Like any object you can drag on the handles of the shape to resize it (Fig 2.90).

You can use the Line Style, Line Color and Fill Color tools with any autoshape.

Once you have changed the Autoshape so that it is the right shape and size to represent a chair, you will need several copies of it. Use Copy and Paste to create these copies and then move each one into place on the drawing (Fig 2.91).

Fig 2.90 *An Autoshape inserted on a drawing*

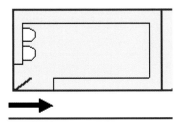

Fig 2.91 *Some of the Autoshapes in place on the drawing.*

Reflecting and rotating a shape

Any object that you create in Draw can be reflected (flipped) or rotated. You will reflect and rotate some of the chair images so that they can be placed around the plan of the room.

Click on the object that you want to change. Click on Draw in the Drawing toolbar, then click on Rotate or Flip (Fig 2.92). You can then choose Flip Horizontal or Flip Vertical. You will also want to rotate some of the chair images to the left or right (Fig 2.93).

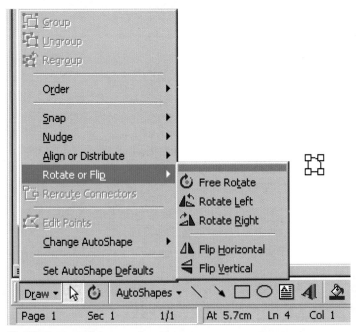

Fig 2.92 *Rotate or Flip commands*

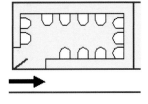

Fig 2.93 *More chairs in the room*

Adding text objects

You can add a text object to the drawing. Click on the Text Box tool in the Drawing toolbar:

 the Text box tool

Click inside the drawing frame on your page, and a text box will appear. The cursor inside will be blinking and waiting for your input (Fig 2.94). You can change the size of the text box object by dragging on its handles.

Fig 2.94 *A text box*

Notice that the Formatting toolbar now has the text formatting buttons on it.

You can change the font type, style and size. Highlight the text in the text box and use the buttons in the Formatting toolbar as usual.

You can move a text box so that it lies in front of other objects. Text boxes do not have fill colours to begin with. That means that you can see whatever is behind the text box (Fig 2.95).

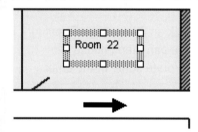

Fig 2.95 *A text box in place*

Add further text boxes to the drawing.

Using colours with text objects

You can change the colour of the text in a text box. Highlight the text then use the Font Color button on the Drawing toolbar:

 the Font color button

You can also fill the text box with a background colour. Click on the text box, then use the Fill Color button on the Drawing toolbar.

Finally you can add a line border to a text box by using the Line Color and Line Style buttons on the Drawing toolbar.

Completing the drawing

Some extra objects have been added to the drawing (see Fig 2.96). Can you work out how they were done?

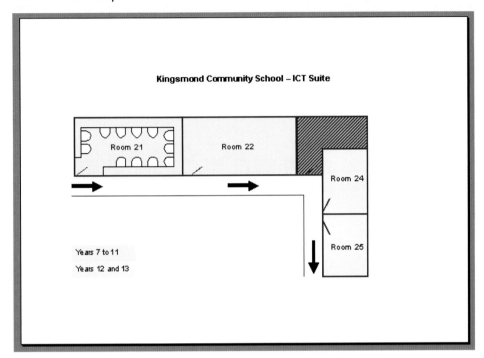

Fig 2.96 The completed drawing

Practice questions

Foundation

1 A leisure centre wants to use a software package to design leaflets to advertise the facilities on offer.
   List three features of a software package that would be particularly helpful for this task.

2 Where could each of the following types of output be used? Give one example of each.
   a LCD screen.
   b Plasma screen.
   c Multimedia projector.

3 What kind of document could be produced with each of these printers?
   a Laser printer.
   b Dot matrix printer.
   c Plotter.

4 In business, which of these best describes a presentation?
   A A folder containing lots of pictures.
   B A talk with computer-generated illustrations.
   C A film.
   D A comedy act.

5 In business, explain the difference between a report and a leaflet.

6 List three health problems that could arise from using a computer. In each case, explain how you could prevent the problem occurring.

7 Outline the main Health and Safety regulations that affect people who use computers in the UK.

Higher

8 Word processing and desktop publishing packages have many features in common. Why do we need both types of package? Identify some features in each type of package which do not appear in the other.

9 Describe the factors that should be taken into consideration when designing an office that will be used by six people, each using their own networked computer.

3 Storing data

Case study: Oakcroft youth centre

Oakcroft youth centre is very popular with 13–19-year-olds in the town. It has a general-purpose hall with a servery and kitchen, a sports hall with a basketball pitch and several other smaller rooms. One of the rooms is used as an ICT room with three rather old and slow standalone computers.

The senior youth leader is Mandi Patterson. She shares an office with other youth leaders and volunteers. They have another old standalone computer system. This is used for keeping records of the club's activities, writing letters, keeping track of spending, etc.

The members of the youth centre are planning a dance marathon. They hope to raise funds to buy some new computers for the members to use. A number of members have volunteered to help organise the event, including Jason Smith.

Storage: internal memory

Let's look again at part of the picture of a computer system (Fig 3.1).

The storage components hold the data that make the hardware work. Some forms of storage hold data permanently, whilst others only hold it temporarily. Some forms of storage let you access data extremely fast, whilst others work much more slowly.

By far the most important storage is known as internal memory, but you will not be very familiar with it because it is hidden away inside the main computer case.

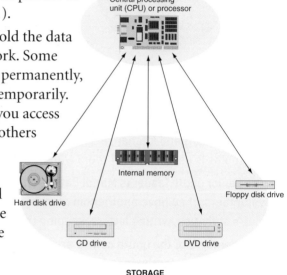

Fig 3.1 Storage in a computer system

Internal memory

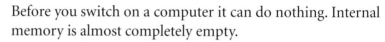

Before you switch on a computer it can do nothing. Internal memory is almost completely empty.

But one small part of internal memory does hold data all the time. It holds the permanent instructions that are needed to wake up the computer when it is switched on. These instructions are a tiny part of the whole operating system and are known as the boot system (Fig 3.2).

When you switch the computer on you can see quite a bit of activity on the screen for the first few minutes. During this time the computer loads up the operating system software (Fig 3.3).

This could be a version of Microsoft Windows, or it could be one of the many alternative operating systems that are available.

You will then probably choose to load some applications software, such as a word processor (e.g. Word – Fig 3.4).

Finally, you will start working on a document (Fig 3.5).

At each stage, data is being stored in the internal memory of the computer system. The internal memory holds the operating system, the applications software and the data about any documents that you are working on.

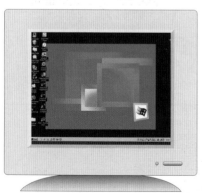

Fig 3.2 Internal memory is empty (apart from the boot system)

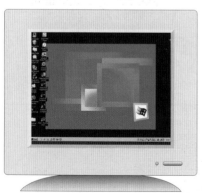

Fig 3.3 Internal memory holds the operating system software

Fig 3.4 Internal memory holds the operating system software plus the applications software

Volatile memory

When you switch off the computer almost all the data stored in internal memory disappears. So when you next switch it on you have to start the process all over again.

We say that most of internal memory is 'volatile', which means that it only holds data whilst it is being supplied with electrical power.

One very small section of internal memory is not volatile. This section holds the boot system which has to be ready to work as soon as the power is switched on.

Fig 3.5 *Internal memory holds the operating system software plus the applications software plus the data about the document*

Integrated circuit

Internal memory is made out of integrated circuits. An integrated circuit is an extremely small electronic circuit. It is created out of silicon. Silicon is a material that is a semiconductor, which means that sometimes it conducts electricity and sometimes it doesn't. Sometimes you will see the term 'semiconductor memory' – that is simply another way of referring to a silicon integrated circuit.

These tiny pieces of silicon that contain the electronic integrated circuits are often known as chips (Fig 3.6). An integrated circuit is always held in a protective plastic case, which has pins leading from it. The pins are used to connect an integrated circuit to the rest of the computer system.

Fig 3.6 *A silicon chip*

RAM integrated circuit

A RAM integrated circuit is volatile. It does need electrical power to hold on to the data, but when it is working the data can be accessed very quickly. Almost all the internal memory of a computer is made out of RAM integrated circuits (Fig 3.7).

Fig 3.7 *A RAM chip*

ROM integrated circuit

A ROM integrated circuit is not volatile. It holds data permanently. A ROM integrated circuit is used in internal memory to hold the boot system (Fig 3.8).

RAM

Random Access Memory is a method for storing data so that it can be deleted and changed. Any data stored on RAM can be accessed immediately.

ROM

Read-Only Memory is a method for storing data permanently. The data on ROM storage cannot be changed.

Fig 3.8 *ROM chip*

Storage: magnetic media

The RAM integrated circuits that make up most internal memory are volatile. That means they do not hold data when the computer is switched off.

When a computer is switched on it has a tiny boot system already in place on a ROM integrated circuit. The rest of the operating system must be loaded into internal memory. But where is it loaded from?

Backing store

The answer is that a copy of the operating system software is kept on backing store. This usually means that it is stored on a hard disk.

Fig 3.1 on page 96 shows a number of different forms of storage – internal memory, hard disk drive, floppy disk drive, CD drive, DVD drive. All, except for internal memory, count as backing store.

Backing store is where data is kept safely, ready to be loaded into internal memory. Usually, the backing stores in a computer system hold far more data than can be fitted into internal memory, so data is loaded only when it is needed.

Backing store is not volatile.

Loading and saving data

Remember that a computer needs many types of data, including operating systems software, applications software and all kinds of data files, such as documents and images.

When data is loaded it is copied from backing store into internal memory. When data is saved it is copied from internal memory to backing store (Fig 3.9).

Storage device

A storage device is a machine that handles the storage of data. For example, a disk drive is a storage device.

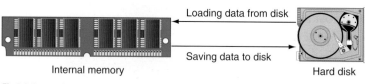

Loading data from disk

Saving data to disk

Internal memory

Hard disk

Fig 3.9 *Internal memory*

Storage media

Storage media are the actual disks and tapes on which the data is stored. (Note that 'media' is the plural of 'medium.')

Magnetic media

Hard disks, floppy disks and tapes are magnetic media. Tiny spots on the surface of the tape or disk are set up as individual magnets. The magnetic field of each spot is set in one of two directions. Thousands, or millions, of magnetic spots together create the codes that computers work with.

Hard disk

A hard disk (Fig 3.10) is a magnetic storage medium. It is a RAM medium so the data on it can be changed. The disk is usually made of metal or glass with a layer of a magnetic material on the surface.

A hard disk is placed in a hard disk drive (HDD). This case protects the disk from dust and damp (Fig 3.11).

Fig 3.10 *A hard disk*

Almost all computer systems use hard disks as their main backing store. You cannot normally see the hard disk or the drive as they are kept inside the computer case. But you can often hear it whirring when the computer is running.

Although we usually talk about the hard disk in a computer system, in practice two or more disks are normally stacked on top of each other inside the hard disk drive. Several disks can hold more data than a single disk.

Fig 3.11 *A hard disk drive*

Floppy disk

A floppy disk is also a magnetic medium. The disk itself is made of a flexible plastic with a magnetic surface (Fig 3.12).

Unlike a hard disk, a floppy disk can be carried around. It is useful for taking data from one computer to another. It can also be used to store copies of important data safely.

Fig 3.12 *A floppy disk*

Floppy disks are also RAM media, but they do not hold a great deal of data, so they are not used as much today as they were in the past. You should treat a floppy disk with care. They can easily get dirty, which damages the data and makes them unusable.

The floppy disk drive (Fig 3.13) has a slot at the front of a computer case so you can insert or remove a disk whenever you need to.

Magnetic tape

Tapes are magnetic media and are mainly used for security purposes. The complete contents of a hard disk may be copied to tape daily, and the tapes stored carefully in case the hard disk is damaged (Figs 3.14 and 3.15).

Fig 3.13 *A floppy disk drive*

Digital audio tapes (DAT) are commonly used, although other formats are available.

Fig 3.14 *Digital tape*

Fig 3.15 *A digital tape drive*

Storage: optical media

Optical media are disks made out of metal and coated with a clear plastic. Like magnetic media, they also use millions of tiny spots on the surface of the disk to create the computer codes. In optical media the spots are either tiny pits on the metal surface or flat areas. The light from a laser reflects cleanly from a flat area but is scattered by a pit, so a laser beam is used to tell which is which.

Optical disks are quite tough, but you should still be careful not to damage them. They should be kept in their boxes when not in use.

CD

Compact Disks have been used for many years for audio. They are optical media, and can be used successfully for storing computer data as well. There are three main types – CD-ROM (Fig 3.16), CD-R and CD-RW. CDs hold much more data than floppy disks.

A CD drive on a computer (Fig 3.17) can also play audio CDs.

Fig 3.16 *A CD-ROM disk*

Fig 3.17 *CD drive*

CD-ROM

The data on a CD-ROM cannot be changed in any way. Most computer systems are equipped with a CD-ROM drive these days.

When you buy some new software it is usually provided on a CD-ROM. You can then insert it into your own computer and install the software. When software is installed the files are copied from the CD-ROM on to the hard disk of the computer.

Other data is sometimes provided on a CD-ROM. For example, you can buy encyclopaedias and other reference works on a CD-ROM. You can also buy disks of Clip Art images, or you can arrange for the photographs on a film to be copied on to a CD.

CD-R

CD-Recordable disks are CD disks that you can write data on. You need to have a special CD drive that can write data as well as read it.

Recording (writing) data on a CD-R disk is often referred to as 'burning' the CD, as the tiny pits have to be burnt out of the surface.

Once some data has been written on the surface of the CD-R it cannot be altered in any way.

A CD-R drive can read any CD-ROM as well.

CD-RW

CD-ReWritable disks are CD disks that can be both erased and written to. That means you can add and delete data as much as you like. Once again, you do need to have a specific CD drive that can write data as well as read it, as well as suitable software.

A CD-RW drive can work with CD-R disks as well. It can also read CD-ROMs and audio CDs.

DVD

Digital **V**ersatile **D**isks were developed because CDs were not very good for storing video. In computer systems they are the best media for storing software that uses a lot of moving images. They also hold much more data than CDs.

A DVD drive on a computer can also play video DVDs.

DVDs and DVD drives look very similar to CDs and CD drives.

DVD-ROM

DVD-ROM disks are similar to CD-ROM disks as the data on each cannot be changed. The main advantage of a DVD-ROM over a CD-ROM is that it holds more data, so can be used to hold software that uses a lot of images, sounds or video.

DVD-R

DVD-Recordable disks are similar to CD-R disks.

Of course, you do need a DVD-R or DVD-RW drive in order to record data on to a DVD-R.

DVD-RW and DVD-RAM

DVD-ReWritable and DVD-RAM disks are two types of DVD disks that can be both erased and written to. That means you can add and delete data as much as you like. Once again, you do need to have a DVD drive that can write data as well as read it, as well as suitable software.

How much data?

Bit

A bit (binary digit) is the smallest piece of data that a computer can handle.

Bits and bytes

Data is stored on magnetic and optical media by marking tiny spots on the surface. Each spot represents one bit.

Bits are usually arranged in groups of eight, known as a byte. Computers need a combination of eight bits to create many of the codes they use. For example, each character that you use on the keyboard has a computer code that uses eight bits, or one byte.

Byte

One byte is 8 bits.

Kilobytes, megabytes and gigabytes

You already know that 'kilo' means one thousand. So 1 kilometre = 1,000 metres. In ICT one kilobyte is approximately 1,000 bytes. In fact, a kilobyte is slightly more than 1,000 bytes – but for all practical purposes you can think of it as 1,000 bytes.

'Mega' means one million, so a megabyte is near enough one million bytes. 'Giga' means one thousand million, so a gigabyte is approximately one thousand million bytes:

Capacity

Capacity is the amount of data that can be stored. Capacity is measured in bytes, kilobytes (KB), megabytes (MB) or gigabytes (GB).

1 byte (B) = 8 bits
1 kilobyte (KB) = 1,000 bytes (approximately)
1 megabyte (MB) = 1,000 KB = 1,000,000 bytes (approximately)
1 gigabyte (GB) = 1,000 MB = 1,000,000 KB = 1,000,000,000 bytes (approximately)

Capacity of media

Table 3.1 Storage capacities

Medium	Capacity	Capacity in bytes (approximately)
Internal memory (RAM)	512 MB	512,000,000
Hard disk	120 GB	120,000,000,000
Floppy disk	1.44 MB	1,440,000
Tape	10 GB	10,000,000,000
CD	650 MB	650,000,000
DVD	4.7 GB	4,700,000,000

Integrated circuits, disks and tapes can hold vast amounts of data. But they can get full.

Table 3.1 shows the typical capacities of storage for computers on sale at the time of writing (early 2004). The capacity of media is increasing all the time, so you might like to buy a computer magazine to check the current figures.

Give it a go

You can find out the capacity of the storage media that you use.

1 Internal Memory – On the desktop, right-click on My Computer, then select **Properties**. In Fig 3.18, the capacity of the internal memory (RAM) is 512 megabytes.

2 Backing stores – Double-click on My Computer from the desktop. You will see a list of all the drives. Right-click on one of them, then click on Properties. In Fig 3.19, the hard disk in drive D has a capacity of 27.9 GB, of which 5.14 GB has been used.

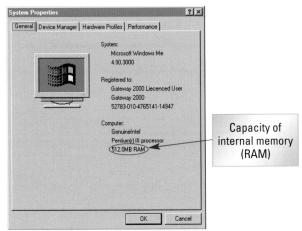

Fig 3.18 The capacity of internal memory

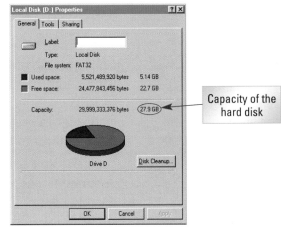

Fig 3.19 The capacity of a hard disk drive

Size of files

All the data in a computer file is coded and then stored in bytes. We measure the size of files in bytes and kilobytes (KB).

Give it a go

You can find out the size of files saved on your hard drive.
Open My Documents, click on the Views icon and select **Details**
(Fig. 3.20). Now check the size of the files on your computer.

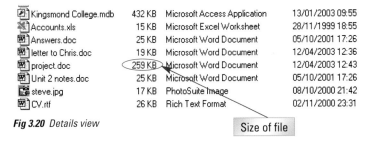

Fig 3.20 Details view

Compressing files

Some files are very large. Video, movie, photograph and sound files can all take up many megabytes of space.

A large file can be reduced in size by compressing it. Compressing removes any empty space in the file and avoids repeating the same data over and over again. A compressed file can be considerably smaller than the original file.

One popular method of compressing a file is to create a 'zip' file (Fig 3.21). The zip software can reduce a file by up to 90%. The new zip file can then be placed on a disk or sent by email.

The zip file cannot be used as it is. The zip software is used to expand it back to its original size so it can be used again.

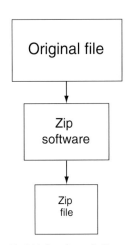

Fig 3.21 Creating a zip file

Transferring data

Copying and pasting

You already know that you can copy and paste images from graphics software to word-processing software. In fact, you can paste images into most applications software.

You can also copy and paste documents and parts of documents from one applications software to another (see Fig 3.22).

Fig 3.22 *Spreadsheet data copied to a word-processed document*

Transferring data within a software family

The Microsoft applications include Word, Excel, PowerPoint, Access, Publisher and FrontPage. These have been designed so that data can be transferred from one application to another, so you can copy and paste from one to the other. They form a software family – so called because they are related to each other.

Other software suppliers have also developed software families, including Adobe and Corel.

You can usually only copy and paste successfully between documents in the same family.

Inserting image files

Image files are used in all kinds of software and across all the software families. Almost all applications software allows you to insert or import an image file, no matter how the image was first created.

You don't actually need any graphics software to do this; you simply need an image file.

Standard file formats

You are able to insert an image into almost any application because images are stored in standard file formats. Applications software is designed to handle all the common file formats. There are several image file formats, and each has its own filename extension, such as .bmp, .jpg, .gif, .tif and .png.

There are a number of other standard file formats that you may come across:

.htm or .html – files created in **H**yper**T**ext **M**arkup **L**anguage, which is the standard format for web pages.

.txt – files that contain simple text characters only.

.rtf – files saved in **R**ich **T**ext **F**ormat, which is a simplified word processing format.

Case study

Jason Smith is helping to organise the disco at Oakcroft youth centre. He has a computer at home and has used a word-processing application to create a poster.

Jason wants to share the poster with the other members of the group so they can check it and suggest improvements. He could:

◎ print it out then show it to them when they next meet;
◎ print it out then post it to them;
◎ put the file on a floppy disk or a CD and take the disk when they next meet, or even post it to them; or
◎ send the file by email to them.

Which methods should he use, and why?

Transferring files between computers

A data file can be transferred from one computer to another, either on a disk or by email. But the second computer will only be able to use the data file if:
◎ the applications software that was used to create the file on the first computer is also installed on the second computer; or
◎ the file is in a standard file format.

Transferring files between different software versions

When new software is released it is often referred to as Version 1. After a year or so, Version 2 may be released. This version will have new features, and it will also have corrected any errors in Version 1. For example, Version 2 of a particular word processing software may allow you to add a fancy border to a page, whereas Version 1 may not have this feature.

Suppose you create a document in Version 2 which uses one of the new features that are not in Version 1. You now transfer the document file to another computer that only has Version 1. What happens? The second computer will not be able to display the border. It might even not be able to handle the file at all.

Give it a go

You can check which version of the software you are using. If you click on the Help menu you will usually see **About** followed by the name of the software. Click on this to find the version number.

Evaluating hardware and software

Evaluate

When we evaluate something we assess how suitable it is for its intended use.

If someone asks you to help him or her to choose a computer system, you should ask this person these questions:

◎ What do you want to use the computer for?

◎ How much do you want to spend?

◎ Do you have any special requirements?

You may wonder why there are so many computer systems and peripherals on the market. The reason is because people do many different things with their computers, so they all have different needs.

So when you plan a new computer don't imagine there is one perfect computer system that will suit everyone.

Hardware

You can evaluate hardware by thinking about these factors:

◎ *Capacity*   Internal memory has to be large enough to store the operating system, plus any applications software and data files as they are used. The hard disk has to be large enough to store all the files that you might need at any time. Remember that image and sound files can be very large.

◎ *Transferability*   If you are going to transfer files *from* somewhere else you need a floppy disk, CD or DVD drive. If you are going to transfer files *to* another computer you need a drive that can write data as well as read it.

◎ *Speed*   CD and DVD drives work at different speeds. A fast drive is useful if you are going to use it a lot, but is more expensive than a slower one.

◎ *Ease of use*   The mouse and keyboard should be easy to use.

◎ *Quality of output*   The screen should be large enough and clear enough. The printer should produce output of the quality that you need. Generally speaking, the more expensive the peripheral is, the better the quality.

◎ **Robustness**   Peripherals have to be quite tough to cope with daily use. Flimsy cases, paper trays and keyboards do not last very long.

◎ **Cost**   Complete computer systems come in a wide range of prices. It is best to go for the highest-capacity internal memory and hard disk that you can afford, provided the screen and printer are at least satisfactory.

Software

You can evaluate software by thinking about these factors:

◎ **What it does**   Two similar pieces of software, such as graphics packages, may in fact let you do very different things. The software must be able do what you want it to do.

◎ **Support for standard file formats**   For many applications it is important that the software can handle standard file formats for images, sounds, etc.

◎ **Easy to learn**   The applications software should be easy to learn.

◎ **Support**   There should be help available. This could be in the form of the Office Assistant (in Microsoft software) or in separate Help files.

◎ **Cost**   Software can vary a great deal in price. Some software is even free. Sometimes the cheap software is as good as the expensive software, but you do have to check that the software does what you want it to do.

Case study

The members of Oakcroft youth centre are hoping to raise enough money to buy some new computers that all the members can use. The main uses of the computers will be to play games and to produce posters, notices and leaflets. They want to buy as many computers as they can afford.

◎ Can you suggest what they should buy? Include all the hardware and software – although you don't need to identify the games.

◎ Have a look at computer magazines and advertisements for ideas.

Mandi Patterson, the youth leader, wants to replace the office computer with a new one. She has about £2,000 to spend, and this should cover all the hardware and software.

◎ Can you suggest what she should buy?

Skills: spreadsheets

Workbook

A workbook is a collection of spreadsheets that all relate to the same topic.

Improving your spreadsheet skills

You will probably have used a spreadsheet application, like Microsoft Excel, before. In this section you can revise what you know already, and develop your skills further.

Looking at the Excel window

Open a new workbook in Excel. The window will look as in Fig 3.23. This shows the first worksheet in the workbook.

The worksheet is divided into many cells. In Excel the columns of cells are referred to by letters. The rows of cells are referred to by numbers. The cell that is highlighted has the address E11 (column E, row 11). The cell address is shown in the Name box.

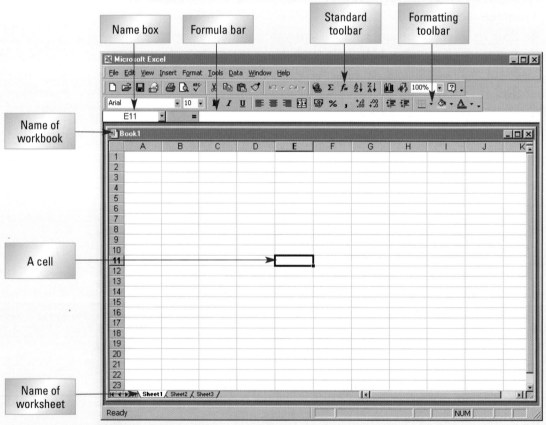

Fig 3.23 The Excel window

Case study

At Oakcroft youth centre, Mandi keeps accounts of all the money raised by events so far. The money will be used to buy new computers for the members to use.

Getting started

First give a name to the worksheet you are working on. Right-click on the tab labelled Sheet 1 at the bottom of the window (Fig 3.24). Select **Rename**, then key in Fundraising as the name of the worksheet.

Next save the workbook by clicking on the Save button. We have called it Youth Centre Events.

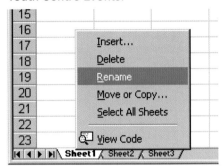

Fig 3.24 *Renaming a worksheet*

Entering data

You can enter text or numbers in any of the cells. We will start by entering a heading in cell A1. Notice that the text appears in the Formula bar as well as in the cell (Fig 3.25). When you have finished entering the text for the cell, either click on the Enter button next to the Formula bar, or press the Enter key:

✔ the Enter button

The text is too long to fit in the cell. The cells next to it are empty, so it appears to overflow across the page, but all the text is held in cell A1.

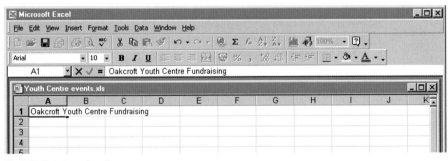

Fig 3.25 *Entering a heading*

You click on a cell to select it and then use any of the buttons on the Formatting toolbar to change the size and colour of the text (Fig 3.26).

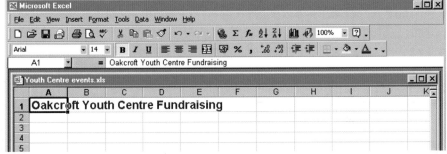

Fig 3.26 *Formatting the text in a cell*

Enter the three headings for the table: Date, Event and Amount Raised.

You can format more than one cell at a time. Click on the cell with the word Date, then hold the mouse button down as you move the pointer over the cells containing Event and Amount raised. This highlights and selects all three cells at once, so you can make all three bold at the same time (Fig 3.27).

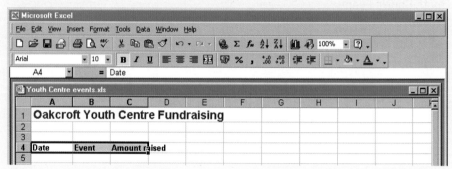

Fig 3.27 *Selecting more than one cell*

Changing the width of a column

If one of the columns is not wide enough, click on the column headings. Click on the line immediately to the right of the column that you want to widen, then drag it to the right (Fig 3.28).

Widen the column here

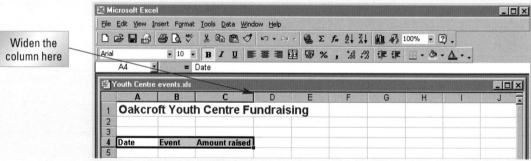

Fig 3.28 *Making a column wider*

Entering dates

Enter a date in the first cell below the heading Date.

Excel recognises several date formats, including:

- 09/02/04 and 9/2/2004 – if you enter either of these it will display it as 09/02/2004.
- 9-February-04 and 9-Feb-2004 – if you enter either of these it will display it as 09-Feb-04.

Important note: In the USA dates are displayed showing the month first, e.g. 2/9/2004 is February 9th, 2004. You computer system should have been set up to display UK date formats. If you have any problems with this, speak to the network administrator.

Deleting data

To delete the data in a cell, click on the cell, then press the Delete key on the keyboard. Alternatively, you can right-click on the cell and select **Clear Contents**.

You can delete the data in several cells by highlighting them all together. Right-click and select **Clear Contents** (Fig 3.29).

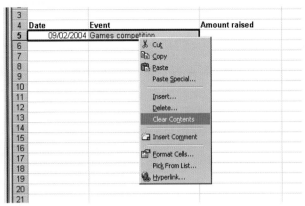

Fig 3.29 *Deleting the contents from cells*

Entering and formatting numbers

Excel recognises numbers when they are entered. But have a look at the numbers in this worksheet. The actual numbers that were entered were 20.40, 25.35 and 136.00, but Excel has removed zeros after the decimal point (see Fig 3.30).

	A	B	C	D	E	F	G
1	**Oakcroft Youth Centre Fundraising**						
2							
3							
4	**Date**	**Event**	**Amount raised**				
5	09/02/2004	Games competition	20.4				
6	14/02/2004	Valentines Party	25.35				
7	25/02/2004	Sponsored cleanup	136				
8							
9							

Fig 3.30 *Entering numbers*

You need to format the numbers in the Amount raised column. Click on the C at the top of the column; this highlights the whole column. Then right-click and select **Format Cells**.

In the Format Cells dialogue box (Fig 3.31), make sure that the Number tab is clicked at the top. In the Category list, select **Number**. In the Decimal places box, select 2. Click on OK.

The numbers now line up neatly, with two decimal places. You have applied this number format to the whole of C column (see Fig 3.32). One cell has text in it and Excel ignores the number formatting in cells that contain text.

Amount raised
20.40
25.35
136.00

Fig 3.32 *Two decimal places number format*

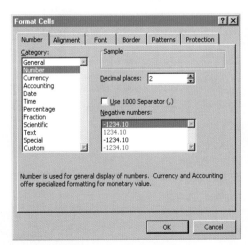

Fig 3.31 *Formatting numbers*

Amount raised
20
25
136

Fig 3.33 *Zero decimal places*

If you wanted to see the amounts in whole numbers only, you should select zero decimal places in the Format Cells dialogue box. That would give the result shown in Fig 3.33.

We will be using two decimal places so that the pence show as well as the pounds.

Alignment

Notice that Excel aligns text to the left of cells, but aligns dates and numbers to the right.

You can change this if you like. Highlight the cells you want to align – in this case we have highlighted the dates. Right-click and select **Format Cells** (Fig 3.34). In the Format Cells dialogue box, select the Alignment tab. Make your choice for horizontal alignment.

The data in those cells is now aligned as required (Fig 3.35).

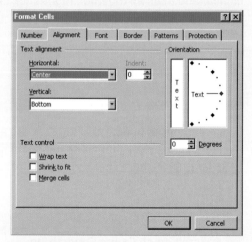

Fig 3.34 *Aligning data in cells*

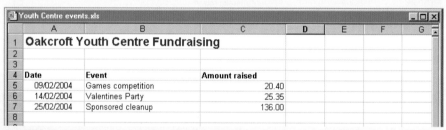

Fig 3.35 *Data aligned in the centre (in the Dates column)*

Using a formula

One of the most powerful aspects of a spreadsheet is its ability to do calculations for you. You will get the spreadsheet to add up the three numbers in cells C5, C6 and C7, and to put the result in cell C9.

All calculations are done by using a formula. In this case the formula will be:

C9=C5+C6+C7

Click on cell C9 then enter the rest of the formula – that is:

=C5+C6+C7

then either click on the Enter button or press the Enter key on the keyboard.

Note that the formula appears in the Formula bar. The formula must begin with =. If you omit the equals sign Excel does not know that it is a calculation.

The result appears in the cell (Fig 3.36). Add some text to the cell next to it to explain what it is.

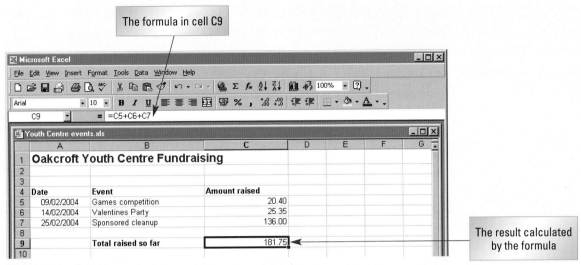

Fig 3.36 A formula and the result

Entering a formula the easy way

There is another way of entering a formula that you will find helpful and much quicker.

1 Click on cell C9, and press the Delete key to remove the formula.
2 Key in =.
3 Next, click on the actual cell C5, which is the first one in the formula. Cell C5 is now given a flashing border, and the text '=C5' appears in C9 (Fig 3.37).
4 Key in +.
5 Now click on cell C6, and its name appears in C9 (see Fig 3.38).
6 Key in +, then click on cell C7.

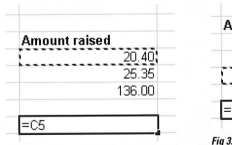

Fig 3.37 Another way to enter a formula

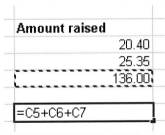

Fig 3.38 The formula taking shape

Click on the Enter button or press the Enter key. The formula is now in place and the calculation is done as before.

Using other formulae

You can use all these operations in a formula:

+

−

* for multiplication
/ for division

You can also use brackets to make the formula clear. For example, if you want to work out the average raised per event, you would use:

=(C5+C6+C7)/3

or

=C9/3 (using the result of the previous formula) (see Fig 3.39).

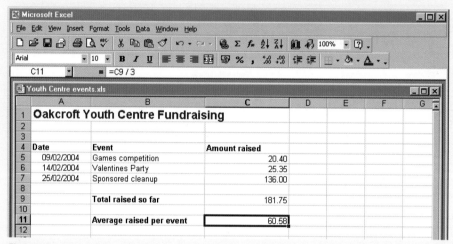

Fig 3.39 *Another formula*

Formatting currency

You can use numbers with two decimal places for money, but it looks better if the currency symbols, such as **£**, are included as well. You don't have to add them in yourself. Simply highlight the column by clicking on the letter C, right-click and select **Format Cells** (Fig 3.40).

This time, select **Currency** under Category. In the Symbol box select **£**, or whichever currency you want.

When you format cells for currency, they act in exactly the same way as any other numbers, except that the symbol is added to each cell (Fig 3.41).

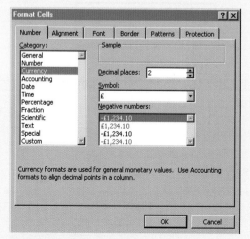

Amount raised
£20.40
£25.35
£136.00
£181.75
£60.58

Fig 3.40 *Formatting as currency*   **Fig 3.41** *Cells formatted as currency*

Case study

Mandi wants to plan ahead for future events at the youth centre. She wants to draw up a calendar for the next two months.

The centre has normal club evenings on Tuesdays, Wednesdays and Fridays. On Mondays it runs a martial arts club, and on Thursdays there is a junior club for 9 to 12-year-olds.

Starting a new worksheet

The calendar can be created on a new worksheet within the same workbook:
At the bottom of the window, click on the Sheet 2 tab to view the next worksheet. Right-click on the name and rename it Calendar.
As before, enter a main heading in cell A1 (Fig 3.42).
In row 3, enter three headings for Day, Date and Event, and widen any columns if necessary.
Enter the first date under the Date heading, in cell B4.

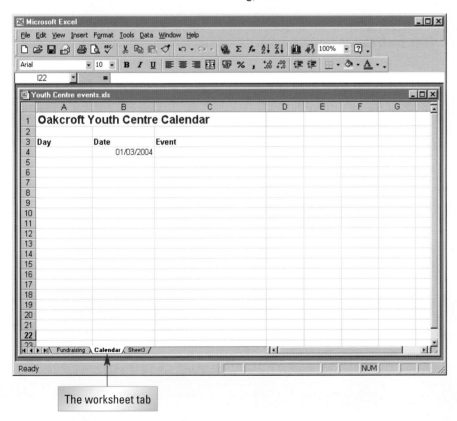

The worksheet tab

Fig 3.42 *A new worksheet*

Using a formula with a date

You want to enter the next date 02/03/04 in cell B5, and so on down the column. Excel can calculate all these dates for you.

You will use the formula: =B4+1

Click on cell B5. Key in =. Click on cell B4, then key in +1.

The correct date appears in B5 (Fig 3.43).

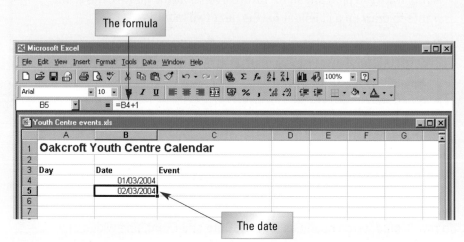

Fig 3.43 *Using a formula with a date*

This works because Excel gives all dates a serial number, starting from 1st January 1900. So when you add 1 to a date it simply adds it to the serial number, then calculates the actual date it would be.

Copying a formula

The next bit is really clever!

Fig 3.44 *The next date*

Click on cell B5. Click on the handle at the bottom right corner of the cell. Drag it down to the next cell. And the next date pops into cell B6 (Fig 3.44).

When you dragged the cell, you were copying the formula from B5 into B6. But it didn't copy it exactly. The formula in B5 is =B4+1. The formula in B6 is =B5+1.

Excel has made an intelligent assumption, which is that in B5 what you really meant was 'take the date in the cell above this one and add one day to it'. So it has done the same in B6, where the date is one more than the previous cell (Fig 3.45).

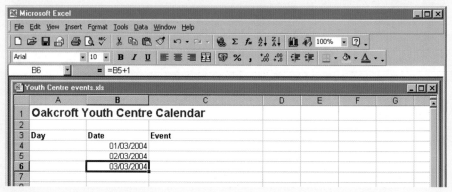

Fig 3.45 *Copying a formula*

You can now use this trick to put in the dates for the next two months. Click on B6, and drag on the handle right down to cell B64 (Fig 3.46).

Date	Event
01/03/2004	
02/03/2004	
03/03/2004	
04/03/2004	
05/03/2004	
06/03/2004	
07/03/2004	
08/03/2004	
09/03/2004	
10/03/2004	
11/03/2004	
12/03/2004	
13/03/2004	
14/03/2004	
15/03/2004	
16/03/2004	
17/03/2004	
18/03/2004	
19/03/2004	

Fig 3.46 *Inserting dates by copying a formula*

Day
Monday
Tuesday
Wednesday
Thursday
Friday
Saturday
Sunday
Monday
Tuesday
Wednesday
Thursday
Friday
Saturday
Sunday
Monday
Tuesday
Wednesday
Thursday
Friday

Fig 3.47 *Days added by dragging down*

1st March 2004 was a Monday, so you can enter that under the Day heading. Now click on A4 and drag down with the handle. Excel even knows the days of the week and fills them in for you! Drag down to A64 (Fig 3.47).

Copying the contents of a cell

You can key in the details of the normal club evening on the first Tuesday, in cell C5. You can then copy that text down to C6 by dragging on the handle (Fig 3.48).

Day	Date	Event
Monday	01/03/2004	
Tuesday	02/03/2004	Club evening
Wednesday	03/03/2004	Club evening
Thursday	04/03/2004	
Friday	05/03/2004	

Fig 3.48 *Copying text down*

This only works for cells that are next to each other.

You can also copy the contents of a cell to another cell anywhere on the worksheet. Click on C5, the cell you want to copy. Then click on the Copy button in the Standard toolbar. A flashing border appears around the cell. Click on C8, the cell where you want to contents to be copied. Click on the Paste button.

The flashing border remains around cell C5 until you press the Escape key on the keyboard (Fig 3.49).

Day	Date	Event
Monday	01/03/2004	
Tuesday	02/03/2004	Club evening
Wednesday	03/03/2004	Club evening
Thursday	04/03/2004	
Friday	05/03/2004	Club evening
Saturday	06/03/2004	

Fig 3.49 *Copying the contents of a cell*

Copying the contents of a group of cells

Now add details of the martial arts club in C4 and the junior club in C7. Leave Saturday (C8) and Sunday (C9) blank (Fig 3.50).

Day	Date	Event
Monday	01/03/2004	Martial Arts
Tuesday	02/03/2004	Club evening
Wednesday	03/03/2004	Club evening
Thursday	04/03/2004	Junior Club
Friday	05/03/2004	Club evening
Saturday	06/03/2004	
Sunday	07/03/2004	

Fig 3.50 More data in the Events list

Click on C4, but *not* on the handle. Then drag down to C10 so that all the cells from C4 to C10 are highlighted (Fig 3.51).

Day	Date	Event
Monday	01/03/2004	Martial Arts
Tuesday	02/03/2004	Club evening
Wednesday	03/03/2004	Club evening
Thursday	04/03/2004	Junior Club
Friday	05/03/2004	Club evening
Saturday	06/03/2004	
Sunday	07/03/2004	
Monday	08/03/2004	
Tuesday	09/03/2004	

Fig 3.51 Highlighting a group of cells

Now click on the handle at the bottom right corner of the highlighted cells. Drag it down to C64, and the contents will be copied down week after week (Fig 3.52).

Oakcroft Youth Centre Calendar

Day	Date	Event
Monday	01/03/2004	Martial Arts
Tuesday	02/03/2004	Club evening
Wednesday	03/03/2004	Club evening
Thursday	04/03/2004	Junior Club
Friday	05/03/2004	Club evening
Saturday	06/03/2004	
Sunday	07/03/2004	
Monday	08/03/2004	Martial Arts
Tuesday	09/03/2004	Club evening
Wednesday	10/03/2004	Club evening
Thursday	11/03/2004	Junior Club
Friday	12/03/2004	Club evening
Saturday	13/03/2004	
Sunday	14/03/2004	
Monday	15/03/2004	Martial Arts
Tuesday	16/03/2004	Club evening
Wednesday	17/03/2004	Club evening
Thursday	18/03/2004	Junior Club
Friday	19/03/2004	Club evening

Fig 3.52 Groups of cells copied down

You can now go through the list and delete the contents of any cells where a club night is cancelled.

Inserting extra columns and rows

If you want to insert a column, click on the letter at the top of the column to the right of where you want it to go. Right-click and select **Insert**.

If you want to insert a row, click on the number at the beginning of the row below where you want it to go. Right-click and select **Insert**.

Deleting rows and columns

To delete a column, click on the letter at the top of the column. Right-click and select **Delete**.

To delete a row, click on the number at the beginning of the row. Right-click and select **Delete**.

Case study

Mandi wants to keep a register of attendances at the club. She will start with the junior club on Thursdays.

Setting up a table

Click on the Sheet 3 tab at the bottom of the window and rename it Thursday Register.

Add a main heading to the worksheet.

The first two columns will contain the names of members, so will be headed Surname and Forename. Enter about ten names. The attendance at the junior club is much higher than this, but you don't need to enter all the names (Fig 3.53).

Oakcroft Youth Centre - Register : Thursdays

Surname	Forename
Winters	Carrie
Patel	Bina
Duggan	Oliver
Lewis	Duncan
Shah	Ahmed
Smith	Sheri
Williams	Josh
Li	Sara
Banks	Ellie
Patel	Harri
Jones	Charlotte

Fig 3.53 The names in the register

119

Sorting data

The names are not in alphabetical order. Click on any of the names in the Surname list. Then click on the Sort Ascending button in the Standard toolbar:

↕ the Sort Ascending button

The names will all be sorted in alphabetical order. Notice that the forenames move with their surnames (Fig 3.54).

Surname	Forename				
Oakcroft Youth Centre - Register : Thursdays					
Surname	**Forename**				
Banks	Ellie				
Duggan	Oliver				
Jones	Charlotte				
Lewis	Duncan				
Li	Sara				
Patel	Bina				
Patel	Harri				
Shah	Ahmed				
Smith	Sheri				
Williams	Josh				
Winters	Carrie				

Fig 3.54 *The names sorted in alphabetical order*

Adding date headings

4th March is the first Thursday in the month, so the date is entered in C3.

You now want to add the dates of each Thursday along this row, as a heading.

Click on D3. You will use the formula =C3+7. This will give the date one week later (Fig 3.55).

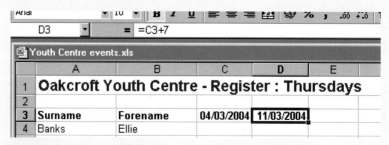

Fig 3.55 *Using a formula for a date*

Now click on D3, and drag on the handle to the right. The dates will once again fill in for you.

If instead you see cells filled with ###### (Fig 3.56), that simply means the cell is not wide enough to display the data. You need to widen the cells (Fig 3.57).

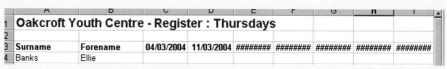

Fig 3.56 *Cells are not wide enough for the data*

Oakcroft Youth Centre - Register : Thursdays							
Surname	Forename	04/03/2004	11/03/2004	18/03/2004	25/03/2004	01/04/2004	08/04/2004
Banks	Ellie						

Fig 3.57 Cells are now wide enough

Rotating content

The problem is now that the date headings do not all fit in the window. You can get round that by making the headings vertical instead of horizontal.

Highlight all the cells containing dates. Right-click, and select **Format Cells**. In the Format Cells dialogue box, click on the Alignment tab (Fig 3.58).

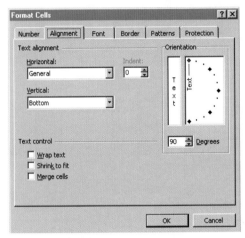

Fig 3.58 Rotating text

Find the Degrees box. Change the value to 90 degrees, then click on OK.

You will now find that the date columns are too wide so you can reduce them to fit on the screen (Fig 3.59).

Oakcroft Youth Centre - Register : Thursdays										
		04/03/2004	11/03/2004	18/03/2004	25/03/2004	01/04/2004	08/04/2004	15/04/2004	22/04/2004	29/04/2004
Surname	**Forename**									
Banks	Ellie									
Duggan	Oliver									
Jones	Charlotte									
Lewis	Duncan									
Li	Sara									
Patel	Bina									
Patel	Harri									
Shah	Ahmed									
Smith	Sheri									
Williams	Josh									
Winters	Carrie									

Fig 3.59 The register ready to be filled in

Filling in the table

Each week the register is filled in with a 1 for an attendance and 0 for an absence.

Make sure you use the numbers 0 and 1, and not the letters O and I (Fig 3.60).

	A	B	C 04/03/2004	D 11/03/2004	E 18/03/2004	F 25/03/2004	G 01/04/2004	H 08/04/2004	I 15/04/2004	J 22/04/2004	K 29/04/2004
1	Oakcroft Youth Centre - Register : Thursdays										
2											
3	Surname	Forename									
4	Banks	Ellie	1	1	0	1	1	0	1	0	1
5	Duggan	Oliver	1	1	1	0	0	0	1	1	0
6	Jones	Charlotte	1	0	1	1	1	0	1	1	1
7	Lewis	Duncan	0	1	1	1	1	0	1	1	1
8	Li	Sara	0	1	1	0	1	1	1	1	0
9	Patel	Bina	1	1	1	1	0	1	1	1	1
10	Patel	Harri	1	1	1	1	0	1	1	1	1
11	Shah	Ahmed	1	1	1	1	1	0	0	1	1
12	Smith	Sheri	1	1	1	1	1	0	1	1	1
13	Williams	Josh	0	0	0	1	1	0	1	0	0
14	Winters	Carrie	1	1	0	1	1	1	1	1	1
15											
16											

Fig 3.60 *The completed register*

Using a function

You can use the spreadsheet to calculate the numbers attending each week.

Click on a cell at the bottom of the first column of attendances. The formula will be

$=C4+C5+C6+C7+C8+C9+C10+C11+C12+C13+C14$

This is very awkward, and would be even more difficult with a really long table. Instead you can use a function.

In cell C16 enter=.

Functions appear where the name box was (Fig 3.61). Click on the arrow to see the drop-down list of functions. Select **SUM**.

The SUM dialogue box appears (Fig 3.62). It very cleverly guesses that you want to add all the numbers from C4 to C15, and it shows it like this: C4:C15. C15 is empty and will be ignored. Click on OK.

The formula in the cell becomes:

$=SUM(C4:C15)$

In C16, all the 1s in column C have been added up (Fig 3.63).

If you want to change the group of cells that are to be included in the SUM function, simply alter the names of the cells in the box labelled Number 1.

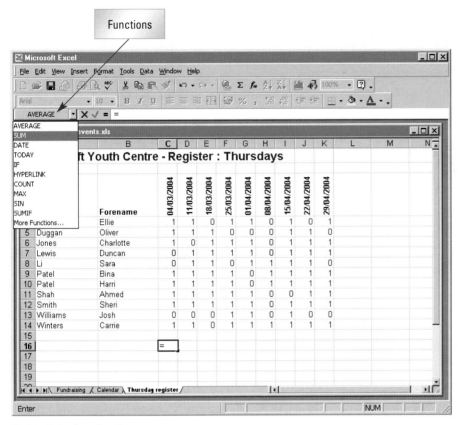

Fig 3.61 *Selecting a function*

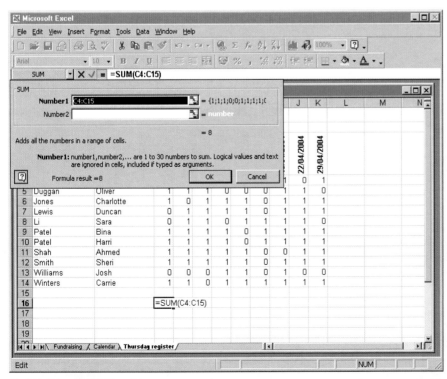

Fig 3.62 *Using the SUM function*

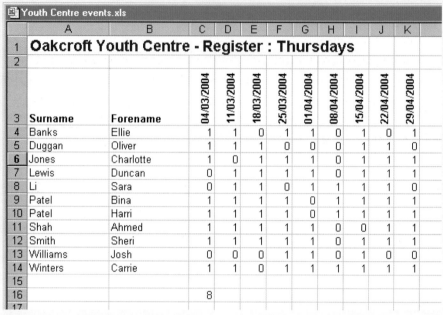

	Surname	Forename	04/03/2004	11/03/2004	18/03/2004	25/03/2004	01/04/2004	08/04/2004	15/04/2004	22/04/2004	29/04/2004
1	**Oakcroft Youth Centre - Register : Thursdays**										
2											
3											
4	Banks	Ellie	1	1	0	1	1	0	1	0	1
5	Duggan	Oliver	1	1	1	0	0	0	1	1	0
6	Jones	Charlotte	1	0	1	1	1	0	1	1	1
7	Lewis	Duncan	0	1	1	1	1	0	1	1	1
8	Li	Sara	0	1	1	0	1	1	1	1	0
9	Patel	Bina	1	1	1	1	0	1	1	1	1
10	Patel	Harri	1	1	1	1	0	1	1	1	1
11	Shah	Ahmed	1	1	1	1	1	0	0	1	1
12	Smith	Sheri	1	1	1	1	1	0	1	1	1
13	Williams	Josh	0	0	0	1	1	0	1	0	0
14	Winters	Carrie	1	1	0	1	1	1	1	1	1
15											
16			8								
17											

Fig 3.63 *The result of using the SUM function*

Copying a formula that uses a function

You can copy the formula in C16 across the row. Click on C16, then drag the handle across to K16.

Once again, it will not simply copy the values in C16 but adjust the formula in each cell so that it adds up the numbers in the column above it. So, for example, the formula in G16 is =SUM(G4:G15) (Fig 3.64).

Give it a go

Can you work out how to make the spreadsheet calculate how many times each person has attended during the two months?

	Surname	Forename	04/03/2004	11/03/2004	18/03/2004	25/03/2004	01/04/2004	08/04/2004	15/04/2004	22/04/2004	29/04/2004
1	**Oakcroft Youth Centre - Register : Thursdays**										
2											
3											
4	Banks	Ellie	1	1	0	1	1	0	1	0	1
5	Duggan	Oliver	1	1	1	0	0	0	1	1	0
6	Jones	Charlotte	1	0	1	1	1	0	1	1	1
7	Lewis	Duncan	0	1	1	1	1	0	1	1	1
8	Li	Sara	0	1	1	0	1	1	1	1	0
9	Patel	Bina	1	1	1	1	0	1	1	1	1
10	Patel	Harri	1	1	1	1	0	1	1	1	1
11	Shah	Ahmed	1	1	1	1	1	0	0	1	1
12	Smith	Sheri	1	1	1	1	1	0	1	1	1
13	Williams	Josh	0	0	0	1	1	0	1	0	0
14	Winters	Carrie	1	1	0	1	1	1	1	1	1
15											
16			8	9	8	9	8	4	10	9	8
17											

Fig 3.64 *Copying a formula containing a function*

Formatting cells

You can change the background colour of a single cell, or of a group of cells.

Click on cell C4 (*not* on the handle) and hold the mouse down as you move it to cell K14. This highlights the complete block of cells (Fig 3.65).

Youth Centre events.xls										
	A	B	C	D	E	F	G	H	I	J	K
1	**Oakcroft Youth Centre - Register : Thursdays**										
2											
3	**Surname**	**Forename**	04/03/2004	11/03/2004	18/03/2004	25/03/2004	01/04/2004	08/04/2004	15/04/2004	22/04/2004	29/04/2004
4	Banks	Ellie	1	1	0	1	1	0	1	0	1
5	Duggan	Oliver	1	1	1	0	0	0	1	1	0
6	Jones	Charlotte	1	0	1	1	1	0	1	1	1
7	Lewis	Duncan	0	1	1	1	1	0	1	1	1
8	Li	Sara	0	1	1	0	1	1	1	1	0
9	Patel	Bina	1	1	1	1	0	1	1	1	1
10	Patel	Harri	1	1	1	1	0	1	1	1	1
11	Shah	Ahmed	1	1	1	1	1	0	0	1	1
12	Smith	Sheri	1	1	1	1	1	0	1	1	1
13	Williams	Josh	0	0	0	1	1	0	1	0	0
14	Winters	Carrie	1	1	0	1	1	1	1	1	1
15											
16			8	9	8	9	8	4	10	9	8
17											

Fig 3.65 *A group of cells highlighted*

Right-click and select **Format Cells**. In the Format Cells dialogue box, click on the Patterns tab, and select a colour (Fig 3.66).

You can use the Borders tab to add borders to single cells or to groups of cells.

Youth Centre events.xls											
	A	B	C	D	E	F	G	H	I	J	K	L
1	**Oakcroft Youth Centre - Register : Thursdays**											
2												
3	**Surname**	**Forename**	04/03/2004	11/03/2004	18/03/2004	25/03/2004	01/04/2004	08/04/2004	15/04/2004	22/04/2004	29/04/2004	
4	Banks	Ellie	1	1	0	1	1	0	1	0	1	
5	Duggan	Oliver	1	1	1	0	0	0	1	1	0	
6	Jones	Charlotte	1	0	1	1	1	0	1	1	1	
7	Lewis	Duncan	0	1	1	1	1	0	1	1	1	
8	Li	Sara	0	1	1	0	1	1	1	1	0	
9	Patel	Bina	1	1	1	1	0	1	1	1	1	
10	Patel	Harri	1	1	1	1	0	1	1	1	1	
11	Shah	Ahmed	1	1	1	1	1	0	0	1	1	
12	Smith	Sheri	1	1	1	1	1	0	1	1	1	
13	Williams	Josh	0	0	0	1	1	0	1	0	0	
14	Winters	Carrie	1	1	0	1	1	1	1	1	1	
15												
16	**Total attendances**		8	9	8	9	8	4	10	9	8	
17												

Fig 3.66 *Formatted cells*

Case study

> Jason is planning the dance marathon Saturday 17th April. He is not sure how much to charge as an entry fee.

Adding a new worksheet

It may look as though you have no more worksheets left in your workbook. You can add a new sheet by selecting *Insert/Worksheet*. It will insert a new worksheet immediately before the one you have open.

Rename the worksheet Dance marathon. Add a suitable heading.

Setting up the values

Add data to the cells as shown in Fig 3.67. Format cells B4 and B6 as currency.

Fig 3.67 *Setting up a spreadsheet for an event*

The formula in B6 is =B3 * B4 (remember that * means 'multiplied by') (Fig 3.68).

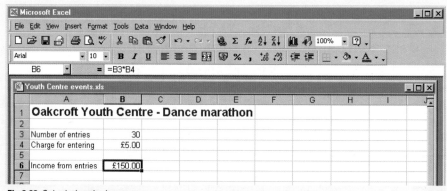

Fig 3.68 *Calculating the income*

Creating a 'what if' scenario

You are not sure how many people will enter, so you want to see what the income might be for different numbers of entries. You are also not sure whether £5 is the right amount to charge, so you want to see what would happen if you charge more or less than this.

A 'what if' scenario lets you try out different values in cells B3 and B4. You could simply make the changes in the cells but, if you use the method described here, you can save all the possible variations and compare them.

Setting up the original values as a scenario

B3 and B4 are the changing cells – you will try out different values in different scenarios.

Highlight cells B3 and B4 together.

Click **Tools/Scenarios**. In the Scenario Manager dialogue box (Fig 3.69), click on the Add button.

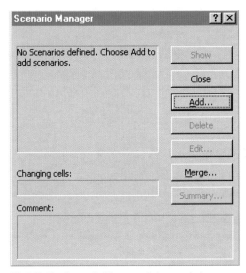

Fig 3.69 *The Scenario Manager dialogue window*

The Add Scenario dialogue box appears (Fig 3.70). Enter the name of the Scenario as 30 entries at £5. Check that the Changing cells box contains B3:B4.

Click on OK.

Fig 3.70 *Adding a scenario*

The Scenario Values box appears (Fig 3.71). Check that the value for $B$3 is given as 30, and the value for $B$4 is given as 5.

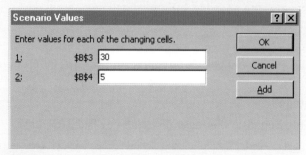

Fig 3.71 *Setting the values of the changing cells*

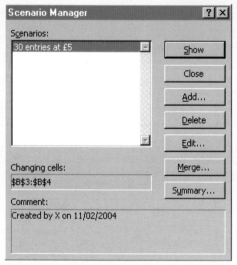

Fig 3.72 *Selecting a scenario*

Notice that cell B3 is referred to as $B$3. This is called an absolute cell address. It stops Excel from doing some of the clever things it did earlier, when you copied a formula to another cell and it guessed which column you were referring to. When the $ signs are included it means cell B3 exactly.

Click on OK.

You are now returned to the Scenario Manager dialogue box, but, this time, the name of the scenario you have just created is shown (Fig 3.72). Click on the Show button.

Make sure you move the Scenario Manager dialogue box so that you can see the entries in the cells.

Nothing seems to happen! That's OK, because all you have done is to save the calculation that you had already done.

Creating a new scenario

In the Scenario Manager dialogue box, click on Add. The Add Scenario dialogue box appears. This time enter the Scenario name 50 entries at £5 (Fig 3.73). Click on OK.

The next dialogue box is the important one, as it is here that you try out a different value. For cell B3 (or, rather, $B$3) change the value to 50 (Fig 3.74). Click on OK.

You are now returned to the Scenario Manager dialogue box. Two scenarios are listed. Make sure that the new one called 50 entries at £5 is highlighted (Fig 3.75). Click on Show.

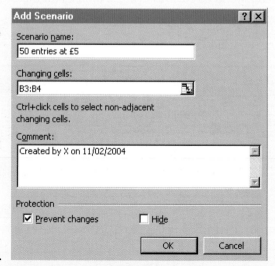

Fig 3.73 *Adding a new scenario*

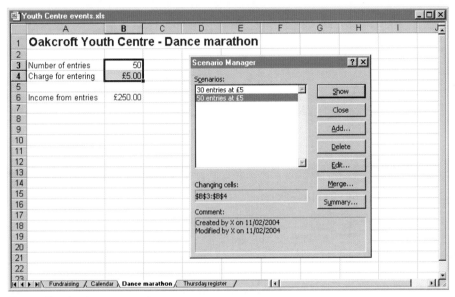

Fig 3.74 *Changing a value*

Fig 3.75 *Showing the new scenario*

The value in cell B3 is now changed to 50. The value in B6 is recalculated as well.

In the Scenario Manager dialogue box, click on the original scenario, called 30 entries at £5. Click on Show. You can now see the original values in B3 and B6.

Adding more scenarios

You can try out all sorts of combinations, changing either the number of entries in B3, or the entry charge in B4, or both.

Just click on Add in the Scenario Manager dialogue box and carry on. Fig 3.76 shows a scenario that sees what happens when you get 40 entries at £3.50.

Creating a summary of the scenarios

When you have created several scenarios you will want to compare them.

In the Scenario Manager dialogue box, click on Summary. The Scenario Summary dialogue box is displayed (Fig 3.77). This confirms the cell where the results of the calculation is shown. This is cell B6, which will have a flashing border.

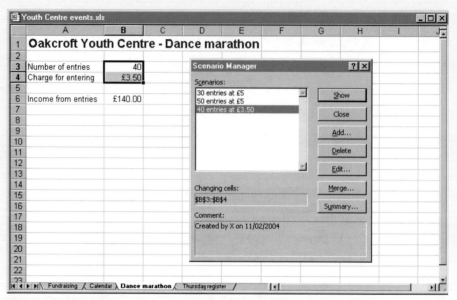

Fig 3.76 *A new scenario*

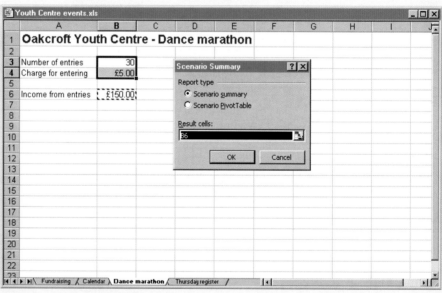

Fig 3.77 *Selecting the Report Type*

Make sure that Scenario summary (not Scenario Pivot Table) is selected as the Report type. Click on OK.

A new sheet, called Scenario Summary, is now created in the workbook (Fig 3.78). It shows the values in your scenarios side by side.

The first column shows the scenario that you have displayed at the moment. The other columns show all the scenarios that you have created.

You may want to print out this summary.

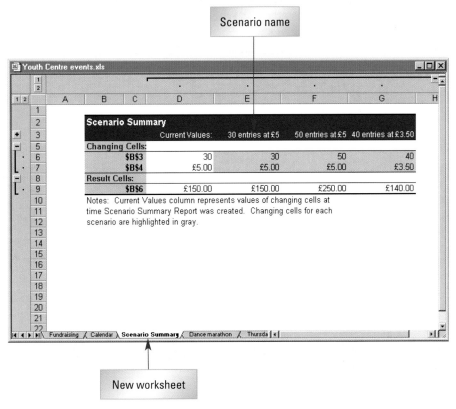

Scenario name

New worksheet

Fig 3.78 *The Scenario Summary*

Skills: charts

You can use spreadsheet software to produce several different types of charts and graphs. But because it is so easy to create a chart, it is also easy to create one that does not give any useful information.

Charts and graphs are diagrams that bring numerical data to life. They let you see at a glance what the important facts are, without having to study tables of figures.

Looking at bar charts and column charts

The two charts in Figs 3.79 and 3.80 display exactly the same information. The only difference between them is whether the bars are horizontal or vertical.

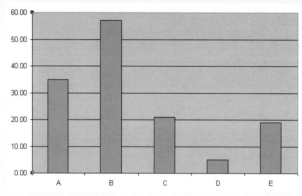

Fig 3.79 A column chart

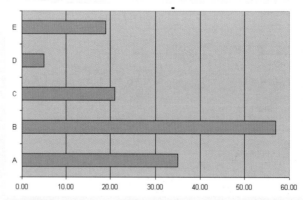

Fig 3.80 A bar chart

Bar charts and column charts always have a gap between the individual bars.

In some books, both types of chart are called bar charts.

Case study

Mandi wants to produce a chart that shows the fundraising in February. She uses the first worksheet in the workbook.

Creating a column chart

You can create a simple column chart using the data on the Fundraising worksheet.

First, highlight the cells containing the details of the events and the amounts raised (Fig 3.81). You should include the headings. Do not include the total.

	A	B	C	D
	Youth Centre events.xls			
1	**Oakcroft Youth Centre Fundraising**			
2				
3				
4	Date	Event	Amount raised	
5	09/02/2004	Games competition	£20.40	
6	14/02/2004	Valentines Party	£25.35	
7	25/02/2004	Sponsored cleanup	£136.00	
8				
9		Total raised so far	£181.75	
10				
11		Average raised per event	£60.58	
12				
13				

Fig 3.81 *Highlight the data to be used in the chart*

Click on the Chart Wizard button in the Standard toolbar:

the Chart Wizard button

Step 1 in the Chart Wizard (Fig 3.82) lets you choose the type of chart you want. In the Chart type list, select **Column**. In the Chart Sub-type options select the top left diagram. Click on Next.

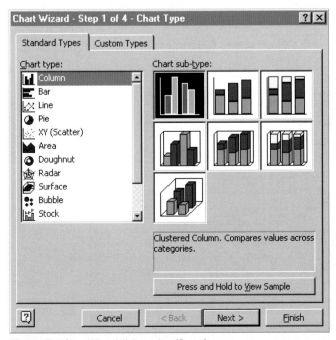

Fig 3.82 *The Chart Wizard dialogue box (Step 1)*

Step 2 in the Chart Wizard (Fig 3.83) displays a small version of the chart so far. Check the box labelled Data range. It should contain

=Fundraising!$B$4:$C$7

This shows that the data is taken from the worksheet called Fundraising, and the cells between B4 and C7.

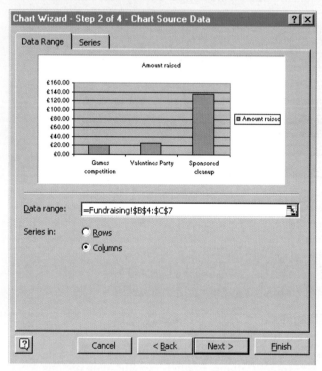

Fig 3.83 *Step 2 of the Chart Wizard*

Step 3 of the Chart Wizard (Fig 3.84) offers you a number of tabs. These let you customise the chart in several ways. You will come back to these later. In the Titles tab, change the Chart title to Oakcroft Youth Centre Fundraising. Click on Next.

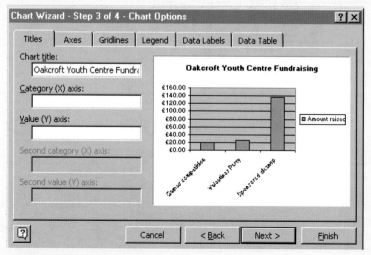

Fig 3.84 *Step 3 of the Chart Wizard*

Step 4 (Fig 3.85) gives you a choice about where the chart will be displayed. You can either insert it on the Fundraising worksheet, or you can create a new worksheet just to hold the chart.

If you want to print the chart from the spreadsheet, it is a good idea to create a separate worksheet.

Click on the As new sheet option. Then fill in the name of the new worksheet, as Fundraising Chart. Click on Finish.

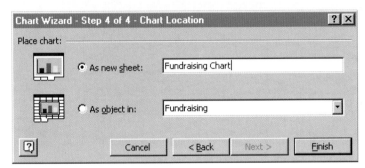

Fig 3.85 Step 4 of the Chart Wizard

The chart now appears in a new worksheet called Fundraising Chart (Fig 3.86).

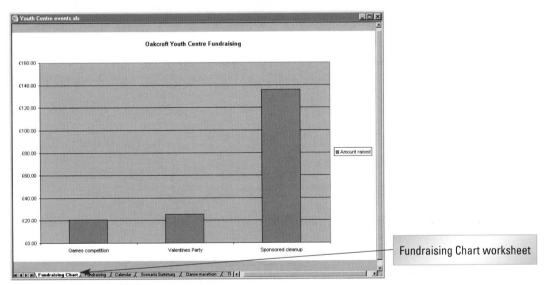

Fig 3.86 The final column chart in a new worksheet

Looking at the chart

As you move your mouse over the chart, helpful screen tips appear. Check out all the parts of the chart mentioned here (Fig 3.87).
- The white area that contains the chart is known as the chart area.
- The grey area that contains the actual chart is called the plot area.
- The vertical axis is called a value axis, because it contains numerical values.
- The horizontal axis is called a category axis, because it contains the categories that describe each item of data.
- The legend describes this series of data.

135

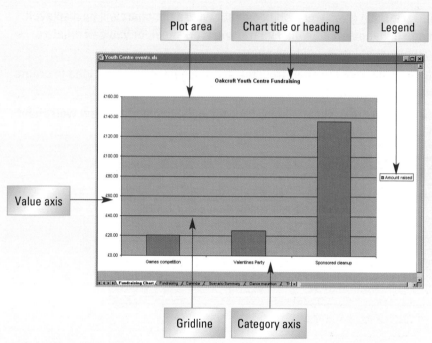

Fig 3.87 *The parts of the chart*

Formatting the chart

If you right-click on any part of the chart you can format its appearance. The aim is to make the chart easier to read and understand. If you overload it with lots of colours and effects it may have quite the opposite effect, so take care.

Here are some ideas:

◎ Right-click on the Value axis, and select **Format axis**. In the Format Axis dialogue box (Fig 3.88), select the Font tab and make the font larger. Repeat this with the Category Axis.

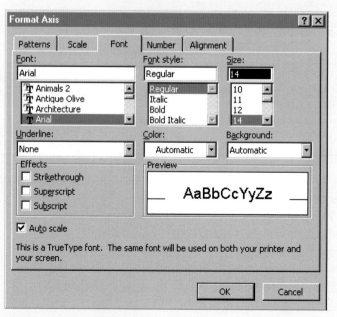

Fig 3.88 *Formatting an axis*

◉ Right-click on the Chart Title and select **Format Chart Title**. In the Format Chart Title dialogue box, change the size and colour of the font. Click on the Patterns tab and, under Border, choose a colour for the border (Fig 3.89). Under Area, select a colour for the fill.

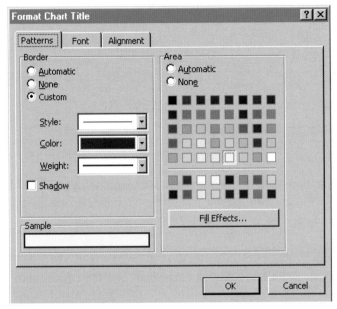

Fig 3.89 *Formatting the chart title*

◉ Right-click on the plot area and select **Format Plot Area**. Select colours for the border and area fill.
◉ Right-click on one of the columns, and select **Format Data Series**. Again, select a colour.

The formatted chart is shown in Fig 3.90.

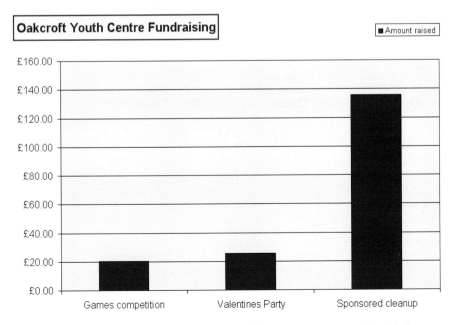

Fig 3.90 *The formatted chart*

Fig 3.91 *Chart area options*

Returning to the Chart Wizard

You can return to any of the steps of the Chart Wizard at any time. Right-click in an empty space in the chart area. The pop-up menu (Fig 3.91) offers options which jump to the Chart Wizard:

Step 1 – Chart Type

Step 2 – Source Data

Step 3 – Chart Options

Step 4 – Location

Printing the chart

Click on the Print button in the Standard toolbar to print out the chart.

Copying and pasting the chart into other documents

You can copy and paste the chart into any other Microsoft software. It will be pasted as a graphic. You can reduce the size of the chart by clicking on it and dragging on the handles.

Case study

Mandi keeps records of the attendances each week. She then adds them up and gets a total for each quarter of the year – January to March, April to June, July to September, October to December. She likes to be able to compare the figures in different years.

Creating a chart with more than one series

You can set up this table of attendances in a new worksheet, called Attendances (Fig 3.92).

A set of data in a table is known as a series. In this case, each column of figures is a separate series. This table has three series, one each for 2002, 2003 and 2004.

	A	B	C	D	E	F
1	**Oakcroft Youth Centre - Total attendances**					
2						
3		**2002**	**2003**	**2004**		
4	January - March	2106	2245	2430		
5	April - June	2287	2436	2517		
6	July - September	1754	1902	2049		
7	October - December	1907	2103	2317		
8						
9						
10						

Youth Centre events.xls

Fig 3.92 *A table of attendances*

It is difficult to make much sense of the data when it is presented as a table, so it is a good idea to put it in a chart.

Highlight all the data cells from A3 to D7. Click on the Chart Wizard button. In the Chart Wizard dialogue box, Step 1 (Fig 3.93), make the same choices as before.

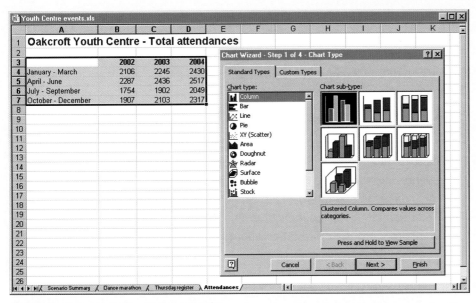

Fig 3.93 *Creating a chart with more than one series*

In Step 2, check that everything is OK, and click on Next.

In Step 3, key in a Chart Title, e.g. Oakcroft Youth Centre Attendances.

In Step 4, you can select the second option so you can see what the chart looks like alongside the data.

The chart is positioned on the worksheet (Fig 3.94). You can immediately make sense of the data. You can see that the attendances have gone up each year. You can also see that attendances drop each year over the holiday period between June and September, but they start picking up again in the autumn.

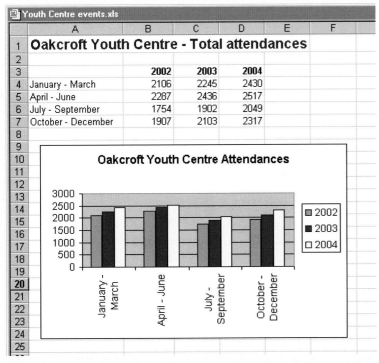

Fig 3.94 *A chart with three series*

You can move the chart to another position by clicking in an empty space in the chart area and dragging it. You can make the chart larger by clicking in the chart area then dragging on the handles.

You can format the chart as before.

Case study

Mandi finally manages to raise nearly £7,500 for new computers for the club members to use. Some of this money was raised from fundraising events, like the dance marathon. She also persuaded some local businesses to sponsor the club. She got some money from a local charity. And finally the local Council gave the club a grant for computers. She wants to show the information about the sources of the funding in an eye-catching way.

Creating a pie chart

A pie chart is used when you want to show proportions. In this case, Mandi is interested in what proportion of the funding came from fundraising, sponsorship, charity and council grant.

Set up a new worksheet called Sources of Funding. Give it a suitable heading.

Enter the data as shown in Fig 3.95. Format column B as currency.

	A	B	C	D	E	F	G
1	**Oakcroft Youth Centre - Sources of funding for computers**						
2							
3	**Source of funding**	**Amount**					
4	Fundraising	£2,195.78					
5	Business sponsors	£1,750.00					
6	Charity	£2,000.00					
7	Local Council	£1,500.00					
8							
9							

Youth Centre events.xls

Fig 3.95 *Table with sources of funding*

Highlight cells A4 to B7. Click on the Chart Wizard button.

In Step 1, select **Pie** in the Chart type list (Fig 3.96).

In the Chart sub-type section you will see pie charts from several different angles. It is actually difficult to make much sense of the pie charts that are angled away from you, or exploded. Click on the top-left option.

At Step 2, check that it looks OK, then click on Next.

At Step 3, give the pie chart a title.

At Step 4, decide whether to place the chart on the same worksheet or on a new one.

Fig 3.97 shows the finished pie chart.

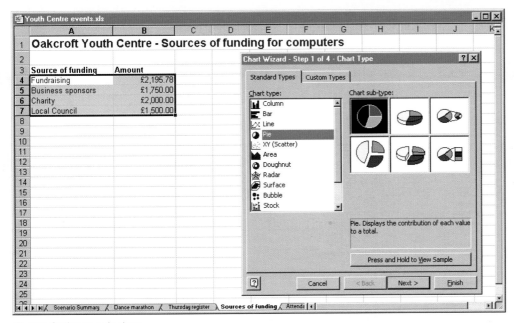

Fig 3.96 *Setting up a pie chart*

Oakcroft Youth Centre computer funding

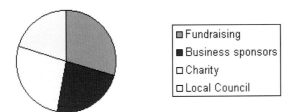

- Fundraising
- Business sponsors
- Charity
- Local Council

Fig 3.97 *The finished pie chart*

Case study

Mandi has noticed that the attendance at the youth centre varies a lot from week to week. She wonders if attendance depends on the weather. There is a thermometer just outside the main entrance to the centre, so for four weeks she notes down the temperature in °C each evening.

Mandi then adds the data about temperature and attendances to the Calendar worksheet. She ends up with a great many numbers, but has no idea what it proves.

Creating a scatter graph

A scatter graph is used if you want to see whether two things are related.

Fig 3.98 shows the data that Mandi has entered on the calendar worksheet.

	A	B	C	D	E	F	G	H	I
1	**Oakcroft Youth Centre Calendar**								
2									
3	Day	Date	Event	Temperature	Attendance				
4	Monday	01/03/2004	Martial Arts	5	30				
5	Tuesday	02/03/2004	Club evening	7	42				
6	Wednesday	03/03/2004	Club evening	8	30				
7	Thursday	04/03/2004	Junior Club	10	25				
8	Friday	05/03/2004	Club evening	7	42				
9	Saturday	06/03/2004							
10	Sunday	07/03/2004							
11	Monday	08/03/2004	Martial Arts	7	33				
12	Tuesday	09/03/2004	Club evening	7	40				
13	Wednesday	10/03/2004	Club evening	10	34				
14	Thursday	11/03/2004	Junior Club	13	39				
15	Friday	12/03/2004	Club evening	14	61				
16	Saturday	13/03/2004							
17	Sunday	14/03/2004							
18	Monday	15/03/2004	Martial Arts	3	15				
19	Tuesday	16/03/2004	Club evening	2	21				
20	Wednesday	17/03/2004	Club evening	5	33				
21	Thursday	18/03/2004	Junior Club	11	30				
22	Friday	19/03/2004	Club evening	11	54				
23	Saturday	20/03/2004							
24	Sunday	21/03/2004							
25	Monday	22/03/2004	Martial Arts	9	32				
26	Tuesday	23/03/2004	Club evening	11	49				
27	Wednesday	24/03/2004	Club evening	9	29				
28	Thursday	25/03/2004	Junior Club	9	29				
29	Friday	26/03/2004	Club evening	10	50				
30	Saturday	27/03/2004						718	
31	Sunday	28/03/2004							

Fundraising Chart / Fundraising / **Calendar** / Scenario Summary / Dance marathon / TI

Fig 3.98 *Data about temperature and attendances*

Highlight the data in the cells from D3 to E31. This includes the headings. Some of the cells have no data in them – this is not a problem as Excel will simply ignore them.

Click on the Chart Wizard button.

In Step 1, select **XY (Scatter)** in the Chart type list. Click on the top diagram in the Chart sub-type options.

In Step 2, check that the data range shows the correct cells.

In Step 3 (Fig 3.99), change the Chart title to Oakcroft Youth Centre. You should give labels to the two axes. The temperatures are shown on the *X* axis, so in the box labelled Value (X) axis enter Temperature. The numbers attending are shown on the *Y* axis, so in the box labelled Value (Y) axis enter Numbers attending.

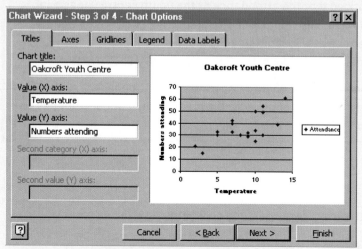

Fig 3.99 *Creating a scatter graph with the Chart Wizard*

In Step 4, decide whether to place the chart on the same worksheet or on a new one.

The final chart will look like Fig 3.100.

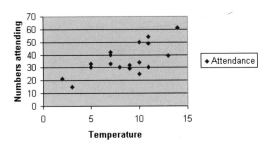

Fig 3.100 *A scatter graph*

Interpreting a scatter graph

If two things are completely unrelated the scatter graph will show a random pattern of dots. For example, suppose that each week you made a note of the number of performers appearing on *Top of the Pops*. This is unlikely to have anything to do with the outside temperature on that day. So if you drew a scatter graph it would show no relationship at all between temperature and the number of performers (see Fig 3.101). You would expect the dots to be scattered about almost at random.

On the other hand, suppose you were to take daily temperature readings at a popular seaside resort during the summer months. You could then count how many people were sitting on the beach at 12 noon each day (Fig 3.102). You would expect the two sets of data to be related – as the temperature rises so the number of people sitting on the beach rises.

The dots on the scatter graph would almost form a straight line.

In the scatter graph that you created for the youth centre the dots look more like a straight line than a completely random arrangment. So that suggests that the temperature does affect the attendance.

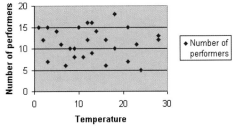

Fig 3.101 *A random arrangement of dots*

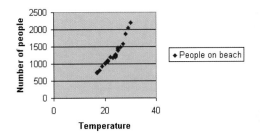

Fig 3.102 *A scatter graph with a strong relationship*

Practice questions

Foundation

1 Which of these statements about the internal memory of a computer is true.
   A Internal memory holds data temporarily, while the computer needs it.
   B Internal memory is another name for the hard disk.
   C Internal memory holds all the data that the computer needs all the time.
   D Internal memory can only hold one program at a time.

2 Internal memory is usually made out of:
   A ROM integrated circuits
   B RAM integrated circuits
   C Magnetic media
   D Optical media.

3 Complete this sentence:
   'RAM integrated circuits are _____ , which means that they need electrical power in order to hold on to data.'

4 Fill in the blanks with phrases chosen from the following list:
   an input device, backing store, a CD-ROM drive, internal memory, a document
   'When data is saved it is copied from _____ to _____.'

5 Give the names of two different types of magnetic media. Explain the difference between them.

6 What can you do with a CD-RW drive that you cannot do with a CD-R drive?

7 One gigabyte is approximately how many bytes?
   A One thousand bytes.
   B One million bytes.
   C One hundred million bytes.
   D One thousand million bytes.

8 Which has the greater capacity – a floppy disk or a hard disk?

Higher

9 Sometimes files are compressed. State two reasons why you might need to compress a file.

10 What are the advantages of using application software packages that all belong to the same software family?

11 Name two file formats for images. Why are there several different file formats for images?

12 In an office, some of the computers are using a more up-to-date version of a standard word processor than others. Explain what problems this could cause for users.

Networks and communications

Case study: Kingsmond Theatre

The theatre in Kingsmond puts on all kinds of events, from plays to rock concerts.

Behind the scenes there are a number of offices, and most of the people who work there need to use a computer. At present various people have desktop computers or laptops, but they are not linked together.

Only one of the computers has access to the Internet through a phone connection. The theatre does not have a website yet.

Emma Bond runs the box office. People either turn up in person or phone the box office to book tickets. She finds out which event they want to attend and how much they are willing to pay. Emma then checks the

ticket booking system on the box office computer to see whether there are any available seats and, if there are, she takes the money and she books the tickets. She then prints out the tickets and either gives them to the customer or posts them.

Joan Chambers is the Programme Manager. It is her job to arrange all the events that will appear at the theatre. She uses her computer to write letters, to send emails and to keep a record of all the events that have been arranged. She is the only person who can use email. She is also responsible for advertising and public relations.

Shaun Maitland is the Theatre Manager. He looks after all the finances of the theatre, so he needs to know how the ticket sales are going. Joan discusses future events with him. Shaun has to decide whether the theatre can make enough money from ticket sales to cover the fees that he must pay to performers and touring companies. He needs to look at the ticket sales and the future planning that Emma and Joan are working on. He also keeps an eye on the sales from the bar.

Networks

Standalone computer systems

Most home computers are standalone systems (Fig 4.1). Many small business computers are also standalone. They cannot communicate directly with other computers.

If you want to share a file that is saved on a standalone system with another computer you will have to copy it on to a floppy disk, CD or DVD.

Fig 4.1 A standalone system

Networks

Computer systems can be connected together in a network. The workstations in a network can:

◎ access the same files held on a central hard disk; and

◎ send messages and files to each other.

One powerful computer acts as the network server, which manages the activity on the whole network. All the workstations in a network can access files that are held on the network server's hard disk.

Local area networks

A local area network (LAN) is a network of computers that are connected by cables over a fairly small area, usually within one building. There are several types of LAN, but most of them look like Fig 4.2.

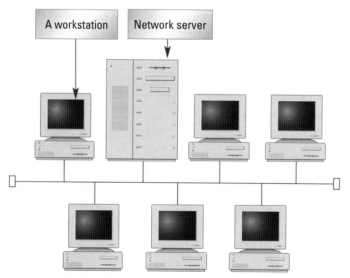

Fig 4.2 A local area network

Network administration

A workstation in a network can access files that are stored on the hard disk of the network server.

On most networks, each person who uses the network is given a username and a password. The software on the network server lists the files that each user has permission to use.

When someone logs on to the network with his or her username and password, the network software makes sure that this user can only use the files for which he or she has permission.

A network administrator is a person who looks after a network. The job includes sorting out the permissions for users.

Sharing files on a LAN

One advantage of using a LAN is that you do not have to store all the applications software on the hard disk of your computer. When you want to use some software you can load it from the network server's hard disk into the internal memory of your computer.

You can also share a file with someone else. If you are working on a report with a group of other people you can save it on the network server's hard disk. Another user can then load it up and make any changes he or she wants to it.

You can also use a file at the same time as other people. This often happens when a large database is used in, for example, a shop.

Wide area networks

Sometimes it is useful to link computers together even when they are too far apart to be connected by a cable. A wide area network (WAN) is a network that connects workstations over a wide area or even across the world.

Instead of normal computer cables, a WAN uses a number of different methods to connect the workstations, including telephone lines, satellite links, broadband connections, etc. (Fig 4.3).

Most WANs are private networks that are run by organisations so that they can share business information.

A WAN lets the members of an organisation share information between all their branches. They can also work on the same files, such as a database, from anywhere in the country. However, it may be possible for a criminal to get into a WAN. The criminal does not have to get into the organisation's building, but he or she may find out how to access the system from any computer.

Give it a go

Are you using a computer connected to a local area network at your school or college? If so, find out as much as you can about it. Here are some questions you could ask:

◎ How many workstations are there on the network?
◎ How far apart are the workstations on the network?
◎ Where is the network server?
◎ What is the capacity of the hard disk on the network server?
◎ Is there just one network, or more than one?

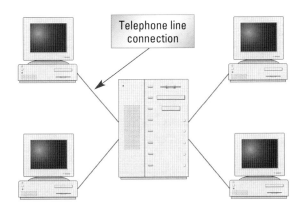

Telephone line connection

Fig 4.3 A wide area network

Communications

What does it mean?

Communication

The word 'communication' in 'information and communication technology' refers to all the ways in which data can be sent from one computer to another through a network. 'Data communications' means the same thing.

Communications in LANs

The workstations in a LAN are usually connected to the server using wire cables. A LAN cannot get very large, as each workstation has to be no more than 1 km from the server.

Large organisations usually have several LANs which are then connected to each other.

You may have heard of wireless networks. Some LANs are now being installed that have very few cable connections, but use radio signals to send data between workstations and the server.

Case study

At the theatre, Shaun, the Theatre Manager, wants to link all the computers into a LAN:
◎ What are the advantages of using a LAN instead of lots of standalone computers?
◎ What are the disadvantages of using a LAN?
◎ How should the computers be connected to the server?

Communications in WANs

In a WAN computers are connected with a server that is a long way away. There are several methods of making these communication links:
◎ dial-up modems
◎ ISDN
◎ ADSL
◎ cable.

ISDN, ADSL and cable are all broadband methods of communication. These carry a lot of signals at the same time and transfer the data much more quickly than is possible using a dial-up modem.

On the other hand, broadband is more expensive to install and run than dial-up.

Dial-up modems

You can connect a computer to a server that is a long distance away by using the normal telephone lines. This means that a stand-alone computer can become a workstation in a WAN during the time that it is connected by telephone.

In order to make the connection the computer has to dial the number of a telephone that is connected to the server.

Computers and telephone lines use different types of signals for sending data. The signals sent by the computer have to be converted

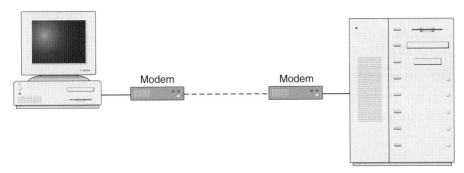

Fig 4.4 *A computer connected to a server using modems*

into another type of signal before they can be sent down a telephone line. When they reach the other end they have to be converted back to the computer format. A modem is a device that converts the signals between the two formats (Fig 4.4).

The connection between a computer and a server through modems is very slow by today's standards.

ISDN (integrated services digital network)

ISDN is another method for connecting a computer to a server in a WAN.

ISDN uses a system of cables that has been constructed across the country. The cables are made of optical fibres instead of wires, and these can carry computer signals directly without the use of a modem. The signals also travel much faster than they do on a telephone line.

If an organisation wants to use ISDN they will need to install a new cable that connects them to the ISDN system.

ISDN has been around for very many years but, today, is being replaced by even faster methods.

ADSL (asymmetrical digital subscriber line)

ADSL is a clever technology that uses ordinary telephone lines to carry broadband communications. It has the advantage that the computer is permanently connected.

When ADSL is used, data is downloaded very rapidly from the server. On the other hand, data sent from the computer to the server travels much more slowly.

Cable

Cable companies now offer television across most of the country. The same cables can be used to provide computer communications. Cable connections are always switched on and so can provide a permanent link between the computer and a server.

Download

You download a file when it is transferred from a server to your computer.

149

The Internet

The Internet connects networks with each other. It is a vast, public, wide area network that creates connections between individual LANs and WANs.

The Internet is available in every country of the world, so is sometimes referred to as a global network. Data can be transferred across the world in seconds using the Internet.

Origins of the Internet

The Internet was originally created by the US military as a way of connecting all the states of America in case of nuclear attack. It was developed further in the 1970s and was used by universities, research institutions and the military. It was mainly used to transfer files from one computer to another over long distances.

Most of these files could be downloaded and read by anyone. But files that were sent from one person directly to another person became known as electronic mail, or email.

Communications in the Internet

The Internet links together many thousands of LANs and WANs (Fig 4.5). Each LAN and WAN in turn consists of many individual workstations.

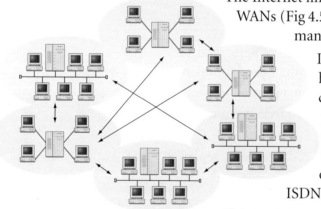

Fig 4.5 *The Internet links networks across the world*

If you use a standalone computer, you will have to connect to a WAN, which is then connected to the Internet. An Internet service provider (ISP) is a company that runs a WAN which gives Internet access. You can connect to the ISP's network in any of the ways listed on the previous pages – dial-up modem, ISDN, ADSL or cable.

If the computer you use is already in a LAN, you will probably be able to connect to the Internet through the LAN. The LAN itself can either have a direct connection to the Internet or may link through to the network of an ISP.

The launch of the World Wide Web

The Internet only became widely used by the general public in the 1990s. The reason for the sudden growth in the use of the Internet was the launch of the World Wide Web in 1991. Before then, you could transfer files across the world, but you had to know where files were stored, and they were not always easy to find.

Web pages can be laid out attractively on the screen and can contain graphics, sound and video clips. Before the Web was invented most files available on the Internet were simple text files. Today all the pages that you visit when you go on the Internet are part of the Web.

But the most important feature of the Web is the use of hyperlinks – the hotspots which allow the user to jump to another page. All the pages on the Web are ultimately linked together through hyperlinks, giving a vast network of information.

The Internet is more than the Web

The Internet includes the Web but has other aspects as well. The main features that the Internet offers are:

- file transfer
- email
- the Web
- instant messaging and chat rooms
- newsgroups
- online voice conversations.

Opportunities

The Internet offers some excellent opportunities to individual users and to businesses:

- You can find vast amounts of information from all over the world.
- You can find other people and organisations that share your interests.
- You can shop online and save lengthy trips to shopping centres or specialist shops.
- You can communicate easily with people wherever they live, using chat rooms, email and newsgroups.
- You can transfer documents and other computer files to another person instantly.

Problems

There are some problems associated with the Internet:

- Offensive material can be found on the Web, and it can also be sent by email or posted in chat rooms. Offensive material would include pornography, as well as text and images that promote racism, sexism, violence, illegal drug use or personal abuse. It is very difficult to control the Internet because each country has its own laws and no laws cover **all** of the Internet.
- Although the Web contains an enormous amount of information, you cannot be sure that anything you read is true. You need to know who provided the information and whether they can be trusted.
- Criminals can obtain details about credit cards and use them to buy goods illegally on the Internet.
- Computer viruses can be transferred from one computer to another through the Internet. Viruses are small programs that can cause a lot of damage to a computer, by deleting or changing files.

The World Wide Web

Web pages and websites

A web page is a single document that can be viewed on the Web. A collection of web pages stored together is known as a website. The home page in a website is the main page that you normally see first of all (Fig 4.6). You should be able to find all the other pages on the website by following links from the home page.

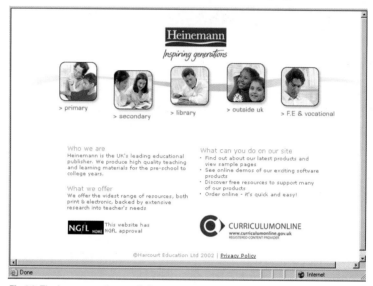

Fig 4.6 *The home page for a website*

HTML

Most web pages are created in a computer language called **H**yper**T**ext **M**arkup **L**anguage (HTML). Web pages are stored as files with the filename extension .htm or .html.

Web browsers

A browser is a piece of software which is used to view pages on the Web. The most-used browsers at present are Internet Explorer and Netscape (see Figs 4.7 and 4.8).

When you visit a web page the HTML code is downloaded to your computer and the browser interprets the code to create the web page

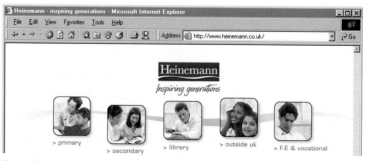

Fig 4.7 *The Internet Explorer web browser*

Fig 4.8 The Netscape web browser

itself. A browser also makes hyperlinks work so that, when you click on a link, the browser will find the correct page and download it.

Domain names

The domain name of a website is something like **www.thisismydomain.co.uk** (see Fig 4.9)

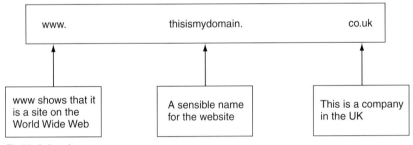

Fig 4.9 A domain name

Domain names have to be registered and can end with any of these:
.com – for a commercial business
.org – for a non-commercial organisation
.info – for a site that provides information
.co.uk – for a commercial business in the UK
.gov.uk – for branches of UK government
.ac.uk – for a university in the UK
.au – for a site registered in Australia
.fr – for a site registered in France
… and many more.

Web servers

All websites are stored on web servers. A web server is a computer that has special web server software and is also connected to the Internet.

When you open a browser and enter the domain name of a website, the browser finds the correct web server and downloads the first page to your computer.

continued ▶   153

URL (unique resource locator)

Every single page on the Web has a special web filename, known as a **U**nique **R**esource **L**ocator (URL). For example, **http://www.thisismydomain.co.uk/news.htm** is the URL for the news page on a website (Fig 4.10).

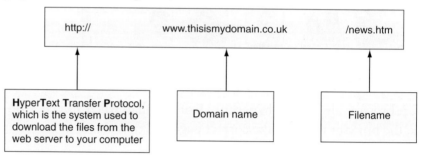

Fig 4.10 *A URL*

Index pages

The index page is the first page that is downloaded from any website. It is called index.htm or index.html. When you enter the domain name such as **www.thisismydomain.co.uk** in a browser it downloads **www.thisismydomain.co.uk/index.htm** or **www.thisismydomain.co.uk/index.html**.

Search engine

A search engine helps you to search the Web for the pages that you need. Google is one of the most widely used search engines and can be found at **www.google.co.uk** (Fig 4.11). You key in some words that describe what you want, for example, 'The history of the World Wide Web'.

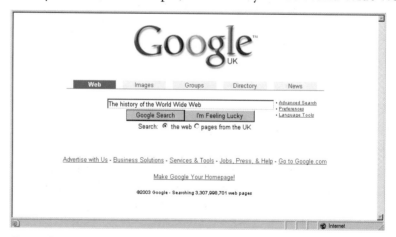

Fig 4.11 *Searching the Web with Google*

The results of the search are then listed for you. In Fig 4.12 you can see that over 3 million web pages were found that seemed to match your search. The results that are listed first are the sites that are used most of all.

Fig 4.12 *The results of a search with Google*

How does Google manage to find 3 million pages in a fraction of a second? Google automatically checks thousands of millions of web pages on a regular basis. It stores the data it collects in a vast index, and it is the index which is used whenever you do a search.

Interactive digital television

Some broadcasters, such as the BBC, provide their own interactive pages that can be viewed on a digital television (Fig 4.13). These have many similarities with web pages but are not part of the Internet.

Fig 4.13 *An interactive digital television image*

But most digital televisions can also give you some access to the Internet. In some cases you need to have a phone line installed alongside the television. You can already send and receive emails in this way. In the future you will be able to view normal web pages through a digital television as well. This method of getting on to the Internet will probably grow quite rapidly as you do not need to buy a separate computer.

Mobile telephones

You can also view smaller versions of web pages on some mobile phones, using a system called WAP (**W**ireless **A**pplication **P**rotocol). At present this is very limited as the screens on mobile phones are so small. In the future, phones will be able to display live video. They will also be able to record video through built-in digital cameras.

Give it a go

Mobile phones are improving all the time. Check on what the latest mobile phones offer. Can you access the Internet with them? Can you send emails? Can you view normal web pages? Can you view video?

Email

Electronic mail, or email, is very widely used by Internet users. You can send an email, receive an email, store copies of all the emails you have sent or received, and send an attachment, which is any kind of computer file, along with an email.

Email client

When you send or receive an email you use a specialist software package, known as an email client, to do this. The most common email clients are Outlook and Outlook Express (Fig 4.14), but there are many others. You must be connected to the Internet in order to send or receive emails. If you use a dial-up modem you make a quick connection, which probably only takes a few seconds. During this time your emails are downloaded from your Internet service provider, and any new ones that you have written are sent off. If you use a broadband connection, emails are sent and received throughout the day.

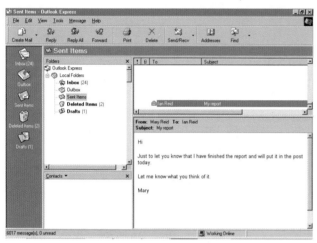

When you receive an email it appears in a folder called the Inbox. When you write an email it is placed in another folder called the Outbox until you are ready to send it.

You can usually create folders so you can organise the copies of the emails that you have sent and received.

Fig 4.14 *Outlook Express is an email client*

Email addresses

An email address usually looks like **myname@thisismydomain.co.uk** (Fig 4.15).

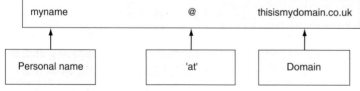

When you send an email you have to enter the email address of the recipient. You can copy an email to several people (Fig 4.16).

Fig 4.15 *An email address*

Recipient

A recipient is the person you are sending an email to.

Address Book

You will collect a number of email addresses, and you can store them in the Address Book in your email client. This means that you can simply click on the address when you want to send the person an email.

Webmail

You can use an online email client, such as Hotmail. The emails are all stored on the web, not on your computer, so you can view them from any computer in the world. This is known as webmail.

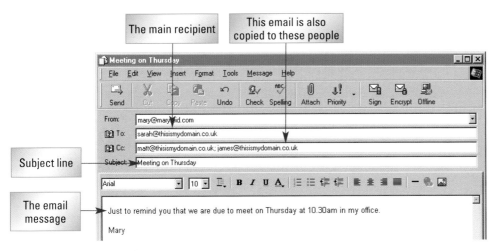

The main recipient

This email is also copied to these people

Subject line

The email message

Fig 4.16 *Creating an email in Outlook Express*

Fax (facsimile communication)

A fax machine scans in a document and turns it into an image file. It then sends the image file through the telephone system to another fax machine, which can print it out. The image file has to be small, in KB, and this means that the image is of poor quality (Fig 4.17). Another problem with sending faxes is that the fax machine you are sending to must be switched on.

Fig 4.17 *A fax*

Advantages of email

If you want to send a message to someone else you can:
◎ send a letter or other document by post;
◎ make a phone call; or
◎ send a fax.
These are still useful for certain purposes, but email has many advantages over them:
◎ Unlike post, emails arrive as soon as they are sent.
◎ You can communicate easily with people wherever they live.
◎ You can communicate cheaply with people wherever they live. It costs the same to email someone whether they live in the United States or England.
◎ You can communicate with people in different time zones. If you send an email the other person can read it and reply when it is convenient for him or her.

Disadvantages of email

There are also some disadvantages with using email:
◎ Up to half of all emails that people receive are unwanted. You can spend several minutes each day removing spam.
◎ If you want to send an original document to someone it has to go by post.
◎ If you want to send someone a document that is not in electronic form, then it can only be sent by email if it is scanned in first. This takes more time than using a fax machine.
◎ Some documents, especially ones that have been scanned in, are too large (in Kb) to be sent by email.
◎ If you have a slow dial-up connection to the Internet some attachments can take a long time to download.

What does it mean?

Spam

Spam is unwanted emails.

157

The Internet and business

Business websites

Most businesses have websites these days. They also use email a great deal. Businesses can sell either goods or services. Goods are actual objects that you can buy, such as a washing machine, cornflakes, soap or a car. Services are all the other things that you pay for, such as entertainment, insurance, holidays and travel. Some services, such as banking, appear to be free but are paid for by the interest that the banks charge on loans.

There are two types of business website:
◎ Informational sites simply give you information about the company and the goods or services they sell.
◎ E-commerce sites give you information and let you buy something from them.

Informational sites

Many small businesses simply want you to know that they are there. They provide basic information about what they do and the things they sell.

Informational sites should always give contact details so you can contact them directly. Contact details should include:
◎ postal address   ◎ telephone number   ◎ email address.

E-commerce sites

An e-commerce site lets you buy something (Figs 4.18–4.21). There are e-commerce sites that sell goods and others that sell services.

Online booking services

Some e-commerce sites let you book a seat at a show or sports event (Fig 4.21). These services have to be carefully designed to make sure that only one person is booked for each seat. They are linked to powerful databases which can check whether a seat has already been booked.

Secure servers

When you order or book anything on the Internet you usually pay for it by credit card. Many people are anxious about giving their credit card details over the Internet. They are afraid that someone else will be able to access their information from the database and then use it to buy goods fraudulently.

The solution is to store all the credit card information in an encrypted form. This is done by using a separate secure web server which stores the personal and financial data and handles the encryption and decryption.When a website is on a secure server you will see a small padlock icon at the bottom of the window (Fig 4.22).

Encryption

Data is encrypted when it is converted into a secret code. Encrypted data is decrypted when it is converted back to ordinary text.

Fig 4.18 *A typical e-commerce website*

Fig 4.19 *Online travel services*

Fig 4.20 *Some e-commerce sites sell both goods and services*

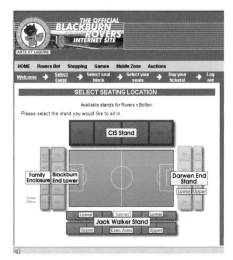

Fig 4.21 *This site allows you to choose your seat for a match*

Fig 4.22 *A site on a secure server*

Global services

When you use the Web you can look at websites stored on web servers anywhere in the world. You can chat online to someone who lives thousands of miles away just as easily as with someone in the next street.

Businesses can make use of this. Suppose you have a problem with your computer and decide to phone the helpline. When someone answers, where do you think he or she is? He or she could be anywhere in the world, and ICT is used to carry your phone call, at no extra cost to you.

A company that designs leaflets using desktop publishing software does not have to be in the same town or even country as their customer. They can create the design, then email it to a printer near the customer.

Skills: web design

You will have visited many websites yourself, and you may have experimented with designing web pages before. In this section you will learn to create a website for a business using Microsoft FrontPage. FrontPage is web-authoring software.

Looking at the FrontPage window

When you launch FrontPage the window looks like Fig 4.23. You should make the window as wide as possible, as it can get quite crowded when you are working on web pages.

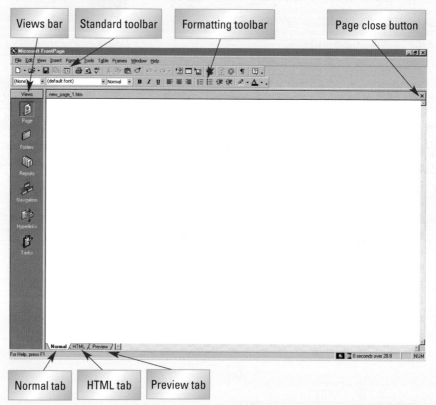

Fig 4.23 The FrontPage window

The Standard toolbar and Formatting toolbar are almost the same as the ones in Word.

The Views bar on the left-hand side is very helpful; we will be using the Page and Navigation buttons to use Page view and Navigation view.

At the bottom of the screen are three tabs – Normal, HTML and Preview. You will be using these as you create web pages.

Webs and websites

In FrontPage you design and create web pages and you save them on your own computer or network. At this stage, FrontPage refers to them as a *web*.

FrontPage will have already created a folder called My Webs in My Documents. You should normally store all your webs in here. You will probably be creating more than one web, so you should give each one its own folder.

When you are happy with a web you then upload it to the web server. It then becomes a proper *website* which anyone in the world can visit.

Starting a web

FrontPage opens in Page view. Notice that in the Views bar, the Page button is pressed.

The page on the screen is called new_page_1.htm. You are going to start a new web so you do not need this page. Close it by clicking on the Page close button.

Now select **File/New/Web**. The New dialogue box (Fig 4.24) will display a number of website templates. Click on the One Page Web template. We will start with one page and add others later.

You also need to give a name to the folder where the web will be stored. Key in the name of the folder – theatre – in the text box (as shown in Fig 4.24). FrontPage will create the folder for you.

Click on OK.

Case study

Kingsmond Theatre needs a website. The site should give information about all the performances and also the ticket prices. Eventually they want a full e-commerce site which will allow people to book tickets online but, for the moment, they simply want a straightforward informational site.

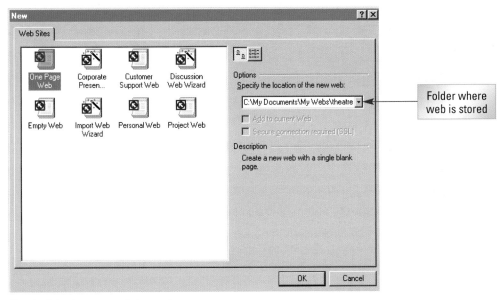

Fig 4.24 Selecting a new website template

The Folder list

The Folder list (Fig 4.25) appears in the FrontPage window. You should make the FrontPage window as wide as possible so that you can see everything clearly.

At the top you can see the name of the folder for this web. FrontPage has also created two extra folders. You will store any images used in the web in the folder called images. The folder called _private is used to store files on a website that will be kept hidden from a visitor.

The theatre web folder already contains one page called index.htm. The first page of any web always has the filename 'index'. This will be the home page for this web.

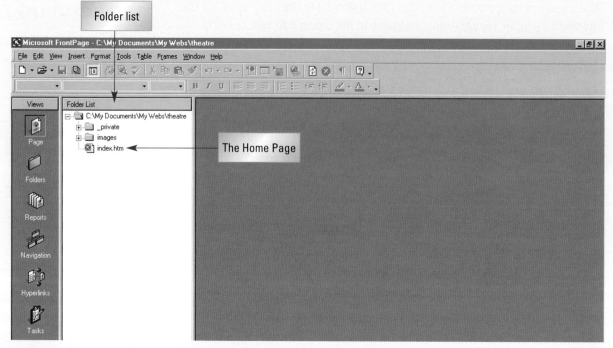

Fig 4.25 *A new one-page web*

Creating the home page

In the Folder list, double-click on index.htm. The page will open, but it will be completely blank.

Notice that the icon for index.htm has changed:

this means that the page is not open

this means that the page has been opened for editing.

You can now start to enter some text on the index.htm page (Fig 4.26).

Save the page by clicking on the Save button in the Standard toolbar. You should save the page whenever you make changes to it.

Aligning text

You can use the alignment buttons on the Formatting toolbar to align text or images to the left, centre or right of the page.

Highlight all the text and align it to the centre.

Creating headings

You will want to turn some of the text into a heading.

At this stage do **not** use the usual font buttons on the Formatting toolbar. With FrontPage there is a very neat way of creating an overall design for a website, and it produces much better results, so be patient for a moment.

Highlight the text, then find the style list at the left end of the Formatting toolbar (Fig 4.27). Click on the small arrow, then select **Heading 1**. You can use any of the other Heading styles for other text (Fig 4.28).

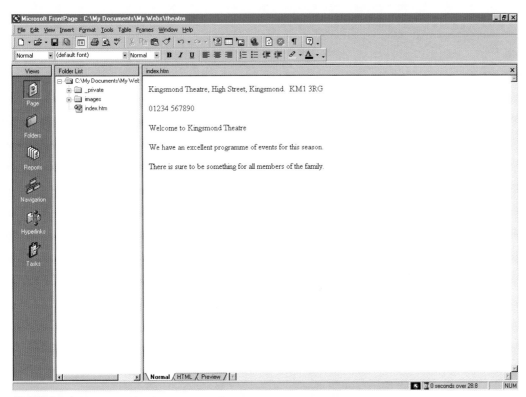

Fig 4.26 *Entering text on a page*

Fig 4.27 *Using the Heading 1 style in the style list*

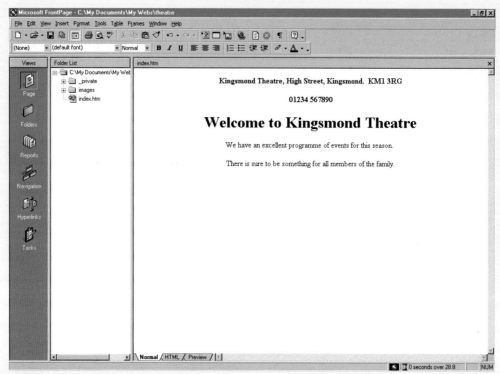

Fig 4.28 *Styles applied to text*

Adding a horizontal line

Click on the page where you want to place a horizontal line. Select **Insert/Horizontal Line** (Fig 4.29).

Fig 4.29 *Horizontal lines added to a page*

Choosing a theme

So far the page looks very boring. You could select the font typeface, size and style, and you could add colours to the background and text. But instead of doing this bit by bit, in FrontPage you can choose an overall theme for your web.

Select **Format/Theme**.

In the Themes dialogue box (Fig 4.30) select the theme you want to use. At the top of the window, click on Apply Theme to: All Pages. Although you only have one page so far, this will give the same theme to any new pages you create.

Choose one of the themes from the list.

You have some choices below the list (Fig 4.30):
◎ Vivid colors – see what effect this has on your choice of theme.
◎ Active graphics – this should be ticked.
◎ Background picture – it is much easier to read text against a plain background, so this should **not** be ticked.
◎ Apply using CSS – do **not** tick this.

Fig 4.30 Choosing a theme

Click **OK**, and you will see an immediate improvement to your page.

In the example in Fig 4.31, we have used the Artsy theme.

Using images on a web page

Images used on a website are usually in one of these two formats:
◎ jpg – mainly for photos, with a large number of colours; or
◎ gif – most other images, including Clip Art, with a smaller range of colours.

Both these formats are compressed. The filename extensions tell you which format has been used, for example, cat.jpg or dog.gif

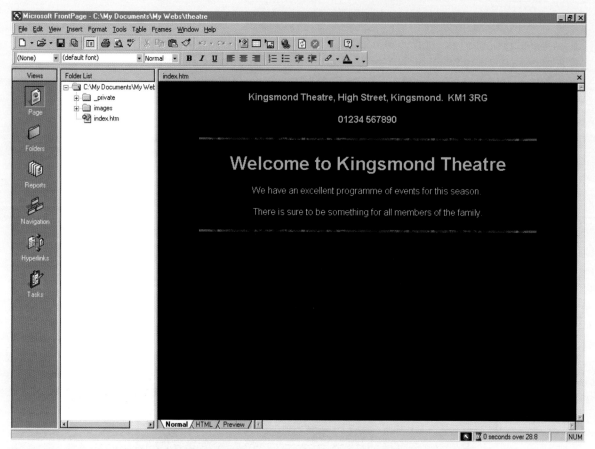

Fig 4.31 *The page with a theme*

Many of the images that you want to use on a web page will be in other formats. FrontPage will convert them automatically for you.

The size of image files

When you download a web page from the Internet, the browser first of all downloads the actual page file. It then downloads all the image files that are used on the page. If there are a lot of images this can take some time, especially on a slow dial-up connection.

Most of the image files that you use in word processing or desktop publishing take a great deal of memory. The size of the image file can vary from a few kilobytes up to several megabytes.

For example, photos taken with a digital camera are often 2 MB or 4 MB in size. If you could put one of these on a website, then tried to download them, they would take many minutes on a slow modem.

For this reason, all images on a website are stored in a compressed format which gives much smaller file sizes.

Inserting Clip Art

You can insert Clip Art on a web page just as you can in word-processed or desktop published documents.

Click on the page where you want the Clip Art to appear. Select **Insert/Picture/Clipart**, then choose the Clip Art image that you want. It will be inserted on the page.

The Clip Art image will probably have to be changed before it is right for your page (see Fig 4.32).

Using the Pictures toolbar

Click on the image, and the Pictures toolbar will appear at the bottom of the window (Fig 4.32).

You can use the buttons on the Pictures toolbar to rotate or flip the image. You can also change the brightness and contrast of the colours.

If you want to go back to the original drawing, click on the Restore button.

Fig 4.32 Clipart inserted on the page, with the Pictures toolbar

Making an image smaller

Sometimes the image is too big for the page. You can make it smaller by dragging the handles around the image.

Fig 4.33 *The handles have been used to resize the image*

If you drag on one of the side handles the image will be squashed in one direction only. If you drag on one of the corner handles the image will get smaller but still keep the same proportions (Fig 4.33).

The image may look a little distorted at this stage.

Resampling an image

When you make an image smaller on the page it does not change the size of the file. This means that the image file uses more kilobytes of memory than it needs to.

You can create a new version of the image file that is exactly the size you want it to be, by resampling it. Click on the image, then click on the Resample button in the Pictures toolbar:

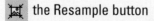 the Resample button

Not only does this reduce the size of the image file but it also improves the appearance of the image.

Fig 4.34 *A case of jaggies in an image that has been enlarged*

It is also possible to enlarge an image in this way, but the resampled file will be larger than the original. Often enlarged images suffer from the 'jaggies', which is the nickname for the jagged edges that you sometimes see on graphics (Fig 4.34).

Saving an image

When you add an image to a page you should then save the page.

The Save Embedded Files dialogue box will then appear. The name of the images folder should appear under Folder, as in Fig 4.35. If the word 'images' does not appear under Folder, then click on Change Folder, and select the images folder.

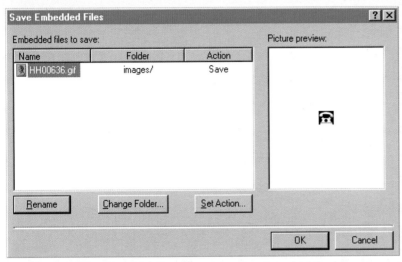

Fig 4.35 *The Save Embedded Files dialogue box*

FrontPage will convert the image to .gif format and then save the image as a separate file in the images folder.

You can check which image files have been saved by clicking on the images folder in the Folder list (Fig 4.36).

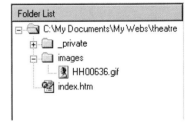

Fig 4.36 *The images folder*

Making parts of an image transparent

The telephone Clip Art has a black background so it fits on the black background of the page. But most Clip Art has a white background, which makes the image looks very odd on the page (Fig 4.37). You need to make the background of the image transparent so that the background colour of the page shows through.

Click on the page where you want the Clip Art to be placed. **Select Insert/Picture/Clip Art**, then choose a Clip Art image that has a differently coloured background from the background on your page.

Click on the image, then align it to the centre.

Click on the image then click on the Set Transparent Color button:

 the Set Transparent Color button

You may get a message at this point – if so, click on OK.

Now click on the background of the image. In our example, you would click somewhere in the white area. The background of the image will become transparent and show the background colour of the page (Fig 4.38).

Save the page and the image as before.

Fig 4.37 *The image has the wrongly coloured background*

Fig 4.38 *The image now has a transparent background*

Checking the size of an image file

You can find out how big an image file is on a web. Click on the images folder in the Folder list.

Right-click on the image file, and select **Properties**. The Properties dialogue box tells you how big the file is in kilobytes (Fig 4.39).

In this example, the image is less than 1 KB in size. The original Clip Art image was at least double that size.

You should aim to keep each of your images under 20 KB. If there are a lot of images on a page, the total size of all the image files should not be more than 60 KB. Any larger, and the page will download very slowly on a slow dial-up modem.

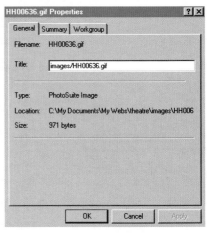

Fig 4.39 The Properties dialogue box

The HTML tab

Whilst you have been creating a web page FrontPage has been writing the HTML code in the background. To see what the HTML looks like for your page, click on the HTML tab at the bottom of the window.

You do not need to learn to read the HTML code but, if you scan through it, you may be able to pick out the text that appears on your page (Fig 4.40).

Professional web designers understand the code and often design the pages by writing the HTML code directly.

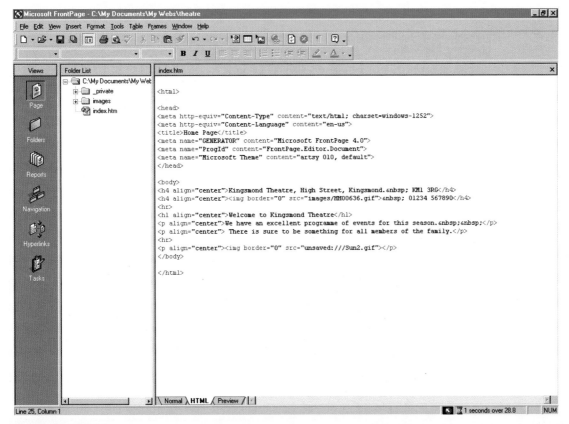

Fig 4.40 The HTML tab

The Preview tab

When you click on the Preview tab you can see what the page will look like when in a browser. You cannot make any changes to the page in Preview.

At this stage the page will look much the same in Preview as in Normal but, as you add extra features to the page, the differences will become apparent.

Using other fonts

You may have noticed the font list in the Formatting toolbar. And you may want to use a fancy font on your web page.

But beware – visitors to a website can only see the fonts that they already have on their own computers. So suppose you highlight some text on a page and select the font called Algerian. It will look as expected on your own computer (Fig 4.41).

WELCOME TO KINGSMOND THEATRE

Fig 4.41 Text in Algerian font

But when the site is up on the Internet, a visitor to your site may just see the font shown in (Fig 4.42). This is because the visitor has not got the Algerian font installed on his or her computer.

Welcome to Kingsmond Theatre

Fig 4.42 The same text seen in a browser on a visitor's computer

The FrontPage themes only use the common fonts that are to be found on all computers, so you should simply stay with them and use the Heading styles in the style list.

Adding a new page

So far your web only has one page. You can add another page. This one will list all the events in the theatre in the next few months.

First, close the page that you were working on.

Click on the New Page button in the Standard toolbar. A page called new_page_1.htm will appear. It will have the same background as the index page, but will otherwise be blank.

Before you do anything else, save the page with the name events.htm

This page will give details about the plays that will be performed. Add some text to the page and save it again (Fig 4.43). You will be adding more later. Close the page.

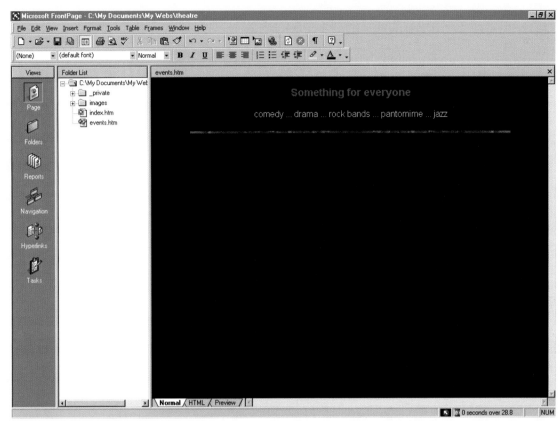

Fig 4.43 *Some text on the new page*

And another new page

Another page in your web will give the dates of all the performances. Create a new page and save it as dates.htm.

Setting up a navigation structure

Now that you have three pages in your web you want people to be able to move from one page to another by clicking on hyperlinks.

Before you can create the hyperlinks, you need to create a navigation structure. This shows how the pages are related to each other.

First, close any pages that are open. In the Views bar, click on the Navigation button. This opens the Navigation view (Fig 4.44). You will see a small rectangle that represents the home page.

From the Folder list, drag events.htm on to the Navigation view and drop it below the home page.

Next, from the Folder list, drag dates.htm on to the Navigation view and drop it to the right of the events page.

You now have a navigation structure for your web (Fig 4.45).

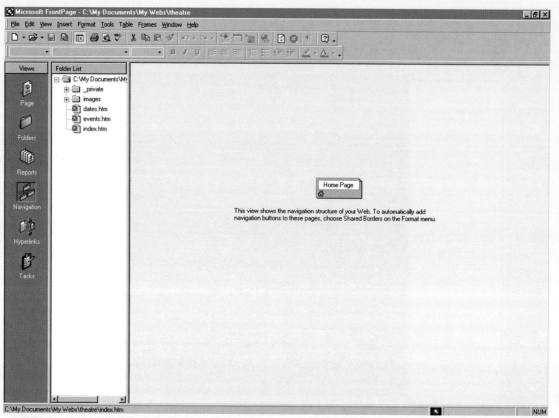

Fig 4.44 *The home page in Navigation view*

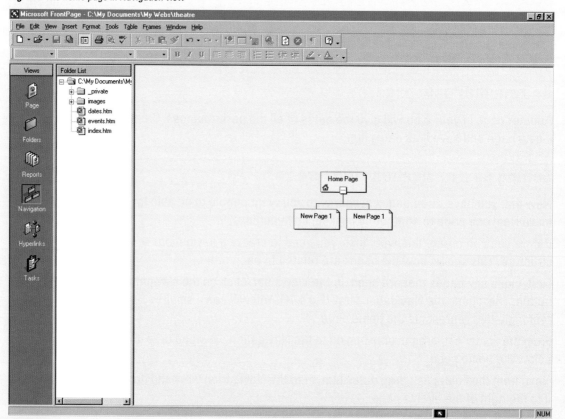

Fig 4.45 *A navigation structure*

Changing page titles

In the navigation structure you will notice that the two new pages are both labelled New Page 1. These are the titles of the pages.

Each page has:

- *a filename*. This is the name of the file and is usually fairly short, for example, index.htm or dates.htm. You choose this when you save the page for the first time;
- *a title*. This is the public name of the page, and it can be longer and more descriptive than the filename, for example, home page, or future events.

In Navigation view, the title of each page is shown. When you click on a page the filename appears in the Status bar (Fig 4.46).

Page titles are important in FrontPage because they are:

- shown on hyperlinks to that page;
- shown in the page banner for a page;
- shown in the Title bar at the top of a browser window; and
- displayed by search engines, such as Google, in the list of results.

You can change the title on any page. In Navigation view, right-click on the page that has the title New Page 1 and select **Rename**. Give it the title Future events (Fig 4.47). Rename the title of the other page as Dates and times.

Navigation and navigation structure

Navigation means getting around a website by clicking on hyperlinks that link to other pages. A navigation structure is a diagram showing how the pages are linked together.

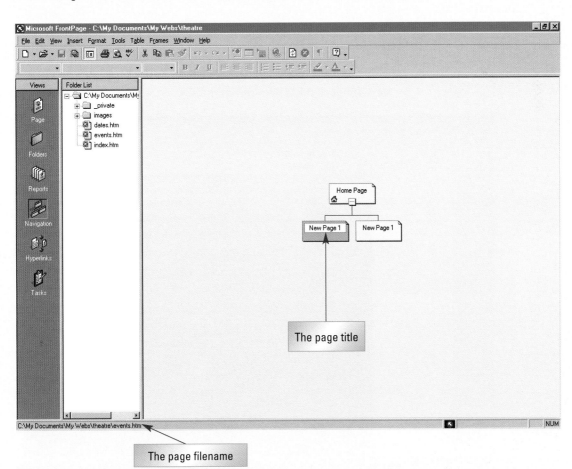

Fig 4.46 The page title and the page filename

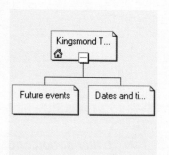

You should also give the home page a title which describes the whole web. Change the home page title to Kingsmond Theatre. Even with this new title we still refer to this important page as the home page.

Looking at the navigation structure

In the navigation structure, the events and dates pages are both at the same level. The home page (with the title Kingsmond Theatre) is known as the parent of the other two pages. Each of the other two pages is a child of the home page.

You can open any page from Navigation view by double-clicking on the page in the navigation structure.

Fig 4.47 *The navigation structure showing the new titles of the pages*

Setting up page banners

A page banner is the main heading for a page. Each theme has its own distinctive style of banner. In the Views bar click on Page. Then open index.htm.

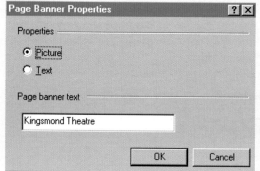

Click at the top of the page. You will probably have to press the Enter key to make space for the banner. Click in the very top row.

Then select **Insert/Page Banner**. In the Page Banner Properties dialogue box (Fig 4.48), select **Picture**. You will see the title of the page in the text box. Click **OK**.

The page will now have a graphical banner at the top. It should be aligned to the centre (see Fig 4.49). If it isn't, click on the banner and use the Center button.

Fig 4.48 *The Page Banner Properties dialogue box*

Fig 4.49 *A banner on the home page*

Save and close the page.

Then open the other two pages in turn and insert a banner on each. Save and close each page.

Setting up a navigation bar on the home page

Open the index.htm page. Click just below the banner – you may have to press Enter to do this.

Then select **Insert/Navigation Bar**. The Navigation Bar Properties dialogue box appears and has many options (Fig 4.50).

On the home page you will want to see navigation buttons for all the pages that you have created so far. They are all child pages of the home page, so select **Child pages under Home**.

Under orientation select **Horizontal** and **Buttons**. Click **OK**.

A navigation bar appears on the page (Fig 4.51).

Save and close the page.

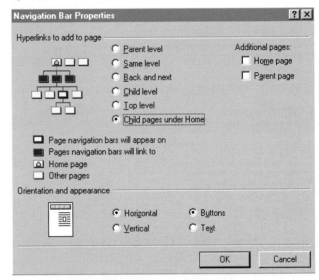

Fig 4.50 *The Navigation Bar Properties dialogue window*

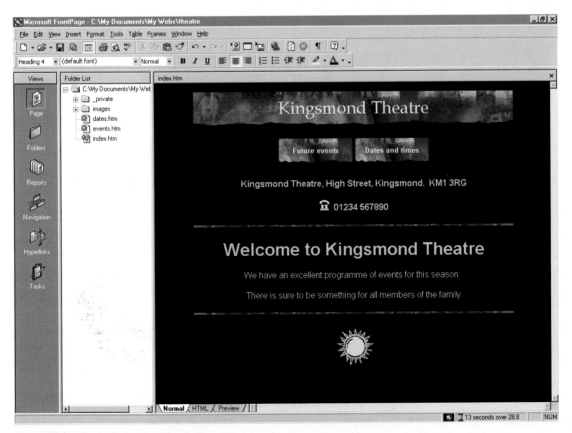

Fig 4.51 *The navigation bar on the Home Page.*

Navigation bar

A navigation bar is a row
or column of hyperlinks to
other pages on a web.

Setting up a navigation bar on other pages

Open the events page. Select *Insert/Navigation Bar* as before. Select **Child pages under Home**.

All pages on a website (apart from the home page itself) should have a link to the home page. So this time select **home page** as well.

Save and close the page.

Now add a navigation bar to the dates page. Make sure you include the home page (Fig 4.53).

Previewing in a browser

You should now check that the navigation on your web works properly. The best way to do this is to open the web in a normal browser.

First, close all the pages that are open. This makes sure that everything has been saved.

In the Folder list, click once on the index.htm file. Now click on the Preview in Browser button in the Standard toolbar:

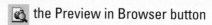 the Preview in Browser button

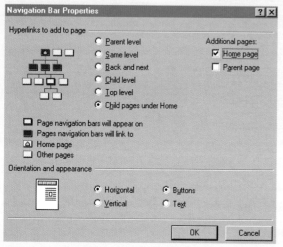

Fig 4.52 Home Page also selected this time

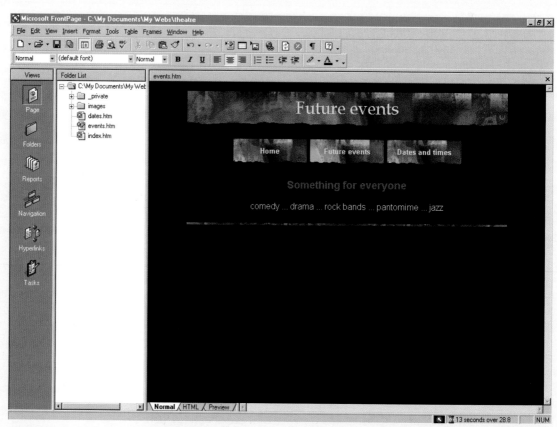

Fig 4.53 The navigation bar on the events page

You will be able to see the home page of your web in your usual browser. Click on the buttons in the navigation bar and check that they take you to the correct pages.

You should notice two interesting things about the navigation buttons.

First, as you pass the pointer over a button the button changes colour. This is known as a hover button.

Secondly, the navigation buttons appear differently on different pages. For example, on the dates page the navigation bar looks like Fig 4.54.

Fig 4.54 *The navigation bar on the dates page*

The button marked Dates and times does not work – as you are already on that page – so it is a slightly different colour from the other two.

Adding content to the pages

You can now add the content to the pages you have created. You will learn new techniques on each page:
- The home page will have extra hyperlinks.
- The dates page will give the dates of all the events, laid out in a table.
- The events page will give details about each of the events that are being staged.

Creating extra hyperlinks

The navigation buttons are the basic hyperlinks on each page, but you can add extra hyperlinks of your own. You can create hyperlinks to pages on your web and hyperlinks to other websites.

Hyperlinks can be made out of text or images.

Text hyperlinks are very useful as you can insert them into the text on a page. In the past all text hyperlinks were underlined, but today they sometimes use a contrasting colour instead.

A *button* is simply an image hyperlink. The navigation bar created using your chosen theme is made of image hyperlinks.

Creating a hyperlink to a page on your web

Open the home page. Key in some text as shown in Fig 4.56.

Highlight the text that you want to turn into a hyperlink. Then click on the Hyperlink button in the standard toolbar:

 the Hyperlink button

The Create Hyperlink dialogue box appears (Fig 4.55). Click on the page that you want to link to. Its filename appears in the URL box. Click on OK.

The hyperlinked text is now underlined (Fig 4.56). Save the page, and then use Preview in Browser to check that the link works.

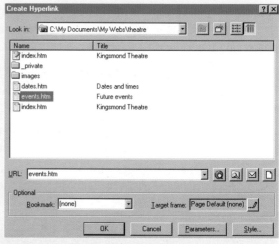

Fig 4.55 The Create Hyperlink dialogue box

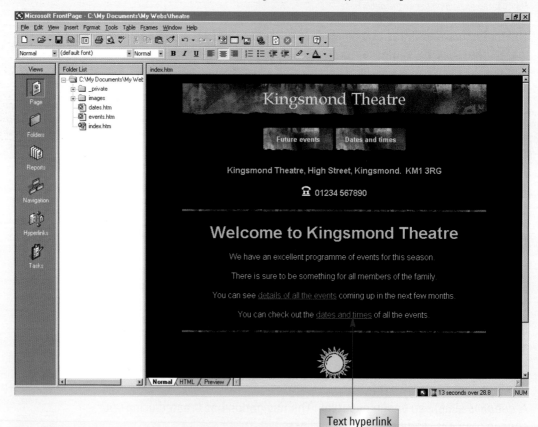

Text hyperlink

Fig 4.56 The home page with text hyperlinks to other pages in the web

Creating a hyperlink to another website

You might want to give a hyperlink to another website. Suppose a reviewer has written a good review of one of the plays that is on at the theatre. The review is on the website **www.thisismydomain.co.uk**.

Write some suitable text, highlight it as before and click on the Hyperlink button.

In the Create Hyperlink dialogue box (Fig 4.57), enter the full URL of the website in the URL box. In this case it would be **http://www.thisismydomain.co.uk**

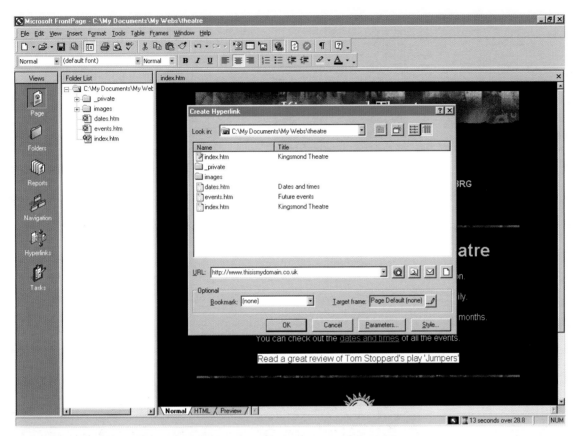

Fig 4.57 *Creating a hyperlink to another website*

You can now test this hyperlink in a browser, by clicking on the Preview in Browser button. The link to the website will only work if you are connected to the Internet.

Creating an image hyperlink

You can turn any image into a hyperlink. Insert the image on the page. Click on the image, then click on the Hyperlink button. Now select the page, or key in the URL as before.

You should think carefully before creating an image link. It should be obvious to the visitor that the image really is a link and what it means.

Close and save the home page.

Inserting a table

Open the dates page.

You are going to create a table that displays the details of all the events this season. It will have three columns to hold the date, time and event.

Click on the page where you want the table to appear. Click on the Insert Table button. A small grid drops down below the button (Fig 4.58). As you pass the pointer over the grid the individual cells are highlighted. Highlight three cells across and four cells down. Then click again.

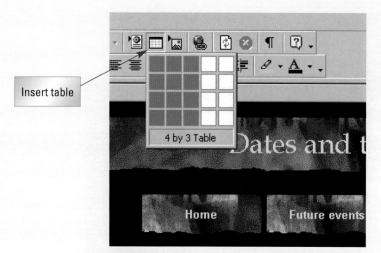

Insert table

Fig 4.58 *Insert Table button with cells highlighted*

The outline of a table with three columns and four rows is now shown on the page (Fig 4.59). You will be needing more than four rows but you can add more later.

On a light background, the outline of the table will appear as a dotted line, like Fig 4.60.

Fig 4.60 *Table outline on a white background*

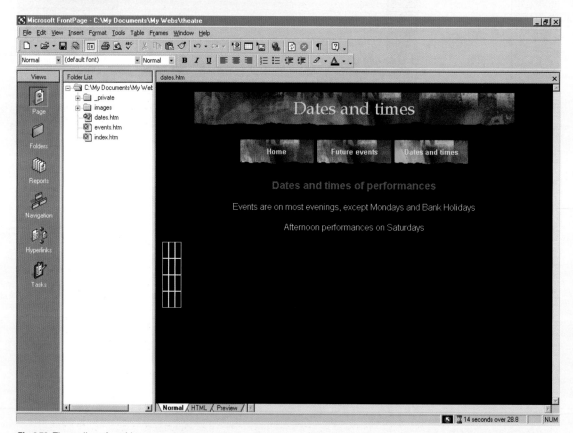

Fig 4.59 *The outline of a table*

Adding data to a table

In the top left cell, key in the date for the first performance. The cell expands to hold the text.

In the next cell in the top row, key in the time of the first performance. Then key in the name of the play in the third cell.

Add more data into the next two rows (see Fig 4.61).

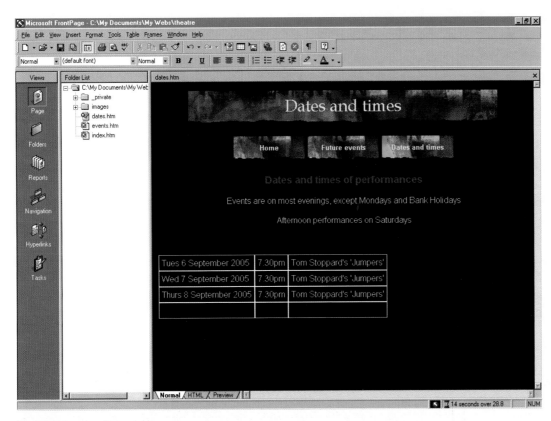

Fig 4.61 *Data entered into a table*

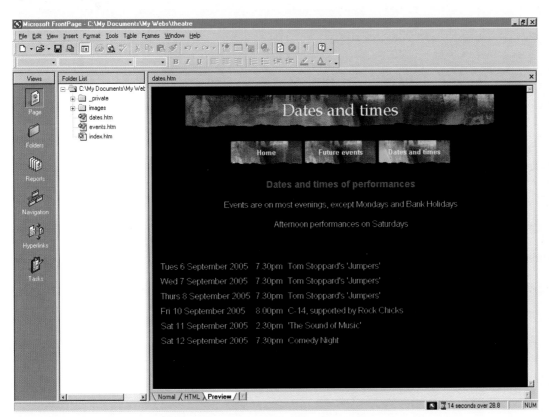

Fig 4.62 *The table in Preview*

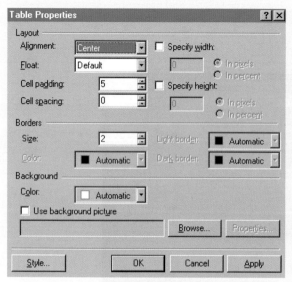

Fig 4.63 The Table Properties dialogue box

You can add extra rows to the table. Right-click anywhere in the bottom row of the table. Select **Insert Row**. This adds an extra row to the table above the row that you have clicked on. Keep adding more rows and data.

Click on the Preview tab. This gives you an idea how the page will look without having to launch a browser. You will see that the outline of the table does not show up on the page (Fig 4.62).

Aligning and adding a border to a table

Click on the Normal tab to continue.

You should now align the table in the centre. Right-click anywhere inside the table. Select **Table Properties**. In the Table Properties dialogue box (Fig 4.63), in the Alignment text box select **Center**.

You can also add an outline to the table to make it clearer.

Under Borders, the Size is given as 0. Change this to 2.

Click **OK**.

The table will now be centred. All its cells will now have a border, using colours from the theme you have chosen (Fig 4.64).

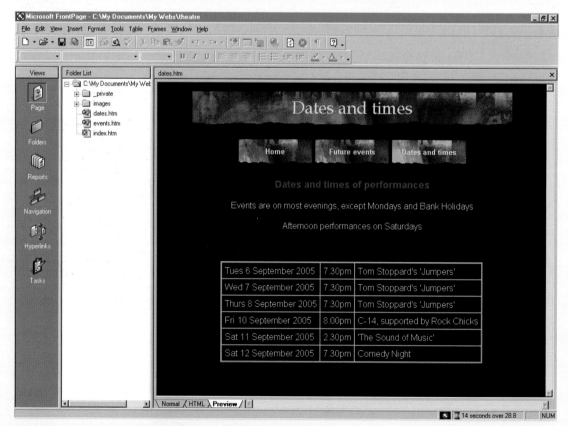

Fig 4.64 The table in Preview with a border and centred

Using a table for layout

Close and save any pages that are open, then open the events page.

A table can be used to space text and images on the page. It is best to keep the border invisible for this.

You will place some information and an image about each event on the page. Create a table with two columns and four rows. Align it in the centre. In the first row the text will be in the left-hand cell and the photo in the right-hand cell. In the second row the photo will be on the left and the text on the right – and so on (see Fig 4.65). Click in the left-hand cell in the top row and key in the name of the event. Highlight this and use one of the Heading styles in the style list. Then key in some information about the event. In the second row, insert text about another event in the right-hand cell. Add information about two more events in the next two rows. Save the page.

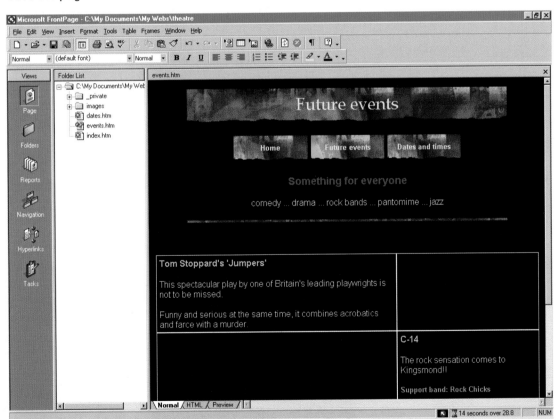

Fig 4.65 Text entered into the table on the events page

Using photos

Photos are very effective on websites. You can insert any photo that you already have in a digital format. These could be:

○ taken with a digital camera then uploaded to the computer;

◉ scanned in from a normal printed photo; or

◉ on a photo CD.

Some photos are stored as bitmapped images. Others are already compressed in .jpg format. In both cases the image files take up a great deal of memory – up to 4 Megabytes. It is essential that photos are resampled once they have been placed on a page.

You should have some photos saved and ready to use before the next step.

Inserting photos

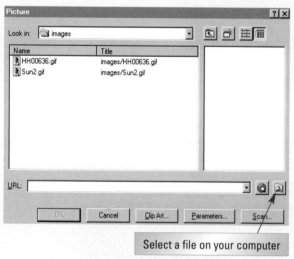

Fig 4.66 *The Picture dialogue box*

You are going to insert photos in the second column of the table.

On the events page, click on the second column of the first row. Click on the Insert Picture From File button in the standard toolbar:

🖼 the Insert Picture from File button

The Picture dialogue box (Fig 4.66) shows the files already in the images folder. You do not want to insert any of these, so you need to browse My Documents to find your own image. Click on the Select File button, then find the photo and load it in the usual way.

When you have inserted the photo (Fig 4.67), you may need to make it smaller. If you do make it smaller, don't forget to resample it.

Save the page. You will be prompted to save the image in the images folder.

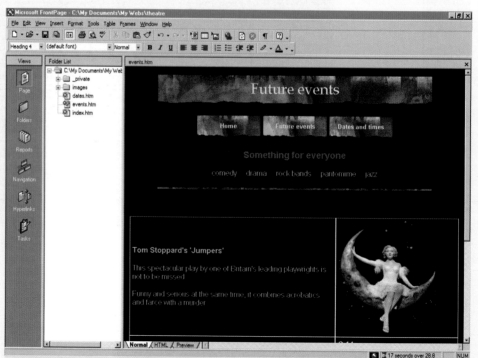

186

Fig 4.67 *A photo inserted in the table*

Cropping an image

You may want to cut out parts of an image – this is known as cropping.

Insert a new photo on the second row. If you need to, make it smaller and resample it.

Click on the photo and then click the Cropping button in the Pictures toolbar:

⊹ the Cropping button

This places a cropping box on the image (Fig 4.68). Everything outside the cropping box will be removed. You can change the shape and size of the cropping box by dragging on the handles around its edges.

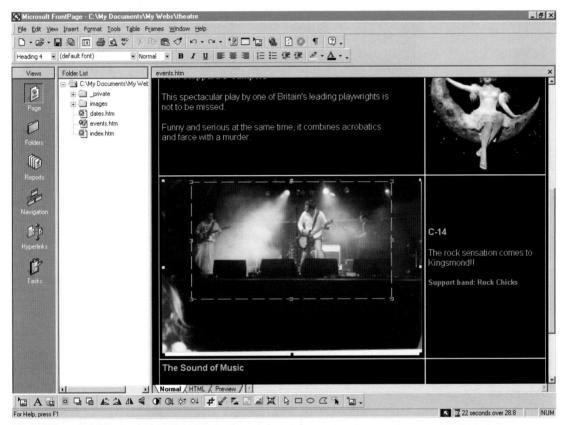

Fig 4.68 *The cropping box on the image*

When the cropping box is correct, click on the Cropping button again.

Then save the page and save the image file as before. This saves the cropped version of the image (Fig 4.69).

Resizing a table

You may find that the table is too large. It should not be any wider than the banner at the top of the page.

You can drag the right-hand edge of the table to make it narrower. You may have to resize and resample some of the images to make them fit (Fig 4.70).

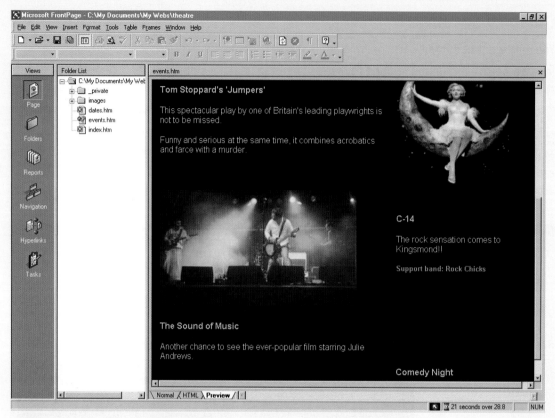

Fig 4.69 *The cropped image in Preview*

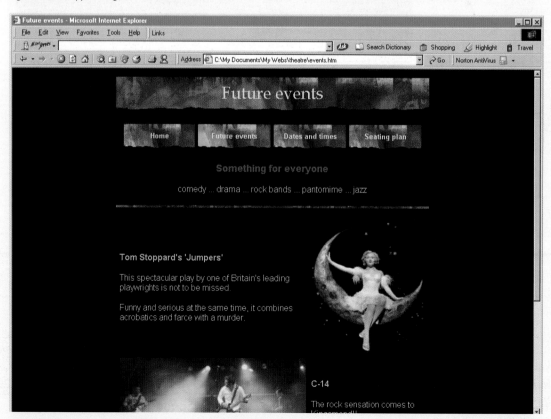

Fig 4.70 *The final version of the events page, viewed in a browser*

Adding an extra page

You want to give some information about the seating in the theatre.

You can add extra pages to the web at any time. As you create a page you should add it to the navigation structure: Close and save any pages that are open. Click on the New Page button to create a new page.
Save the page as seating.htm and close it.
Click on Navigation in the Views bar. Now drag the seating page and place it to the right of the dates page.
Change the title of the page to Seating plan (Fig 4.71).
Now click on Page in the Views bar, and open the seating page again.
Add a banner as before.
Add a navigation bar, once again selecting Child pages under Home and Home page in the Navigation Bar Properties dialogue box.
Align the banner and navigation bar to the centre.
Save the page and close it.

Click on the Preview in Browser button and see what has happened to the navigation bars on all the pages – a link to the new page has been added automatically to each navigation bar (Fig 4.72).

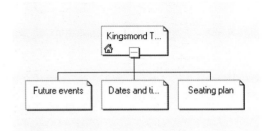

Fig 4.71 *Adding a new page to the navigation structure*

Fig 4.72 *The navigation bar now has a new button*

Drawing an image for the web

On a web page you can insert images that you have designed yourself and saved as bitmapped images.

You are going to draw a plan of the seating at the theatre, like Fig 4.73.

The blue seats are the Front Stalls and the red seats are the Back Stalls. The tickets for all performances cost £20 in the Front Stalls and £10 in the Back Stalls:
Launch **Paint**. Start by making the image a suitable size. Select **Image/Attributes**.
You will see the Attributes dialogue box (Fig 4.74). In the Units section select **pixels**.

Fig 4.73 *Seating plan*

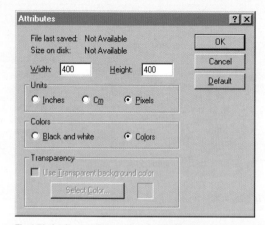

Fig 4.74 Attributes dialogue window in Paint

An image that is 400 pixels wide will fit on to the screen easily. Enter a Width of 400 and a Height of 400. Click **OK**. Draw a plan of the seating. Save it as seatplan.bmp. Close **Paint**.

Go back to FrontPage. Open the seating page.

Click on the page at the point where you want the image to be placed. Click on the Insert Picture from File button in the Standard toolbar. Find the image and insert it (Fig 4.75). The image has a white background. If the background to your page is any colour other than white, you will have to use the Set Transparent Color button in the Pictures toolbar. Save the page, and save the image in the images folder. Close the page.

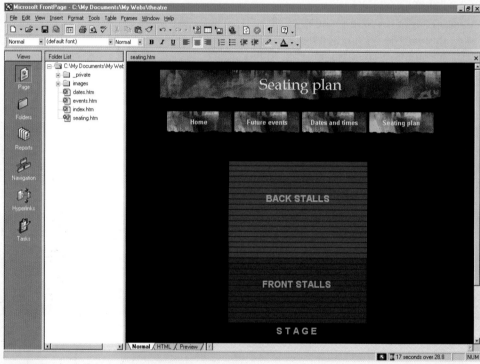

Fig 4.75 The seating plan image on the page

Adding extra pages below an existing page

You are going to create two final pages. One will give information about the seats in the Front Stalls and the other will give information about the Back Stalls:

Create two new pages and save them as front.htm and back.htm. Save and close both pages.

Add the front.htm page to the navigation structure, below the seating page. Add the back.htm next to the front.htm page.

Change the titles of the pages to Front stalls and Back stalls (Fig 4.76).

Add a banner and navigation bar to each page, as before.

Fig 4.76 The new navigation structure.

Creating an image map

You can create hotspots on an image. On the seating plan you will create one hotspot on the blue area, and this will link to the Front stalls page. Another hotspot on the red area will link to the Back stalls page.

An image that has hotspots on it is known as an image map.

Close any pages that are open. Open the seating page. Click on the seating plan image.

In the Picture bar there are four hotspot buttons:

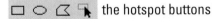 the hotspot buttons

Click on the Rectangular Hotspot button. On the seating plan image, draw an outline around the blue area (Fig 4.77). When you lift up the mouse button the Create Hyperlink dialogue box appears. From the list click on front.htm and click **OK**.

Hotspot

A hotspot is an area of an image that acts as a hyperlink.

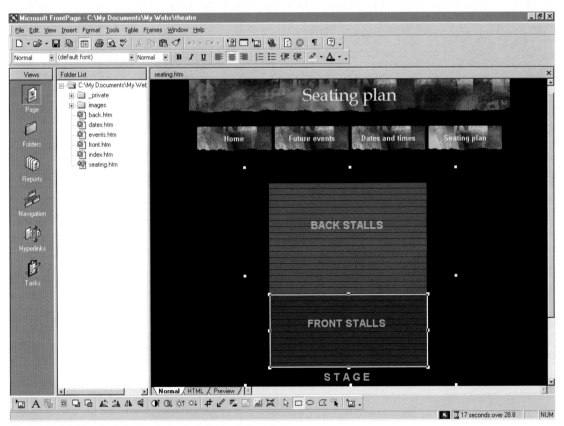

Fig 4.77 *Highlighting the hotspot with the Rectangular Hotspot button*

Now do the same with the red area, this time selecting back.htm.

Add some text to explain to your visitors what to do.

Save the page.

Use the Preview in Browser button to check how this works.

If you click on the blue area in Fig 4.78 you link to the page in Fig 4.79.

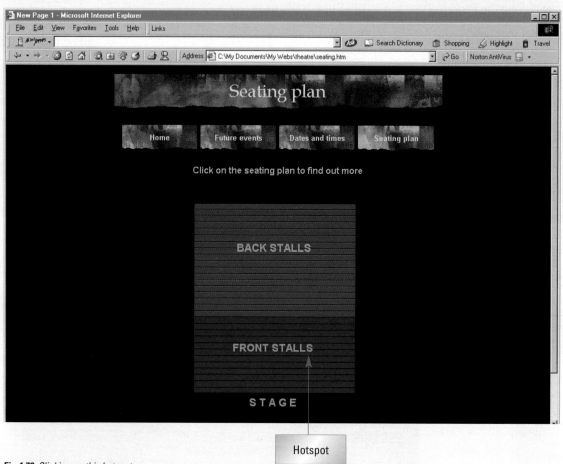

Fig 4.78 *Clicking on this hotspot …*

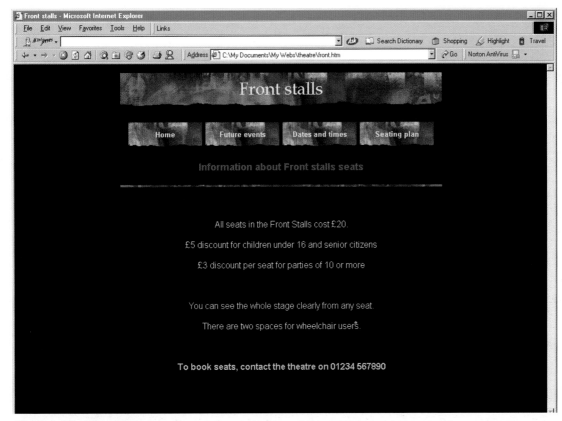

Fig 4.79 ... links you to this page

Finishing the web

Your web is now almost finished. You can add extra information to any of the pages.

Practice questions

Foundation

1 The computers used by staff in a school are networked together. Give two advantages of having a network instead of standalone computers.

2 Which of these statements best describe a network server?
   A A network server is a person who looks after a network.
   B A network server is a computer that spies on all the computers in a network.
   C A network server is the name given to the cables that link all the computers together.
   D A network server is a computer that lets other computers access files on a shared hard disk.

3 Which of these methods of communication can be used to connect the workstations on a wide area network?
   A Telephone lines.   B Satellite links.
   C Broadband cable.   D Radio frequencies.

4 Give one advantage and one disadvantage of using a WAN.

5 What is the main service offered by an Internet Service Provider?

6 What is a web browser?

7 *www.thisismydomain.co.uk*
   What do each of these parts of this name tell us?
   a www   b co   c uk

8 What is the index page of a website?

9 Here are four methods of communication:
   A Fax   B Email   C Telephone (voice)   D Post
   For each of these situations suggest the best method to use from the list.
   a You want to get a message urgently to a colleague working on the other side of the world.
   b You want someone in another town to comment on a diagram drawn in black ink.
   c You want to send a digital photo to a website designer to include on a website.

10 What is encrypted data?
   A Date which can be read by anyone.   B Very long data.
   C Data which is hidden inside other data.
   D Data which has been converted into a secret code.

Higher

11 Why are people switching from dial-up modems to broadband connections in order to use the Internet?

12 Although the Internet had been in use for twenty years before, it only became widely used after the World Wide Web was invented in the 1990s. Explain the reasons for this, and the new opportunities that it has given.

13 Describe, with examples, two problems associated with the Internet.

14 Name two devices, other than a computer, that could be used to display web pages.

15 A cinema lets you book a ticket online and allocates you a specific seat. How does the booking system avoid selling the same seat to someone else as well?

5 Managing data

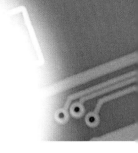

Case study: Kingsmond Autos

Kingsmond Autos sells second-hand cars. It stores them in the forecourt in front of the shop.

The cars are all made since 1980; cars made before that are handled by a sister company that sells classic cars.

Charlotte Mann works for Kingsmond Autos as a car salesperson. Her job is to watch out for people who arrive at the shop to look at cars. She then answers their questions and tries to find a car that will suit their needs. If a customer decides to buy a car, Charlotte sorts out all the details.

The database

Kingsmond Autos has a database on its computer system. It contains information about all the cars it has for sale, as well as data about each salesperson. When a car is sold it also keeps a record of the order made by the customer. The order identifies the actual car that has been sold and the salesperson who has sold it.

Selling a car

One day, Charlotte meets Julian Ferris who is looking around the forecourt for a reasonably priced family car. He spots a 2002 Skoda Octavia which seems just right. Charlotte shows Julian all the features in the car, then offers him a test drive in the car. Julian decides to buy it.

Charlotte takes Julian into the office where she uses the computer to store the data about Julian's order for the car. She has to enter today's date as the date of the order. The computer already has information about all the cars for sale, so she finds the Octavia on the database.

They then sort out the finance. Charlotte helps Julian to apply for a loan to pay for the car. He will have to wait several days until the money has been sorted out before he can collect the car.

Commission

Charlotte is paid a certain amount for every car she sells – this is known as commission. She makes sure that Kingsmond Autos knows which cars she has sold – if she doesn't do this she doesn't get the commission. The computer contains data about each salesperson, and Charlotte is able to enter data that links her with the sale of the Octavia.

Databases

A database is a collection of data. It is organised so that you can search for and read the data that is stored in it.

There are two main types of database:
◎ flat-files
◎ relational databases.

Record

A record is the data in a database about a single object or person in the real world.

Field

A field is a category used for data in a database.

Flat-files

A flat-file is a simple database in which the data can be written down as a single list or table.

You will already be using flat-files, such as:
◎ the phone book on your mobile phone; or
◎ the address book in your email system.

Your email Address Book contains *records* about a number of people. It stores the data in *fields*, such as name (Fig 5.1).

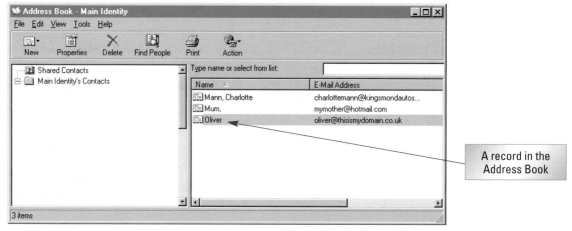

Fig 5.1 *An email Address Book*

Creating your own flat-file

You cannot change the field names in a built-in database like an Address Book. But many software applications let you create your own databases and to define your own fields:
◎ In Excel, a flat-file database is known as a list.
◎ In Word and Publisher, a flat-file database is known as a data source.

Flat-files are usually printed out in rows. Each row is one record. The headings at the top of the columns are the field names (Fig 5.2).

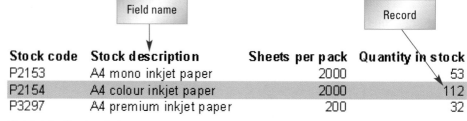

Stock code	Stock description	Sheets per pack	Quantity in stock
P2153	A4 mono inkjet paper	2000	53
P2154	A4 colour inkjet paper	2000	112
P3297	A4 premium inkjet paper	200	32

Fig 5.2 *A flat-file set up in Excel*

Primary key

A flat-file will have one special field, the *primary key field*. This field holds data that identifies each record. The data in a primary key field should be unique – that is, no other record should have the same data in that field.

For example, if you open an account in a bank or building society you will be given an account number. You will be the only person with that number, so it identifies your bank account. In the database, the account number is the primary key field.

Names

In a database, we usually split a person's name into two fields – Surname and Forename (first name). We often search databases for people by their surname and we sort address lists by surname. We could not do that if the surname was part of a larger field that included both forename and surname.

Creating a primary key field

Some flat-files do not seem to have a primary key field.

In a flat-file of all your friends, the fields could be surname, forename and address. You may have two friends with the same surname, or two friends with the same forename, or two friends at the same address, so none of these fields could be the primary key field.

You must add an extra field that will be the primary key field. You could give each friend a number, starting with 1 for the first person you add to the database.

If you were simply keeping this list on paper there would be no point in giving each friend a number. But on a computer database it is important that you do have a primary key field, even if you have to create it.

The data in primary key fields are often numbers or codes. We sometimes give the primary key field a name like Friend ID or Book ID. ID means identification.

What does it mean?

Primary key field

A primary key field is the field in which the data uniquely identifies each record.

Give it a go

Which field should be the primary key field in the database shown in Fig 5.2?

Which field could you use as the primary key field in these flat-file databases?

1   Membership database for a club – the fields are membership number, surname, forename, address.

2   A database of books for sale in a bookshop – the fields are title of book, author, ISBN. (The ISBN is the International Standard Book Number and is the long number that can usually be found on the back cover of a copy of a book.)

3   The database of cars for sale at Kingsmond Autos – the fields are car registration, make, model, year of manufacture.

Relational databases

Table

A table in a relational database is a set of records, just like a flat-file database.

Flat-files are useful if the data is quite simple.

A relational database has two or more tables that it links together.

Creating a relational database

A relational database is created using a relational database management system (RDMS), such as Access.

You must design the database before using the software.

The database at Kingsmond Autos could hold all sorts of data, but we are going to concentrate on the cars they have for sale, the people who sell the cars, and what happens when someone orders a car.

Designing the Cars for Sale table

The Cars for Sale table has these fields: car registration, make, model, year of manufacture. Registration is the primary key field, and is underlined (Fig 5.3).

When data is put in this table it will look like Fig 5.4.

Cars for Sale table
Registration
Make
Model
Year

Fig 5.3 *Fields in the Cars for Sale table*

Registration	Make	Model	Year
V123 ABC	Nissan	Micra	1999
Y456 XYZ	Fiat	Punto	2001
LD03 LMN	BMW	3 Series	2003
AB51 PQR	Skoda	Octavia	2002
R456 CDE	Volkswagen	Polo	1997
T789 JKL	Honda	Civic	1999

Fig 5.4 *The Cars for Sale table*

Designing the Salesperson table

The Salesperson table will have these fields: surname, forename (Fig 5.5).

The table must have a primary key field. You can create an extra field called Salesperson ID. Each salesperson is given a Salesperson ID, which is made up from his or her initials. The table now looks like Fig 5.6.

When data is put in this table it will look like Fig 5.7.

Salesperson table
Surname
Forename

Fig 5.5 *Fields in the Salesperson table*

Salesperson table
Salesperson ID
Surname
Forename

Fig 5.6 *Salesperson table with an extra field*

Salesperson ID	Surname	Forename
CM	Mann	Charlotte
DJ	Jones	Daniel
LM	Mackenzie	Lucy
SL	Liu	Sarah
SLV	Livingstone	Sean
TH	Heseltine	Thomas

Fig 5.7 *The Salesperson table*

Designing the Orders table

When a salesperson sells a car, he or she enters the details about the order on the database, starting with today's date. Then the salesperson enters the car registration – that is enough to identify which car has been sold. Finally the salesperson enters his or her own salesperson ID, to make sure that the commission is paid.

The Orders table has the fields shown in Fig 5.8.

When data is put in this table it will look like Fig 5.9.

Order number	Date ordered	Registration	Salesperson ID
1	23/06/2004	GR52 PTY	SL
2	30/06/2004	AB51 PQR	CM
3	01/07/2004	JQ52 HNG	DJ

Fig 5.9 The Orders table

Orders table

Order number

Date ordered

Registration

Salesperson ID

Fig 5.8 Fields in the orders table

Give it a go

Can you spot Julian's order in the Order table?

Designing the relationship between two tables

The Cars for Sale and Orders tables now look like Fig 5.10.

The Registration field appears in the Cars for Sale table and in the Orders table. When an order is created the database can look up the details about the car by searching for the registration in the Cars for Sale table.

To make the two tables work together you must set up the relationship between them.

Draw an arrow between the two fields with the same name. The arrow always starts at the field which is a primary key. The relationship is *from* the Cars for Sale table *to* the Orders table (Fig 5.11).

Relationships are always *from* the primary key field *to* the field in the other table.

Fig 5.10 The Cars for Sale and Orders tables

Fig 5.11 The relationship between the Cars for Sale and the Orders table

Designing another relationship

There is also a relationship between the Salesperson table and the Orders table (Fig 5.12).

The Salesperson ID field appears in the Salesperson table and in the Orders table. The database can look up the surname and forename of the person who sold a particular car.

Salesperson ID is the primary key in the Salesperson table. The relationship is *from* the Salesperson table *to* the Orders table (Fig 5.13).

We can now combine the three tables, and the two relationships, into one diagram (Fig 5.14).

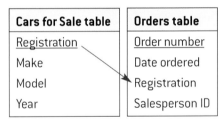

Fig 5.12 A relationship exists between the Orders and the Salesperson tables

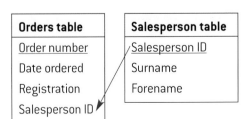

Fig 5.13 The relationship between the Orders and the Salesperson table

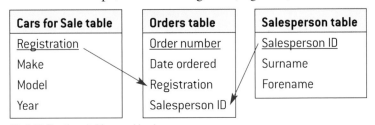

Fig 5.14 The three tables combined

Data validation

We all make mistakes when we are keying in data. There are two types of mistake:

◎ Keying-in errors – when we hit the wrong keys by mistake, or spell words wrongly.
◎ Incorrect data – when we enter false data.

An error in a database could mean that your ticket for an event is sent to the wrong address, or that you get someone else's mobile phone bill.

Valid data

Valid data is data which makes sense when it is input. In the Kingsmond Autos database, there is a Year field. In this field, 2003 is valid data, but 3.9 isn't.

You can't assume that all valid data is correct. You can enter the data 1995 or 2003 in the Year field – both are valid, but only one of them can be correct. But if all data is checked to see whether it is valid then at least some of the errors can be removed.

Data validation

If you enter data that is not valid the database should tell you that you have made an error, and ask you to try again. This is known as data validation. The database carries out several data validation checks on each piece of data.

Presence check

A presence validation check checks that data has been entered in important fields.

Fig 5.15 The presence check for a primary key

You can leave data out of some fields in a record, but you must always have data in the primary key field. In Access you will see an error message like the one in Fig 5.15 if you forget to put data in the primary key field. A Null value is simply 'nothing'.

You can also set up the database so that it carries out a presence check on any other fields that you think are important. For example, you want to make sure that the Make of a car is entered in each record. You set up the presence check in the database. If you then leave out the Make for a car you will get the error message shown in Fig 5.16.

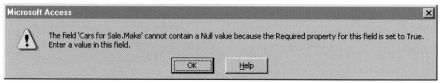

Fig 5.16 An error message produced by a presence check

What do you think?

Can you think of ways in which errors in a database could affect your life?

Data type check

A data type validation check checks that the data entered in a field is the correct data type for that field.

When you set up a table in a database you say what the data type is for each field (Fig 5.17).

Access lets you choose between these data types for each field:

◎ Text – this is used for words and phrases with up to 255 characters.
◎ Memo – this is used for text that is longer than 255 characters.
◎ Number – this is used for whole numbers or decimals.
◎ Date/Time – this is used for dates, such as 23/06/2004, or times, such as 15:30:00 (for 3.30 pm).
◎ Currency – this is used to store money values with a currency symbol, such as £34.89.
◎ AutoNumber – this is a special data type which automatically gives a number to a field.
◎ Yes/No – this is used for tick boxes, where a tick means 'yes' and a blank means 'no'.

Fig 5.17 Some of the data types in Access

If you try to enter the wrong type of data in a field you will get an error message like the one shown in Fig 5.18.

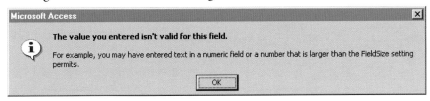

Fig 5.18 An error message produced by a data type check

Range check

A range validation check checks that the data you enter lies between sensible limits.

For example, suppose you had a table in a database that stored data about people. Under a field called Age, you would normally enter a number between 0 and 110. If you entered an age outside these limits by mistake, the range check would spot it (Fig 5.19).

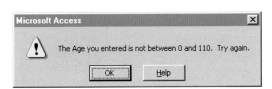

Fig 5.19 An error message produced by a range check

Check digit

A check digit is an extra digit added to the end of long number codes, such as credit card numbers. A complex calculation is carried out on all the other digits in the number, and the check digit is the result.

People often make mistakes when keying in long numbers. If a mistake is made the calculation doesn't produce the same check digit result, and you are told to key the whole number in again. The last digit of an ISBN is a check digit.

Forms, reports, filters and queries

Forms

Databases let you view and browse through the data. You can also add, delete or change individual records.

If you look at data in a table that has lots of fields you may find they can't fit across the screen. Then if there are a great many records you will have to scroll down to view them all. This can be very awkward.

A much neater way of looking at the data is by using an on-screen form. This can display one record at a time.

Fig 5.20 *A form for viewing data*

Fig 5.20 shows a form that has been created to look at the data in the Cars for Sale table in the Kingsmond Autos database.

Forms can be set up to display all the data from one table in all the fields, certain fields only, or data from more than one table.

You can also improve the appearance of a form to make it more understandable.

Fig 5.21 is an example of a form that displays data from more than one table at the same time.

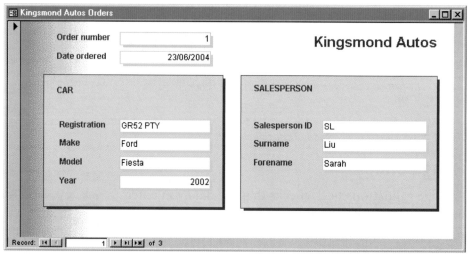

Fig 5.21 *A form that displays data from three tables*

Reports

A report is any printed output from a database. These are often printed out as lists of records. You could create a report like the one for Kingsmond Autos shown in Fig 5.22.

Reports can be set up to show:

◎ all the data from one table;
◎ the data in certain fields only;
◎ data from more than one table; or
◎ only the data that resulted from a search of the records.

Fig 5.23 shows a report with data from three tables.

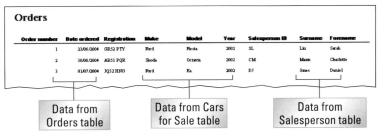

Cars for Sale

Model	Registration	Make	Year
3 series	LD03 LMN	BMW	2003
Accord	LG02 WSL	Honda	2002
Anglia	C567 RST	Ford	1986
Civic	T789 JKL	Honda	1999
Clio	LM53 KHV	Renault	2004

Fig 5.22 *A report showing all the cars*

Orders

Order number	Date ordered	Registration	Make	Model	Year	Salesperson ID	Surname	Forename
1	23/06/2004	GR52 PTY	Ford	Fiesta	2002	SL	Lin	Sarah
2	30/06/2004	AB51 PQR	Skoda	Octavia	2002	CM	Mann	Charlotte
3	01/07/2004	JQ52 HNG	Ford	Ka	2002	DJ	Jones	Daniel

Data from Orders table — Data from Cars for Sale table — Data from Salesperson table

Fig 5.23 *A report with data from three tables*

Filters

A coffee filter lets the coffee flow through into the jug and keeps back the unwanted coffee grounds. A data filter does the same job – it lets you see the records that you want and hides the rest. For example, a filter in the Kingsmond Autos database might pick out all the Ford cars, or all the cars made since 1997.

Of course, you have to find a way of explaining to the database what it is you want. You have to create a criterion (or rule) which selects certain records. You can have more than one criterion in a filter. You create a filter when you want to search for data in a database.

Criteria in filters

Here are some examples of criteria that you could use to search the Kingsmond Autos database:

◎ *Make = "Ford"* – finds all the cars made by Ford.
◎ *Year > 1999* – finds all the cars made after 1999.
◎ *Model like "C*"* – finds all cars whose model names begin with C.
◎ *NOT "Ford"* – this finds all the cars which are not Fords.

You can combine two or more criteria to form a complex criterion. You need to use the words AND, OR or NOT to combine the criteria. Here are some examples:

◎ *Year > 1998 AND Year < 2003* – this finds all the cars made after 1998 and before 2003.
◎ *Make = "Ford" AND Year < 2000* – this finds all the Fords that were made before 2000.
◎ *Make = "Honda" OR Make = "Nissan"* – this finds all the cars which were made either by Honda or by Nissan.
◎ *Make = "Ford" AND Model like "S*" AND Year < 2000* – this finds all the cars made by Ford before 2000 whose Model begins with S.

Queries

A filter is usually created for a one-off search. But in a database you can also save a filter so you can use it again. A saved filter is known as a query.

A report can be based on a filter or a query. If you think you will want to produce a report from a filter again in the future, you should save it as a query so it is ready for use.

> **What does it mean?** **Criterion**
>
> A criterion is a rule that selects some of the data in a database. Note that the plural of criterion is 'criteria'.

> **What does it mean?** **Logical operators**
>
> AND, OR and NOT are known as logical operators, and they are often written in capital letters in criteria.

Data capture

At Kingsmond Autos, Charlotte inputs data into the database through a keyboard. This is the simplest way of getting data into a computer but there are many other ways in which data can be input. Any method of inputting data into a computer system is known as data capture.

Magnetic stripe cards

Fig 5.24 *The magnetic stripe on a plastic card*

On the back of many plastic cards you can find a magnetic stripe (Fig 5.24). Data can be stored on the stripe, just as it can on magnetic tape. Magnetic stripes can be found on these cards:

◎ Various types of bank cards – cash cards, debit cards, credit cards.
◎ Travel tickets for trains and buses.
◎ Car park tickets.
◎ Identity (ID) cards which let you into a building.

When you push the card into a slot the data on the stripe is read by a card reader. In some shops the sales assistant will slide the card through the card reader – this is known as swiping.

Smart cards

Fig 5.25 *A smart card*

Some plastic cards now have a microprocessor and internal memory chip on them. They can hold more data than a magnetic stripe.

Smart cards (Fig 5.25) are used for the same purposes as magnetic stripe cards. They are not found on cards that are only used once, such as car park tickets. The data on a smart card is read by a smart card reader. Increasingly credit and debit cards include a chip which stores data about the owner of the card as a security measure. The Pin number unlocks the card (Chip and PIN).

Bar codes

Fig 5.26 *A bar code*

A bar code (Fig 5.26) is a pattern of black stripes printed on a document. The stripes vary in width, and each digit from 0 to 9 has its own pattern. Bar codes are used for items for sale in a shop and concert and event tickets.

The stock code is the primary key for an item in the shop's database. The bar code holds the stock code, but not the price. The database looks the price up once the stock code has been input.

A bar code is read by a bar code scanner. The scanner shines light at the bar code, then catches the reflected light. It can tell whether the light fell on a black bar or a white space, and can work out the numbers that the bar code represents.

Fig 5.27 *A flat-bed bar code scanner*

Most supermarkets use flat-bed scanners at the checkouts (Fig 5.27). Some shops use hand-held scanners which are waved over the bar code (Fig 5.28). These are also known as wands.

Questionnaires and data capture forms

You have probably filled in a form which has boxes for you to tick, or spaces where you can write. You might see something like this:

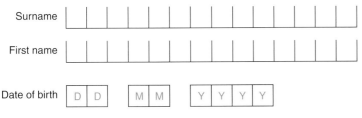

Surname

First name

Date of birth D D M M Y Y Y Y

Fig 5.29 A questionnaire

Fig 5.28 A hand-held bar code scanner

The vertical lines force the writer to space out the letters so they are easier to read. The letters DD, MM and YYYY tell the writer the format that should be used for the date. This makes it easy for someone to read the data on the form and to key it in.

Optical mark recognition (OMR)

Sometimes on a form you are asked to draw a careful line or mark across a box. Optical mark recognition reads these marks and inputs the data into a database. Optical mark recognition is used for National Lottery forms and multiple-choice tests. The completed documents are passed through a document reader. This shines a light at the marks and records where the marks are placed.

Optical Character Recognition

Some documents are printed using a special font which can be read using optical character recognition. Optical character recognition is used to read postcodes printed on envelopes, personal information on a passport and printed text on a document.

Fig 5.30 A multiple-choice answer sheet

Magnetic ink character recognition (MICR)

Information is printed along the bottom of a cheque. A special font is used, and the characters are printed using a magnetic ink (Fig 5.31). Most of the data is already printed on a blank cheque – the cheque number, the branch code and the account number.

When a cheque is written the amount is filled in. At the bank that figure is also printed on the cheque. The data in magnetic ink on the cheque is read automatically by a magnetic ink character reader.

Data logging

Data can also be captured automatically by sensors and then transmitted to a computer system. This is covered in more detail on pages 296–7.

Fig 5.31 The magnetic ink characters on a cheque

The Data Protection Act 1998

How much information do other people hold about you? Do these organisations have your data?

- School or college.
- Mobile phone company.
- Bank or building society.
- Local council.
- Youth club.
- Clubs that you belong to.
- Shops.
- Doctor, dentist and hospital.
- Police.

Do you ever worry about what they do with all that information? Who is allowed to see it? Is it accurate?

The law

The Data Protection Act 1998 is a very important law that applies in the UK. Similar laws are to be found in all the countries in the European Union, and in many other countries beyond.

The Data Protection Act is concerned with personal data. Personal data is information about living people.

The first Data Protection Act only applied to data held on a computer database. The latest Act covers all personal data whether it is stored on a computer or written on paper. These are the main ideas behind the Act:

- Personal data should only be collected from people with their permission.
- People who store personal data should only hold data that they need to know.
- Personal data should be stored securely.
- You have the right to see any data that someone else has about you.

Anyone who is responsible for the personal data held is known as a *data controller*. The person the data is about is called a *data subject*.

Notification (or registration)

The Information Commissioner is the government official who is responsible for making sure that the Data Protection Act is followed. Any organisation or individual who uses personal data must complete a notification form. On the form data controllers should explain:

- what data they intend to collect;
- how they intend to collect it;
- what they want to use the data for;
- whom they may pass the information on to; and
- how they will keep the data secure.

The form is then sent to the commissioner for approval.

Data protection principles

There are eight data protection principles.

1 *Personal data shall be obtained and processed fairly and lawfully.* Data controllers must complete a notification form. The data subject must give permission for any data to be used.

2 *Personal data shall be obtained and processed for only one or more specified purposes.* The organisation must only use the data in the way they described on their notification form and they must not use it for any other purpose.

3 *Personal data shall be adequate, relevant and not excessive.* The data must be just what is needed and nothing more.

4 *Personal data shall be accurate and, where necessary, kept up to date.* The organisation has to try to ensure that the data is correct, although it cannot be held responsible if the data subject made a mistake when he or she gave the information in the first place.

5 *Personal data shall not be kept longer than necessary.*

6 *Personal data shall be processed in accordance with the data subject's rights.* Any data subject is entitled to read the information that is held about him or her.

7 *Personal data shall be made secure.* The data must only be available to people within the organisation who need to know it.

8 *Personal data shall not be transferred to countries or territories outside the European Union, unless that country ensures adequate protection.* This is because all the countries in the European Union (EU) have similar data protection laws, but countries outside the EU vary a great deal.

Exemptions

There are some cases where the Data Protection Act does not apply – these are exemptions from the Act.

The law does not apply to data held:

◎ For 'personal, family or household purposes', so you do not have to worry about declaring your personal address book or mobile phone.

◎ About examination scripts and marks, e.g. by GCSE examination boards.

◎ For national security, e.g. by the armed forces.

◎ For the investigation of crime, e.g. by the police.

◎ For taxation purposes.

◎ On lists that are required by law, such as the register of electors (those who can vote in elections).

For more information about the Data Protection Act see **www.dataprotection.gov.uk**

Give it a go

Consider how the Data Protection Act affects you:

◎ If anyone holds any data about you (apart from your name and address), you are a data subject. What are your rights as a data subject?

◎ If you store any personal data about other people you are a data controller.

Skills: databases

Case study

The database at Kingsmond Autos holds data about the cars for sale, the salepersons and the orders.

Cars for Sale table
Registration
Make
Model
Year

Fig 5.32 Fields in the Cars for Sale table

To begin with you will set up a single table with information about the cars that are for sale. This is very much like a flat-file. Later this will become one of the tables in a relational database.

You will start by setting up a table, with the fields shown in Fig 5.32.

Registration is the primary key field.

Starting a database in Access

When you launch Microsoft Access the first dialogue box asks you whether you want to open an existing database or start a new one (Fig 5.33).

Select **Blank Access database**.

Fig 5.33 Selecting Blank Access database

You will be asked to save your database straightaway. All Access databases are given the filename extension .mdb. Call the database Kingsmond Autos. Click **Create**.

The Database window appears (Fig 5.34). Note the list of objects to the left. We will be using Tables, Queries, Forms and Reports.

Access will prompt you to save your work whenever you add a new object.

Fig 5.34 The Database window

Creating a table

The database opens in the Tables window. Double-click on Create table in Design view (Fig 5.34) and the Design view appears (Fig 5.35).

On the first line enter this information about the first field, exactly as shown:

Under **Field Name** enter **Registration**

Under **Data Type** enter **Text**

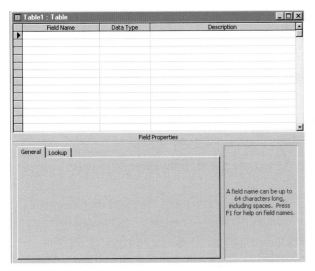

Fig 5.35 Design view for a new table

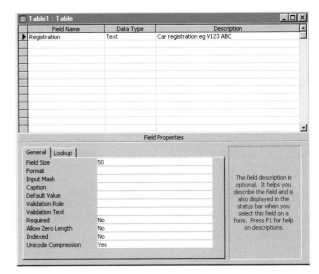

Fig 5.36 Adding a field to the table

Under **Description** enter **Car registration eg V123 ABC**

When you click under the Data Type the word 'Text' will appear without you having to key it in.

You enter a Description to give you a hint about the contents of the field (Fig 5.36).

Now add these fields on the next two rows:

Make   **Text**   **Make of the car eg Nissan**

Model   **Text**   **Model eg Micra**

The next field will be a numeric (number) field:

Year   **Number**   **Year of manufacture**

When you click under Data Type, you can click on the down arrow and select **Number** from the list of data types (Fig 5.37).

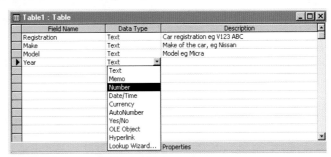

Fig 5.37 Selecting Number as the Data Type

Deleting a field

If you make a mistake and want to delete a field, click on the grey box to the left of the Field Name. This will highlight the whole row. Then press the Delete key on your keyboard.

Creating the primary key for the table

The table must have a primary key, which in this case is the car registration.

Click anywhere on the row containing the Registration field name. A pointer will appear at the beginning of the row.

Fig 5.38 Primary key defined

Now click on the Primary Key button in the main toolbar at the top of your screen (Fig 5.38):

 the Primary Key button

Save the table by clicking on the usual Save button in the main toolbar. When prompted name it Cars for sale.

Close the window.

Entering data into a table

You should still be in the Tables window. If not, click on the Tables button in the Objects list.

You will see the Cars for Sale table listed in the Tables window.

A table that has already been created can be viewed in Design view or Datasheet view. So far you have been looking at the Design view. You can open a table in Datasheet view by clicking on the Open button, or in Design view by clicking on the Design button (Fig 5.39).

You will now look at the Datasheet view of the Cars for Sale table.

Click once on the Cars for Sale table. Click on the Open button.

This opens the table in the Datasheet view, which allows you to enter data.

Enter your own choice of data for six cars. Only enter years after 1980 (Fig 5.40).

When you click in a field the Description that you gave it appears in the Status bar at the bottom of your screen (Fig 5.41).

Save the data by clicking on the Save button in the main toolbar. If you forget to do this Access will automatically save the data when you close the window.

Close the Datasheet view window.

Sorting the data

Every time you close the table Access makes sure that the data and any changes are saved.

The next time you open the table the data will also be sorted for you. Access uses the primary key to sort the data.

In the Tables window, click once on the Cars for Sale table, then click on Open. Registration is the primary key. The records are now sorted by putting the registrations in alphabetical order (Fig 5.42).

You can sort the data using any field you like. You may want to sort the data in alphabetical order of makes.

Click on the field name Make at the top of the column. The whole column will be highlighted with a black background.

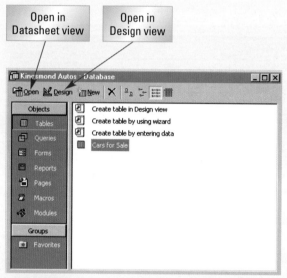

Fig 5.39 Selecting the Cars for Sale table in the Table window

Fig 5.40 Data entered in the table in Datasheet view

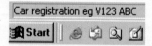

Fig 5.41 The field description in the Status bar

Fig 5.42 Data sorted by the primary key

Find the Sort buttons in the main toolbar:

Sort in ascending order

Sort in descending order.

Click on the first button to sort the records into ascending order. This creates a list sorted alphabetically in the normal way (Fig 5.43).

You could also sort the records by Year of manufacture, putting the newest cars at the top of the list. The Years will be in descending order.

Click on the field name Year, then click on the second Sort button for the reverse order (Fig 5.44).

Close the table. You will be prompted to save it. Next time you open the table it will be sorted in the way you last sorted it.

Registration	Make	Model	Year
LD03 LMN	BMW	3 series	2003
Y456 XYZ	Fiat	Punto	2001
T789 JKL	Honda	Civic	1999
V123 ABC	Nissan	Micra	1999
AB51 PQR	Skoda	Octavia	2002
R456 CDE	Volkswagen	Polo	1997
			0

Record: 6 of 6

Fig 5.43 *The data sorted in ascending order by Make*

Registration	Make	Model	Year
LD03 LMN	BMW	3 series	2003
AB51 PQR	Skoda	Octavia	2002
Y456 XYZ	Fiat	Punto	2001
T789 JKL	Honda	Civic	1999
V123 ABC	Nissan	Micra	1999
R456 CDE	Volkswagen	Polo	1997
			0

Record: 6 of 6

Fig 5.44 *The data sorted in descending order by Year*

Validation checks

It is easy to make a mistake when entering data in Access. You should build in tests which check whether the data 'makes sense' when it is input. These tests are known as validation checks.

Access does some validation checks automatically. When you enter data it checks that the data is of the correct data type. You will have noticed that several different data types can be selected, including text and number.

You can add some further validation checks of your own by checking that data falls within acceptable ranges.

Validation checks help to make the database user-friendly.

Checking the data type

Open the Cars for Sale table in Datasheet view.

Enter a new record, but enter a letter instead of a number into the Year field, then press the Enter key. You will get an Access error message.

When you created the table in Design view you set the Data Type for the Year field as Number. Access has checked the data and found that you entered a letter. This fails the validation check, so it tells you about the error (Fig 5.45).

Click **OK** on the message. Correct the data and the close the table. The new data will be saved automatically.

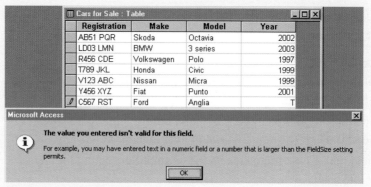

Fig 5.45 *A data type error message*

Adding your own validation check

If you are not in the Tables window, click on Tables in the Objects list:

Click once on the Cars for Sale table and click on the Design button. This opens the table in Design view (Fig 5.46).

Click somewhere in the Year row. Look at the Field Properties at the bottom of the Design view window.

Next to Validation Rule key in: >1980; this means that only years from 1980 onwards will be considered valid.

Next to Validation Text key in: Please enter a year from 1980 onwards; this is the message that will appear if an invalid Year is entered.

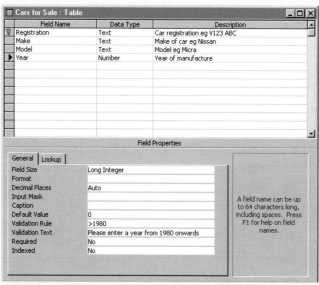

Fig 5.46 *Validation rule and text in the Year field*

Close the table. You will be warned that the new validation (or data integrity) rule may make some existing data invalid. Click on Yes.

Open the table in Datasheet view. Add a new record with an invalid Year (e.g. 1066) to see how it is handled (Fig 5.47).

Click on OK then correct the data.

In future you should always add validation rules *before* entering any data.

Registration	Make	Model	Year
AB51 PQR	Skoda	Octavia	2002
C567 RST	Ford	Anglia	1986
LD03 LMN	BMW	3 series	2003
R456 CDE	Volkswagen	Polo	1997
T789 JKL	Honda	Civic	1999
V123 ABC	Nissan	Micra	1999
Y456 XYZ	Fiat	Punto	2001
P345 TUV	Jaguar	X-type	1066
*			0

Microsoft Access

⚠ Please enter a year from 1980 onwards

OK   Help

Figure 5.47 *Validation text appears in an error box when the validation rule is broken*

Deleting records

If you want to delete a record, click on the small grey square to the left of the record (Fig 5.48). This highlights the whole record. Then press the Delete key on your keyboard.

Click on this grey square to highlight the record →

Registration	Make	Model	Year
AB51 PQR	Skoda	Octavia	2002
C567 RST	Ford	Anglia	1986
LD03 LMN	BMW	3 series	2003
R456 CDE	Volkswagen	Polo	1997
T789 JKL	Honda	Civic	1999
V123 ABC	Nissan	Micra	1999
Y456 XYZ	Fiat	Punto	2001
P345 TUV	Jaguar	X-type	1996
▶ TG53 PRT	Ford	Fiesta	1981
*			0

Record: 9 of 9

Fig 5.48 *Preparing to delete a record*

Creating a form

If you have a lot of fields in a table, you may find it difficult to see all the data in Datasheet view. It is quite useful to create a form that will let you enter one record. This form will be used on the screen – it's not for printing out.

If the table is open in either Design view or Datasheet view, close it before you go to the next step.

In the Objects list, click on Forms , then click on Create Form by using Wizard. The Form Wizard dialogue box appears (Fig 5.49).

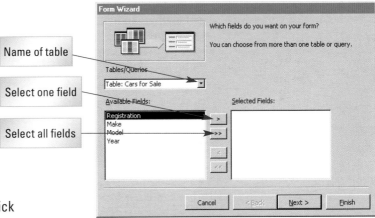

Name of table

Select one field

Select all fields

Fig 5.49 *The Form Wizard dialogue box*

The name of the table Cars for Sale appears in the Tables/Queries box, and the fields in this table are listed in the Available Fields box. Click on the >> button to select all the fields (Fig 5.50). (You could select individual fields by clicking on the > button.)

Click on Next. In the next dialogue box, select **Columnar** layout. This will arrange all the fields in a column on your form (Fig 5.51).

Click on Next. In the next dialogue box, select a style. In the example in Fig 5.52 we have selected a style called Blends.

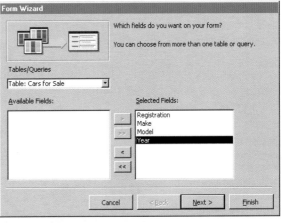

Fig 5.50 *All fields selected in the Form Wizard dialogue box*

213

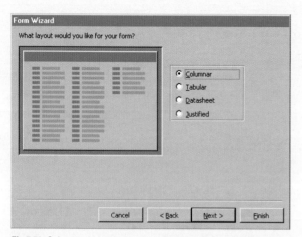

Fig 5.51 *Columnar layout selected in the Form Wizard dialogue box*

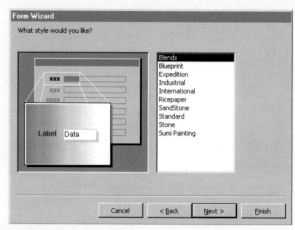

Fig 5.52 *Selecting a style in the Form Wizard dialogue box*

Click on Next. In the next dialogue box, click on Finish.

Using a form

A form appears with all the fields in it (Fig 5.53). The first record in the table is displayed.

At the bottom of the form you can see some navigation buttons (Fig 5.54). Try them out.

Fig 5.53 *A form created using the Form Wizard*

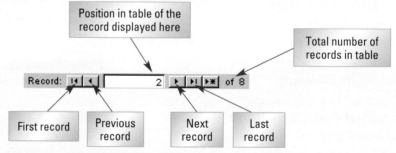

Fig 5.54 *The navigation buttons on a form*

Using a form to edit data in a table

You can change the data held in a table by changing it on a form.

Try changing the data in one or two records. Close the form.

Click on Tables in the Objects list. Open the Cars for Sale table and check that the changes have been made to the data.

Using a form to add a new record to a table

You can add a new record to the table.

Close the table if it is still open. Click on Forms in the Object list.

Click on the Cars for Sale form, then click on Open.

Click on the New Record button (Fig 5.55). You will be given a blank form to complete.

Fig 5.55 The New Record button

Fig 5.56 Entering a new record

Add data in the first field (Fig 5.57). When you press the Enter key on your keyboard you will jump to the next field. Complete all the fields for one record.

Use the form to add several new records. When you close the form all the new data will be saved.

Creating a report

A report is a printed document of data in the database.

Close any tables or forms that may be open.

In the Objects list, click on Reports. Double-click on Create Report by using Wizard.

The Report Wizard dialogue box appears (Fig 5.57).

The name of the table Cars for Sale appears in the Tables/Queries box, and the fields in this table are listed in the Available Fields box.

Select all the fields by clicking on the $>>$ key (Fig 5.58), then click on Next.

In the next dialogue box (Fig 5.59), do not make any changes. Just click on Next.

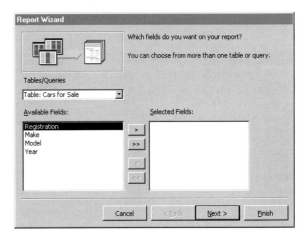

Fig 5.57 The Report Wizard dialogue

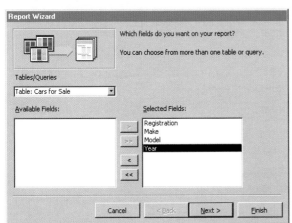

Fig 5.58 All the fields selected

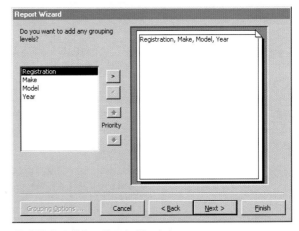

Fig 5.59 Just click on Next in this window

In the next dialogue box (Fig 5.60), you can choose how you want the records sorted in the report. Click on the down arrow in the first text box. A list of fields will drop down. Select the one that you want to use to sort the records. In this example, the records will be sorted by the Model field.

The records will be sorted in ascending order of Model names. If you want to sort them in descending order click on the Sort button to the right of the field name.

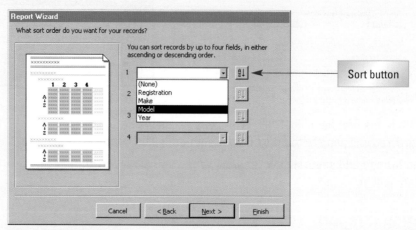

Fig 5.60 *Sorting the records for the report*

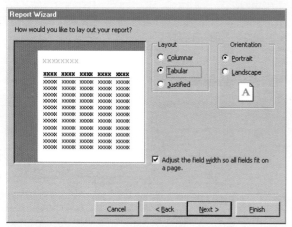

Fig 5.61 *Selecting the layout for a report*

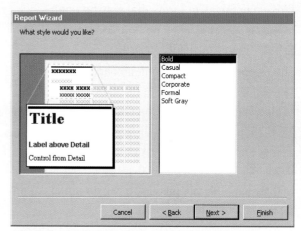

Fig 5.62 *The Bold style chosen for the report*

Click **Next**.

In the next dialogue box (Fig 5.61), you can choose the layout of the report. It can be printed portrait or landscape. The records can be printed out one record at a time (Columnar) or laid out in a table (Tabular). Select **Tabular**.

Make sure that there is a tick beside Adjust the field width so all fields fit on a page.

Click on Next. You can now choose a style for your report. In the example in Fig 5.63 we have selected a style called Bold.

Click on Next. In the final dialogue box click on Finish.

You will then view a preview of your report (Fig 5.63). You can print this out by clicking on the Print button in the main toolbar.

Close the Preview window. The report is saved so you can print it out again later if you like.

Selecting fields for a report

You can create a report that only lists some of the fields. Look at the report shown in Fig 5.64.

Cars for Sale

Model	Registration	Make	Year
3 series	LD03 LMN	BMW	2003
Accord	LG02 WSL	Honda	2002
Anglia	C567 RST	Ford	1986
Civic	T789 JKL	Honda	1999
Clio	LM53 KHV	Renault	2004
Corsa	GT52 FRT	Vauxhall	2002
Fiesta	S497 RFT	Ford	1998
Fiesta	GR52 PTY	Ford	2002
Focus	KM04 HTC	Ford	2004
Ka	JQ52 HNG	Ford	2002
Micra	V123 ABC	Nissan	1999
Mondeo	RD03 TYG	Ford	2003
Octavia	AB51 PQR	Skoda	2002
Polo	R456 CDE	Volkswagen	1997
Punto	Y456 XYZ	Fiat	2001

Fig 5.63 A report showing all the cars sorted by Model

Cars for Sale, sorted by Make

Make	Skoda
Registration	AB51 PQR
Make	Ford
Registration	C567 RST
Make	Ford
Registration	GR52 PTY
Make	Vauxhall
Registration	GT52 FRT
Make	Ford
Registration	JQ52 HNG
Make	Ford
Registration	KM04 HTC
Make	BMW

Fig 5.64 Another report created in the database

To create this report, you start by picking out only two fields in the first dialogue box (Fig 5.65).

Can you work out what you should do next?

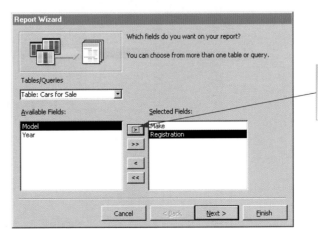

Fig 5.65 Selecting only two fields

Creating filters to search for records

You create a filter when you want to search for data in a database. To carry out the search you have to enter a criterion.

Close any tables, forms or reports that are open.

Open the Cars for Sale table in Datasheet view. Make sure you have enough records to make it worth your while doing a search (Fig 5.66).

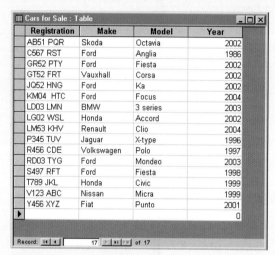

Fig 5.66 The records in the table

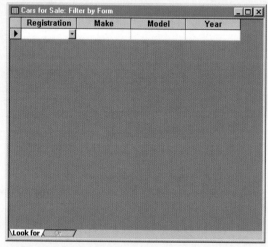

Fig 5.67 The Filter by Form window

You are going to search for all the cars made by Ford.

Click on the Filter by Form button in the main toolbar:

 the Filter by Form button (this looks like a coffee filter with a form)

The table changes to the one shown in Fig 5.67.

You can now enter a criterion in one of the fields. Since you are looking for a particular Make, click in the Make field.

If you click on the down arrow in this field (Fig 5.68), you will see a list of all the data stored in this field. Select **Ford**.

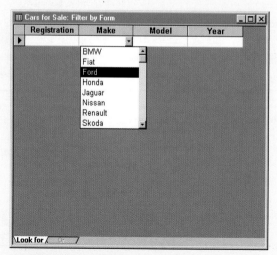

Fig 5.68 Selecting a criterion

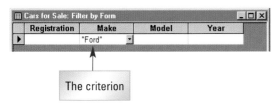

The criterion

Fig 5.69 The criterion in place

The criterion you have selected appears in the field with double quotation marks, like this: "Ford" (see Fig 5.69). This means that it is going to search for all the records in which Make = "Ford".

Now click on the Filter button in the main toolbar:

 the Filter button

The table now shows only the records that have Ford in the Make field (Fig 5.70).

Restoring the full set of records

Click again on the Filter button in the main toolbar. You can now see all the records again.

Click once more on the Filter button and the filtered records are displayed.

Searching for words beginning with a given letter

You will now search for all the cars with a Model name that begins with C.

You are going to create a new filter. The new filter will search the whole of the Cars for Sale table, even if only a few are showing at the moment.

Click on the Filter by Form button.

The previous filter will still be displayed, so delete "Ford" from the Make field.

This time key in the following in the Model field (Fig 5.71):

Like "C*"

Don't forget to include the *, which means 'anything'.

That will find anything that begins with C in that field. Click on the Filter button and you should see the correct list of records in the table (Fig 5.72).

Searching for data that is less than or greater than a value

You can use these symbols in a criterion:

< for less than

> for greater than

You want to find all the cars manufactured after 1999 – that is, all the records for which the Year will be greater than 1999.

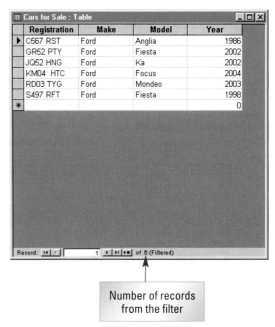

Number of records from the filter

Fig 5.70 The filtered records

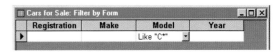

Fig 5.71 The new criterion

Fig 5.72 Records within Model beginning with C

219

Click on the Filter by Form button. Delete the previous filter.

In the Year field key in >1999 (Fig 5.73).

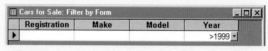

Fig 5.73 A criterion using the > symbol

Click on the Filter button. You should now see a list of all the cars with Years from 2000 onwards (Fig 5.74).

Registration	Make	Model	Year
AB51 PQR	Skoda	Octavia	2002
GR52 PTY	Ford	Fiesta	2002
GT52 FRT	Vauxhall	Corsa	2002
JQ52 HNG	Ford	Ka	2002
KM04 HTC	Ford	Focus	2004
LD03 LMN	BMW	3 series	2003
LG02 WSL	Honda	Accord	2002
LM53 KHV	Renault	Clio	2004
RD03 TYG	Ford	Mondeo	2003
Y456 XYZ	Fiat	Punto	2001
*			0

Fig 5.74 The table filtered for cars manufactured after 1999

Creating a report from a filter

Save the table before you go any further. This saves the latest filter you were using.

When you have searched your data with a filter you may want to create a report that lists the results of your search.

Make sure the list of filtered records is displayed (as in Fig 5.74).

Find the New Object button on the main toolbar. This button can change so it may look like any of these:

or or or something different again! The image it shows depends on whether you have used it before.

This may seem very confusing but, when you pass the pointer over the button the screen tip will say **New Object**.

To help you find it, the New Object button is usually next to the Help button (Fig 5.75).

New Object

Fig 5.75 The main toolbar (as displayed when using a filter)

Fig 5.76 Selecting Report from the New Object drop-down list

Click on the down arrow next to the New Object button, and select **Report** from the drop-down list (Fig 5.76).

The New Report dialogue box will appear (Fig 5.77).

Select **Report Wizard**. Check that the name of the table appears in the box at the bottom of the dialogue box. When you click on OK, the Report Wizard will take you through your options as before.

In the final Report Wizard dialogue box (Fig 5.78), make sure you give the report a suitable title.

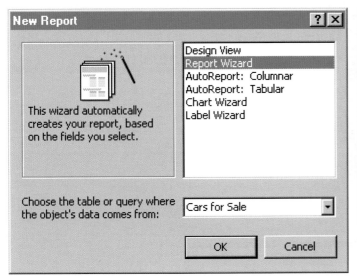

Fig 5.77 Selecting the Report Wizard

Fig 5.78 Giving the report a suitable title

The report now displays only the records that were found using the filter (Fig 5.79).

Cars manufactured after 1999

Registration	Make	Model	Year
AB51 PQR	Skoda	Octavia	2002
GR52 PTY	Ford	Fiesta	2002
GT52 FRT	Vauxhall	Corsa	2002
JQ52 HNG	Ford	Ka	2002
KM04 HTC	Ford	Focus	2004
LD03 LMN	BMW	3 series	2003
LG02 WSL	Honda	Accord	2002
LM53 KHV	Renault	Clio	2004
RD03 TYG	Ford	Mondeo	2003
Y456 XYZ	Fiat	Punto	2001

Fig 5.79 A report based on a filter

Using AND in a criterion

You can carry out more complex searches by using filters. Suppose you want to find all the cars that were made between 1998 and 2003. You could say:
I want all the cars where the Year is greater than 1998 AND less than 2003.

Click on the Filter by Form button. Delete the previous filter.

You should enter this criterion in the Year field (Fig 5.80):

>1998 and <2003

Cars for Sale: Filter by Form			_ □ X
Registration	**Make**	**Model**	**Year**
▶			>1998 and <2003

Fig 5.80 A criterion using AND

If the Year field is not wide enough you can drag on its side to enlarge it.

This filter lists any cars made in these years: 1999, 2000, 2001, 2002 (Fig 5.81).

The results do not include cars made in 1998 or 2003. If you want to include those you would have to key in:

>1997 and <2004

Registration	Make	Model	Year
AB51 PQR	Skoda	Octavia	2002
GR52 PTY	Ford	Fiesta	2002
GT52 FRT	Vauxhall	Corsa	2002
JQ52 HNG	Ford	Ka	2002
LG02 WSL	Honda	Accord	2002
T789 JKL	Honda	Civic	1999
V123 ABC	Nissan	Micra	1999
Y456 XYZ	Fiat	Punto	2001
			0

Fig 5.81 *The filtered table*

Using NOT in a criterion

You are now going to search the table for all the records where the Make is NOT a Ford.

Click on the Filter by Form button. Delete the previous filter.

Click on the Make field. Select **Ford** from the drop-down list. Then key in the word NOT in front of it, so that it reads **not "Ford"** (Fig 5.82).

Registration	Make	Model	Year
	not "Ford"		

Fig 5.82 *A criterion that uses NOT*

The result of this search is a list of all the cars that are not Fords (Fig 5.83).

Registration	Make	Model	Year
AB51 PQR	Skoda	Octavia	2002
GT52 FRT	Vauxhall	Corsa	2002
LD03 LMN	BMW	3 series	2003
LG02 WSL	Honda	Accord	2002
LM53 KHV	Renault	Clio	2004
P345 TUV	Jaguar	X-type	1996
R456 CDE	Volkswagen	Polo	1997
T789 JKL	Honda	Civic	1999
V123 ABC	Nissan	Micra	1999
Y456 XYZ	Fiat	Punto	2001
			0

Fig 5.83 *Cars which are not made by Ford*

Searching for data using a filter with two criteria

You can also search for records using more than one criterion. Suppose you want to find all the Ford cars made before 2000. We could say that we want to find all the cars which are made by Ford AND are also manufactured before 2000. This requires two separate criteria.

Click on the Filter by Form button, and enter criteria as in Fig 5.84.

Cars for Sale: Filter by Form			
Registration	**Make**	**Model**	**Year**
	"Ford"		<2000

Fig 5.84 *Two criteria in a filter*

Cars for Sale : Table			
Registration	**Make**	**Model**	**Year**
C567 RST	Ford	Anglia	1986
S497 RFT	Ford	Fiesta	1998
*			0

Fig 5.85 *Ford cars made before 2000*

When you click on the Filter button you see the list given in Fig 5.85. Compare it with the complete list of Ford cars in Fig 5.70.

Using the Or tab

There is another way of entering two criteria.

When you click on the Filter by Form button you may have noticed two tabs at the bottom of the window. One of them says Or (Fig 5.86). You use that one if you have two criteria and you want to search for records that match either the first criterion OR the second.

Fig 5.86 *The tabs at the bottom of the Filter by Form window*

This time we are going to search for cars that are made either by Honda OR by Nissan. This will give all the Honda and Nissan cars in one list.

Click on the Filter by Form button and delete the previous criterion. In the Make field select **Honda** from the drop-down list (Fig 5.87). Notice that you are in the Look for tab.

Click on the Or tab. Now select **Nissan** in the Make field (Fig 5.88).

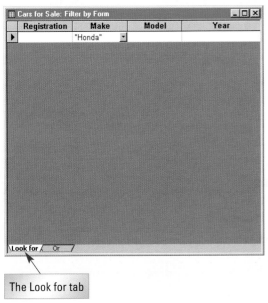

The Look for tab

The Or tab

Fig 5.87 *A criterion entered in the Look for tab*

Fig 5.88 *A criterion in the Or tab*

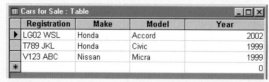

Fig 5.89 *The result of a filter with two criteria using the Or tab*

When you click on the Filter button you will see the results of this filter (Fig 5.89).

The next time you create a filter it is easy to forget that you have already entered a criterion in the Or tab. So check the Or tab before you create a new filter.

Using more than two criteria

You can use as many criteria as you like in a filter. You can put criteria in all the fields. For example, you could set a filter to search for all the cars made by Ford AND manufactured before 2000 and with models beginning with S (Fig 5.90).

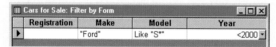

Fig 5.90 *A filter with three criteria*

The problem with this filter is that nothing matches it!

Did you notice that when you use the Or tab another one appears? So you can go on entering OR criteria. Can you work out how you would search for all the cars made by either Honda OR Nissan OR Vauxhall OR Renault?

Using a filter on a form

A form can be used to look at records as well as to enter new ones. You can simply use the navigation buttons to look at all the records one by one.

You can also use a filter on a form.

Close any tables that are open. In the Objects list, click on Forms. Click on the Cars for Sale form that you created earlier, then click on the Open button.

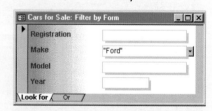

Fig 5.91 *Creating a filter on a form*

Click on the Filter by Form button as before. You can now set up the criteria just as you did with a table (Fig 5.91).

When you click on the Filter button you will only see the first record that matches the search. But you can use the navigation buttons to view all the others in turn (Fig 5.92).

Use the navigation buttons to see the other records in this filter

Fig 5.92 *The results of the filter*

Saving a filter as a query

You have now created a lot of filters. But when you create a new filter, the previous one is wiped. When you save a table or form, it saves the last filter only.

It would be useful to save some of the filters so you can use them again. You do this by saving it as a *query*:

If you have a form open, close it and save it before you go any further. In the Objects list, click on Tables. Open the Cars for Sale table. Click on the Filter by Form button, then set up a filter to find all the Honda cars (Fig 5.93).

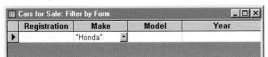

Fig 5.93 A new filter

Click on the Filter button to check that it works properly.
Now click on the Filter button again to view the criterion again. On the main toolbar, find the Save as Query button – it is towards the left end of the toolbar, and shows a filter on top of the usual Save image:

the Save as Query button

Click on this. Give your query a name which explains what the filter does – in this case, Honda cars (Fig 5.94). Click on OK.

Fig 5.94 Save the query with a suitable name

Close the table. Then click on Queries in the Object list, and you will find that the query has been saved for you (Fig 5.95).

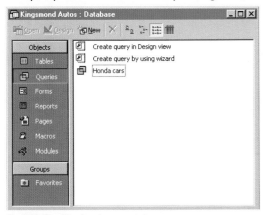

Fig 5.95 The filter has been saved as a query

Opening a query

Open the query by clicking on its name then clicking on the Open button.

The results of the filter are now shown on the screen.

You should save any useful filters as queries.

Creating a report from a query

When you create a report you can use the records in an existing query.

Close anything that is open.
Click on Reports and then double-click on Create Report by using Wizard.
In the Report Wizard dialogue box (Fig 5.96), you will see a box with the heading Tables/Queries. Click on the arrow alongside this and you will see a drop-down list of all the tables and queries in your database. Select the Honda cars query.

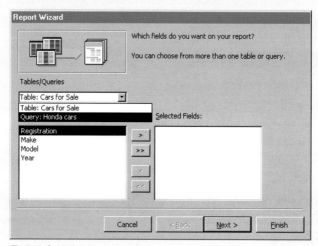

Fig 5.96 *Selecting a query as the basis of a report*

Click **OK** then carry on through the wizard as before.

The report will simply use the data from the query (Fig 5.97).

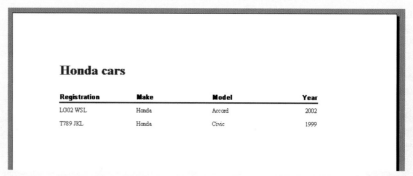

Fig 5.97 *A report based on a query*

Creating a relational database

Although you have learnt a great deal about Access already, the real magic begins when you create a relational database. A relational database has more than one table, and there are relationships between them.

Our database will have the tables shown in Fig 5.98. The reasons for including all these tables and fields are given on page 199.

Cars for Sale table	Orders table	Salesperson table
<u>Registration</u>	<u>Order number</u>	<u>Salesperson ID</u>
Make	Date ordered	Surname
Model	Registration	Forename
Year	Salesperson ID	

Fig 5.98 *Tables for the database*

Adding another table to the database

The Cars for Sale table already exists, so we are going to add two more tables:

Close any tables, forms, reports and queries that are open.
In the Objects list, click on Tables, then click on Create Table in Design View.

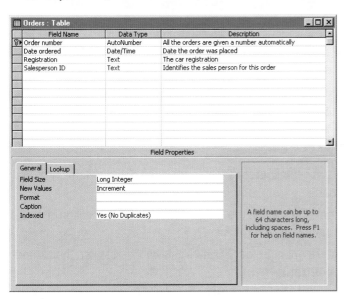

Fig 5.99 *The Orders table*

Start with the Orders table and enter these fields:

Field Name	Data Type	Description
Order number	AutoNumber	All the orders are given a number automatically

You can select AutoNumber from the drop-down list for Data Type. This is a special field type that automatically gives a number to each order, starting from 1 for the first order:

Date ordered	Date/Time	Date the order was placed
Registration	Text	The car registration
Salesperson ID	Text	Identifies the salesperson for this order

Click on the Order number field, then on the Primary Key button, to make it the primary key for this table.
Save the table as Orders then close it. Don't add any data to this table yet.
Now create the Salesperson table, with Salesperson ID as the primary key (Fig 5.100).

Field Name	Data Type	Description
Salesperson ID	Text	The 2 or 3 letters used to identify each salesperson
Surname	Text	The salesperson's surname
Forename	Text	The salesperson's forename

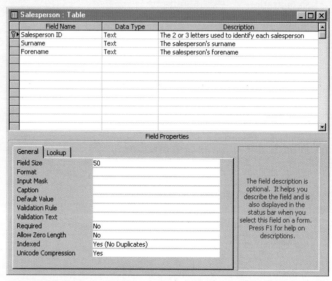

Fig 5.100 *The Salesperson table*

Entering data in the new tables

Kingsmond Autos has six salespersons. They are each given a Salesperson ID, which is simply made up from their initials.

You can now enter some records in the Salesperson table. You will probably find it easier if you create a form for this.

Close any tables that are open. Select **Forms** from the Objects list, then select **Create Form by Using Wizard**.

In the Form Wizard dialogue box (Fig 5.101), select the Salesperson table from the Table/Query drop-down list.

Use the >> button to select all the fields, and carry on as before.

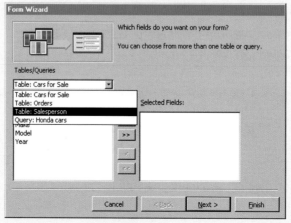

Fig 5.101 *Selecting the Salesperson table*

When the form is ready, use it to enter details of the six salespersons (Fig 5.102).

Fig 5.102 *Using a form to enter records in the Salesperson table*

Do not enter any records in the Orders table. This is where the magic comes in, but we have to set up the relationships first.

Creating the relationships between the tables

The relationships between the tables are shown in Fig 5.103.

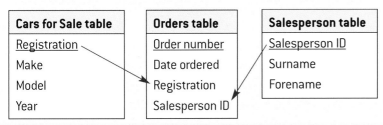

Fig 5.103 *The relationships between the tables*

You can only create a relationship between two fields if they have the same data type.

The Registration field in the Cars for Sale table has text as its data type. The Registration field in the Orders table also has text as its data type, so you can set up that relationship.

The Salesperson ID fields in the Orders and Salesperson tables both have text as its data type, so you can do that one as well.

We normally show a relationship like Fig 5.104.

Fig 5.104 *A relationship*

In Access a relationship looks like Fig 5.105.

Fig 5.105 *A relationship in Access*

To create the relationships, first make sure that all the tables are closed.

In the main toolbar, click on the Relationships button:

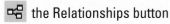 the Relationships button

In the Show Table dialogue box (Fig 5.106), click in Cars for Sale, then click on Add.

Then click on Orders and click on Add. Click on Salesperson and click on Add. Then click on Close.

The Relationships window appears (Fig 5.107). Each table is represented by a box.

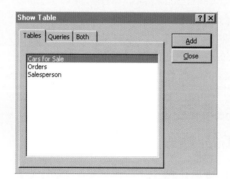

Fig 5.106 The Show Table dialogue box

Fig 5.107 The Relationships window

If you can't see all the fields in a table, drag on the bottom of the box.

The first relationship is between the Registration field in the Cars for Sale table and the Registration field in the Orders table (Fig 5.108). The Registration field is the primary key in the Cars for Sale table, so the relationship is *from* Cars for Sale *to* Orders.

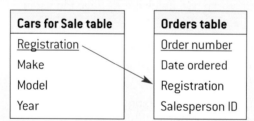

Fig 5.108 The relationship between the Cars for Sale and Orders tables

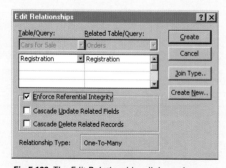

Fig 5.109 The Edit Relationships dialogue box

In the Relationships window, click on the Registration field in the Cars for Sale table then drag it on top of the Registration field in the Orders table. The Edit Relationship dialogue box appears (Fig 5.109).

Check that the Cars for Sale table is shown in the Table/Query box. Check that the Orders table is shown in the Related Table/Query box. The relationship goes *from* the first one *to* the second.

Click on Enforce Referential Integrity. This makes sure that in the Orders table you don't enter a car registration that doesn't exist. Click on the Cascade Delete Related Records box. This will ensure that all related records are removed when you delete a record in any of the tables.

Click on Create. The relationship will appear in the Relationships window (Fig 5.110). A line is drawn between the two Registration fields, with the 1 and ∞ symbols at the correct ends of the line.

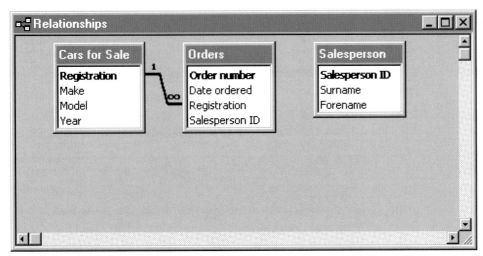

Fig 5.110 The relationship between the Cars for Sale and Orders tables

You are now going to set up the relationship between the Salesperson table and the Orders table (Fig 5.111).

The relationship is *from* the Salesperson table *to* the Orders table. So in the Relationships window you click on the Salesperson ID field in the Salesperson table and drag it on to the Salesperson field in the Orders table.

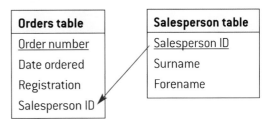

Fig 5.111 The relationship between the Orders and Salesperson tables

Again, in the Edit Relationships dialogue box, check that the Salesperson table is in the Table/Query box and the Orders table is in the Related Table/Query box. Then click on Enforce Referential Integrity and Cascade Delete Related Records, then on Create (Fig 5.112).

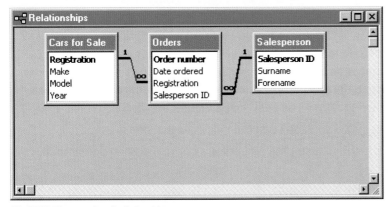

Fig 5.112 The completed relationships

Close the Relationships window. You will be asked if you want to save the layout of the relationships. Click on Yes.

Creating a form to record the orders

When a customer chooses a car and decides to buy it, a salesperson uses a database form to create an order. The car is then held in the showroom until the customer has paid for it.

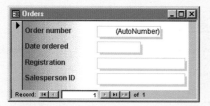

Fig 5.113 *A simple Orders form*

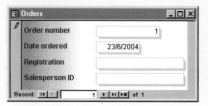

Fig 5.114 *The Autonumber field automatically inserts a number*

Start by using the Form Wizard to create a simple form for the orders (Fig 5.113).

The data type for the Order number field is AutoNumber. To see how this works, don't try to enter anything in the Order number field for the moment.

Enter a date in the Date ordered field. You can enter a date in many different ways, e.g. 23/6/04 or 23 June 2004, but it will convert it to the standard format 23/06/2004.

As soon as you started keying in another field the number 1 appeared in the Order number field (Fig 5.114).

In the Registration field, key in the registration for one of the cars in the Cars for Sale table. Then key in one of the Salesperson IDs in the last field. What happens if you try to key in something else? You may have found out already but, if not, deliberately make a mistake in the next record.

Fig 5.115 *Error message when a registration is keyed in that the database does not recognise*

Fig 5.116 *The relationship between the tables*

In the example in Fig 5.115, the database checked the Registration TH03 XYZ in the Cars for Sale table. It made the check because you set up a relationship between the Cars for Sale table and the Orders table (Fig 5.116). You also ticked Enforce Referential Integrity, which forces the database to check that the Registration already exists in the Cars for Sale table.

This is very helpful – you don't want to sell a car that doesn't exist!

Now go back to the Registration and enter a car registration that actually exists.

Now try making an error in the Salesperson ID field. The same thing happens because you have set up a relationship between the Salesperson table and the Orders table.

This checking only happens when you enter data in a field that is at the ∞ end of a relationship.

Creating a form based on more than one table

The Orders form that you have created displays the data from the Orders table. But it also checks the data against the other two tables. It would be really useful if we could see the data from the other two tables as well.

Close any forms and tables that are open.

Use the Form Wizard to create a new form (Fig 5.117).

You are creating a form for Orders, so you *must* start with the Orders table. Select the Orders table in the Tables/Queries box. Then select all the fields by clicking on the >> button.

In the same dialogue box (Fig 5.118), go back to Tables/Queries and this time select the Cars for Sale table. The first field in the Available Fields list is Registration. But you have already selected the Registration field from the Orders table. So do not select the Registration field again. Instead, click on the next field, Make, and click on the > key to select it. Do the same with the Model and Year fields.

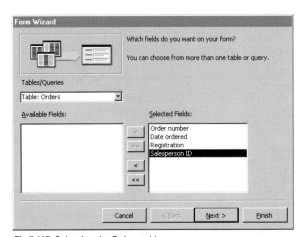

Fig 5.117 *Selecting the Orders table*

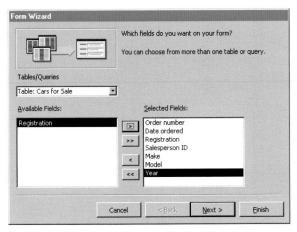

Fig 5.118 *Selecting the fields from the Cars for Sale table in the Form Wizard dialogue box*

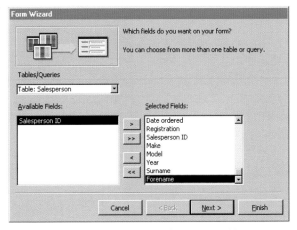

Fig 5.119 *Selecting the fields from the Salesperson table*

Finally go to Tables/Queries and select the Salesperson table (Fig 5.119). Once again, you do not want to select the Salesperson ID field as it has already been selected. Select the other fields.

The next dialogue box (Fig 5.120) asks you how you want to view the data. You want to view it 'by Orders' – that is, you want the information about the Orders to be at the head of the form. So click on Next.

Make your own choices in the next two dialogue boxes. In the final dialogue box (Fig 5.121), key in the title for the form – Orders with full data.

When you click on Finish the form is completed (Fig 5.122).

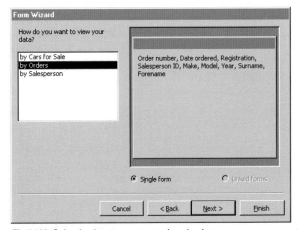

Fig 5.120 *Selecting how you want to view the data*

233

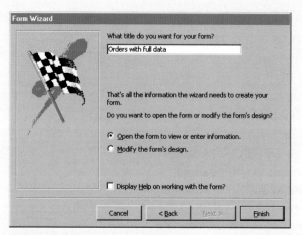

Fig 5.121 *Giving the form a suitable title*

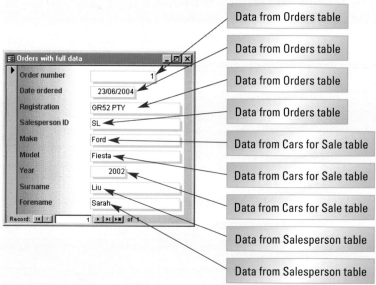

Fig 5.122 *The finished form with data from three tables*

Using the form to add new orders

With the form still open, click on the New Record button at the bottom of the form.

Enter a date in the Date ordered field (Fig 5.123). The next number will appear in the Order number field.

Enter one of the existing car registration numbers in the Registration field. Press **Enter**.

And the data about that car appears, as if by magic, in the Make, Model and Year fields.

Fig 5.123 *The data about the car appears when you enter the Registration*

Now enter the initials of one of the Salespeople – and again the data about that person appears on the form.

Using a filter on a form based on more than one table

You can use a filter on the Orders form in just the same way as you used a filter on the Cars for Sale table earlier.

You can also save the filter as a query.

Creating a report based on more than one table

You can also create a report that contains data from all three tables. Use the Report Wizard to start the report.

In the first dialogue box you make exactly the same selections as you did for the last form. Select the Orders table, then select all the fields in it. Next, select the Cars for Sale table and select all the fields except Registration. Finally, select the Salesperson table and select all the fields except Salesperson ID.

Click **Next** four times.

The next dialogue box (Fig 5.124) asks you 'How would you like to lay out your report?' Click **Columnar**. This will print the individual records one after the other.

Work through the remaining dialogue boxes of the wizard. The finished report is shown in Fig 5.125.

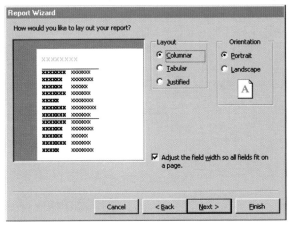

Fig 5.124 Choosing the Columnar layout for a report

Orders

Order number	1
Date ordered	23/06/2004
Registration	GR52 PTY
Salesperson ID	SL
Make	Ford
Model	Fiesta
Year	2002
Surname	Liu
Forename	Sarah
Order number	2
Date ordered	30/06/2004
Registration	AB51 PQR
Salesperson ID	CM
Make	Skoda
Model	Octavia
Year	2002
Surname	Mann
Forename	Charlotte
Order number	3

Fig 5.125 Report with data from three tables

Practice questions

Foundation

Field name	Data type
Surname	Text
Forename	
Date of birth	
Membership number	
Over 16	
Annual subscription	

James has designed a simple database to hold details of all the members of a leisure club. Members over the age of 16 pay a subscription of £90 per year, whilst those under 16 pay £30 per year.

The file design is shown here. Questions 1 to 7 all refer to this.

1 Copy the table and complete the data type column for each of the fields. Choose from: text, number, date/time, currency, Yes/No (also known as Boolean or logical).

2 Name one important field that is missing.

3 Which field could act as the primary key field? Why is it a suitable field?

4 Some of the fields have validation checks.
  a Name one field that should have a presence check.
  b Name one field that should have a range check. Write down a suitable validation rule for this field.

5 James decides to create a report from this data. Which of the following reports could he **not** produce from the data.
  A A list of all the members sorted alphabetically by name.
  B A list of all the members under the age of 16.
  C A list of all the female members.
  D A list of all the members over the age of 65.

6 New members have to fill in an application form. It is sometimes difficult to read their handwriting, so James has designed the form to make people write as clearly as possible. Draw a sketch of the part of the form where applicants fill in their surname.

7 The leisure club wants to make sure that it obeys the law on Data Protection.
  Which of these actions **MUST** the club take in order to comply with the law?
  A Allow anyone to see any of the data it holds.
  B Keep paper copies of all its data.
  C Delete old data from the database.
  D Notify the Information Commissioner.

8 According to the Data Protection Act 1998, personal data is:
  A data that you would want to keep private.
  B data about living people.
  C data about people, living or dead.
  D data held by the police.

Higher

9 A relational database management system (RDMS) is a software package that allows you to create a relational database. Describe three of the features of a RDMS that you would not find in a flat-file management system.

Keeping data safe

Case study: Kingsmond Garden Centre

Kingsmond Garden Centre sells everything that you might need for a garden. That includes plants, of course, and also garden tools, sheds, pools, paving stones, plant pots and garden furniture.

The garden centre is, in many ways, like any other shop. It orders the stock it sells from a number of suppliers, such as nurseries and shed manufacturers. Many of the products are displayed outside, whilst others, such as tools, are on view in the indoor shop. When they have decided what to buy, customers take their purchases to one of the point-of-sale terminals in the shop.

The member of staff

Jenny Smith is the Plant Area Manager at Kingsmond Garden Centre. From her many years of experience, she knows which plants to order from the nurseries, how many she is likely to sell and the best time to buy them. Customers often ask her for advice. Jenny also has to look after the plants whilst they are on display at the garden centre so that they stay in good condition.

Jenny is paid monthly and her salary is paid directly into her bank account. One month she discovered that she had been paid less than she should have received. She arranged to see the Personnel Manager and, before they met, Jenny wrote down some questions that she wanted to ask.

1 Who knows how much I should be earning?
2 What data about me is held on the computer system?
3 Who is allowed to read the data about me?
4 Who can change the data about me?
5 Can someone change the data about me by accident?
6 Is it possible for someone to change the information about me deliberately even if he or she is not allowed to do so?

What do you think?

◎ Before you read the rest of this section, what do you think might be the answers to these questions?

◎ Try again after you have read this section.

Looking after personal information

Personal information before computers

Fig 6.1 *A traditional filing cabinet*

Before computers were widely used in business most information was stored on paper documents. The documents were kept in hanging files in filing cabinets (Fig 6.1).

Most businesses had to be particularly careful about personal information. Remember that personal information is information about a living person, which could be a customer or a member of staff.

At Kingsmond Garden Centre a customer might place an order for a product that was not in stock at the time. All the information about the customer's order would be stored in a filing cabinet in the Sales Office. This information was very important to the business, so the filing cabinets were always locked when the garden centre was closed.

The Personnel Manager, Mark Moran, also had filing cabinets which contained documents and reports about all the staff at the centre. These documents included information about their pay and was considered highly confidential. Not only were the filing cabinets kept locked when not in use, but also the office was always locked when there was no one present.

Personal information with computers

Today most business information is stored on databases on a computer system. Kingsmond Garden Centre has a network of computers, with one on each manager's desk. The point-of-sale terminals in the shop are also linked into the network.

The company's database system holds data about:

◎ all the stock that is on display in the outdoor and indoor areas;
◎ orders for more stock that have been placed with suppliers;
◎ customers who have ordered extra items;
◎ past customers; and
◎ the staff who work at the centre.

Which of these is personal information?

What do you think?

Personal information often has to be changed. For example, if you move house, several organisations will have to change the information they hold about you.

◎ How can you be sure that the new information they hold about you is correct?
◎ How can you make sure that no one changes your information if he or she is not supposed to?
◎ What could happen if your new address on a database was incorrect?

Accessing personal information on a computer system

If information is written down on a piece of paper, it is usually obvious if someone has altered it. But it is not nearly so easy to tell if computer data is changed.

You might think that anyone who works at the garden centre can read and change any of the data stored in the database. But that would not be a good idea as it would breach confidentiality. Also, if the data is personal data, the Data Protection Act applies.

All personal data must be kept safe so that it can only be read by people who have a right to know it, and can only be changed by people who are authorised to change it.

What does it mean? **Authorised**

A person is authorised to do something if he or she has been given permission to do it.

Case study

Louise Mann saw a plant pot she liked at Kingsmond Garden Centre. She wanted two of them to place on her patio, but the centre only had one pot left.

The sales assistant offered to order another one for her from their suppliers. He entered Louise's details in the computer; he asked for her name, address and phone number, and then told her that he would let her know when the pot had arrived.

He also asked her if she would like to be placed on their mailing list to receive news from time to time about new products and special offers at Kingsmond Garden Centre. Louise thought that was a good idea as she did like to buy her garden supplies from them.

But Louise was a bit worried. She had been getting a lot of junk mail recently about credit cards, mobile phones and home improvements, and she was afraid that the Garden Centre would pass on her details to other companies, who would then start sending her even more unwanted letters.

Half-price double glazing windows – While stocks last!

The staff assured her that they would not give her details to another company and that they kept all their data safe.

PHONES 'R' US
750 minutes, 50 texts only £18 per month!

EASY PEASY CREDIT
6 months 0% APR, while offer lasts

She also wondered if someone who didn't work for the garden centre could somehow get his or her hands on the data that referred to her.

◎ Was Louise right to be worried?
◎ What law applies in this case?

In the rest of this section you will learn about ways to prevent computer data being changed improperly and how the law protects it.

Copyright and computer misuse

Copyright

When someone writes a book, composes music or creates a work of art, he or she (or his or her employers) normally owns the copyright to that work. This means that no one else may print, copy, perform or film the work without his or her permission. In Britain, normally, copyright extends for 50 years after the creator's death, and the rights extend to his or her heirs.

This means you should obtain permission from the copyright holder before photocopying books, copying music or videos, performing plays or reproducing photos, etc. You may have to pay the copyright holder for a licence to do so. Sometimes blanket permission is given – for example, to make limited copies of books for educational use.

For many years it was not clear whether software developers could claim copyright for their work. The *Copyright, Designs and Patents Act 1988* made it clear that software should be treated in the same way as books and articles.

When you buy some software most of the price covers the cost of the copyright licence for its use. This usually gives you permission to make one copy for your own use, plus any necessary backup copies.

Software piracy

What does it mean? *Software piracy*

Software piracy refers to the illegal copying and selling of software.

If you worked on your own as a software developer and you created some software that people want to buy, you would expect to make some money from selling it. You would have the copyright to the software, and you would be very unhappy if someone else were to copy it and then sell it.

Software piracy costs the IT industry millions of pounds each year in lost sales. This means that software companies have to put up the price of their products and the customer has to pay more. You may be aware that a similar problem exists in the music industry.

The Copyright, Designs and Patents Act 1988 makes software piracy illegal.

Hacking and the law

The technical term for hacking is 'unauthorised access', and the Computer Misuse Act is the law in the UK that deals with this offence.

Sometimes hackers gain unauthorised access simply out of bravado. But in many cases they have criminal intentions, as they wish either to shut down systems or to steal or alter information.

Hacking

Hacking is the actions of people who gain access to computer systems when they have no right to do so.

Computer Misuse Act (1990)

Someone can break this law in three different ways:

1 *Unauthorised access to computer material without intent to carry out further offence.* Examples of offences under this section include logging on to a system with someone else's username and password, or simply reading programs or data when not authorised to do so.

2 *Unauthorised access with intent to commit or facilitate commission of further offences.* If someone gains unauthorised access to a computer system and does so in order to commit a crime, he or she is guilty of a more serious offence. For example, a person might try to transfer money illegally from one account to another, or might want to find out incriminating information he or she could use to blackmail someone.

3 *Unauthorised modification of computer material.* If a person deliberately alters or deletes information held on a computer system when he or she does not have the authority to do so, he or she is acting illegally. This part of the Computer Misuse Act is also designed to catch people who introduce viruses to systems.

How does the Computer Misuse Act affect me?

The Computer Misuse Act will only affect you if you deliberately try to gain access to a computer system, or to change computer data, when you do not have permission to do so. If you do any of these things by accident, you should not be in trouble.

But to cover yourself, if you do delete some data by accident at school you should admit this straightaway to a member of staff, explaining that it was a mistake. Similarly, if you find that you have been given access to parts of the system that you should not visit, you should report that to the network administrator straightaway.

Also, if you discover that you have passed on a virus, you should apologise and warn the people who received it. But do remember that someone is only guilty of committing an offence if he or she does so with intention, so you need not worry that you may be prosecuted if you pass on a virus accidentally.

Hacker gets three years

Love rat hacked into my e-mails

MP and website shock

Virus wipes out company's records

Give it a go

Have you received any information or warnings about the Computer Misuse Act at your school? If not, you could create a notice telling students about its implications for them.

Protecting data using physical means

Protecting storage media from damage

Computer data can be stored on magnetic storage media such as hard disks, tapes and floppy disks, or on optical media such as CDs and DVDs. These can all be damaged, either deliberately or by accident.

Storage media must be protected from heat and fire, oil and dust, magnetic fields, and water and humidity.

In general, storage media kept in a clean environment at room temperature will last longer than media exposed to heat, dirt and humidity.

The effects of heat on storage media

All storage media should be kept out of direct sunlight. They can all become warped and distorted in excessive heat, and the drive will not be able to read them.

◎ Floppy disks and tapes are particularly vulnerable to heat and should be kept at a temperature between 10 °C and 60 °C.

◎ CDs and DVDs are made out of a plastic material and are easily damaged at temperatures above 40 °C, although they can survive the cold quite well.

◎ Hard disks are held inside protective casings which control the temperature.

Of course, no media can survive fire, so copies of important files should be kept on media in a fire-proof safe.

The effects of oil and dust on storage media

You should never touch the surface of storage media. Oil from fingers can make the surface unreadable. Oil can also transfer to the drive head, causing permanent damage.

The surface of magnetic media should not be exposed to the air because dust particles can settle on them. Dust can also interfere with the data transfer, and can again build up on the drive head.

Optical media are more robust but the surface can become scratched and dirty and this will prevent the data being read properly.

The effects of magnetic fields on storage media

Magnetic fields are created by magnets. Magnetic storage media can be severely damaged if they are placed close to sources of magnetic fields. What you may not realise is that electric motors, audio speakers and many other devices have magnets inside them.

The speakers provided with computer systems can usually be used safely near disks and tapes, but be very careful with other audio equipment.

Never put a magnet, not even a decorative fridge magnet, near magnetic storage media.

The effects of water and humidity on storage media

A wet magnetic disk or tape will simply not work. Sometimes they can be allowed to dry out, but there is no guarantee they will still function, so you should always try to keep storage media dry at all times. Optical storage media can be wiped dry if they become wet.

Humidity (a damp atmosphere) can be just as much of a problem as water. The protective casing on hard disks does prevent the air around the disks from becoming humid, but other magnetic media can easily be affected by humidity in the air.

Protecting storage media from vandalism and theft

If someone gains entry to a building or rooms containing computers without permission, he or she may have criminal intentions.

Here are some ways of protecting storage media from intruders:

◎ Install locks on doors, which should be locked whenever the room is empty.
◎ Install intruder alarm systems.
◎ Employ security guards to patrol the site, especially at night (Fig 6.2).
◎ Keep all removable media in locked boxes and drawers.
◎ Place network servers in a part of the building that cannot be reached easily from outside (for example, not on the ground floor).
◎ Install locks on computers – for example, point-of-sale terminals can be protected with devices that will only unlock the system if a key or swipe card is used (Fig 6.3).
◎ Keep copies of all important files in safes (Fig 6.4).

Unauthorised access is normally deliberate. But if the security in a building is not good enough someone may accidentally wander into a forbidden area.

Fig 6.2 *Employ a security guard*

Fig 6.3 *A lock on a point-of-sale terminal*

Figure 6.4 *A safe*

Case study

Desmond Bonaventure is the Managing Director of Kingsmond Garden Centre. He and all the other managers at Kingsmond Garden Centre have computers on their desks. The main network server is located in the office of the Network Administrator, Christel Jacques. There are also three point-of-sale terminals in the shop which are linked to the network.

Desmond wants to make sure that all the data held on the computer system cannot be damaged. Can you suggest some things he should think about?

Protecting data using software

Usernames and passwords

Whenever you log on to the computer system at your school, you probably have to key in two pieces of information:

◎ your username (sometimes called your user ID); and
◎ your password.

The network administrator will have given you your own username, which may be a number or else a version of your name. Your username is not confidential.

You will also have been given a password, and you should keep it secret. You will probably be allowed to change your password whenever you like, and you should remember it without writing it down anywhere.

If another person tries to log on, pretending to be you, he or she would need to know both your username and your secret password to do so. Never allow anyone else to do this, as he or she could alter your files or even delete them. Even if he or she means no harm he or she could change your work by accident. Someone who does this without your permission is committing an offence under the Computer Misuse Act.

How usernames can control access to data

The network administrator gives usernames to all the users on a network, and each user will also have a password. When someone logs on with a particular username the administrator can be reasonably sure that it is the right person, as only that person should know the password.

The network administrator sets up the network software so that each user is only permitted to read the data he or she is allowed to see. Some users will also be permitted by the software to change data. These permissions are known as access privileges.

The network administrator sets the access privileges for each user, identifying them by their usernames. He or she allocates the right level of access to each user, depending on the work they do.

This means that each user will only be authorised to use certain software and will only be allowed to view certain data. If the user attempts to gain access to anything else, he or she will be breaking the law under the Computer Misuse Act.

Case study

Desmond Bonaventure had to decide which members of staff should be authorised to read each type of data stored in the database. For example, any of the sales staff working at the point-of-sale terminals are allowed to view the data about the products in stock.

Desmond also had to decide which members of staff should be authorised to change the data in any way, either by amending individual items of information or by adding new data. Not everyone who can read the data is given permission to change it. For example, Jenny Smith, the Plant Area Manager, is the only person who is authorised to order completely new products from suppliers.

As far as personal information is concerned, under the Data Protection Act, Desmond had to register with the Information Commissioner. He then had to decide which members of staff should be able to read or change personal data. Managers like Jenny are allowed to read some of the data about members of staff, but only Desmond and the Personnel Manager may read information about salaries. Personal data about staff can only be changed by the personnel team.

You have read something about the work done by the following staff:

◎ Desmond Bonaventure, the Managing Director.
◎ Jenny Smith, the Plant Area Manager.
◎ Mark Moran, the Personnel Manager.
◎ Christel Jacques, the Network Administrator.

For each person, write down a list of the data he or she should be authorised to read. Then put a tick against the data he or she should be authorised to change.

Use of encryption to protect data

Usernames and access privileges can prevent most data from falling into the wrong hands. But a determined criminal may find ways of getting at data. The data can still be protected if it is stored in some kind of secret code. This technique is known as encryption.

When confidential information is stored on a database, it is sometimes encrypted first (Fig 6.5). This means that someone who does not know how to decrypt (decode) the data will not be able to make any sense of it.

To encrypt a file the system needs an algorithm (a set of rules) and a key (a special number). Encryption uses the algorithm and key to convert each character (letter) of the original file into another character, and the encrypted file is saved. Spaces and punctuation marks are also encrypted.

The algorithms used are quite complicated. It is not a simple case of replacing a letter, such as 'a', by the same letter each time it appears. Another key is usually needed to decrypt the file back to its original state. It is virtually impossible for anyone to decrypt the file unless he or she knows the algorithm and key to use.

Encryption

Encryption is the technical term for a secret code.

Mrs Jones, of 12 Station Way, has filed a complaint against one of our sales staff.

↑

Plain text

ajhp r4us rqst xdft 7pkl o04d eety drgh 1ws4 anmk dery qscx einh 5tgh sdft rtyl dvnk sedk y6io plas rdh

↑

Encrypted text

Fig 6.5 Plain and encrypted text

245

Skills: mail merge

You will probably at some time have received a letter which is addressed to you, but you will know that very similar letters will also have been sent to thousands of other people. These letters are generated by a process known as mail merge.

Unwanted letters of this type are sometimes referred to as junk mail. But it can also be a good way of keeping the members of a club informed about activities. Mail-order companies often use it as a way of telling previous customers about new products.

Mail merge takes name and address data and merges it with a standard letter document. The output is thousands of personally addressed letters (Fig 6.6). The name and address data can be stored in a database, in a spreadsheet or in another document.

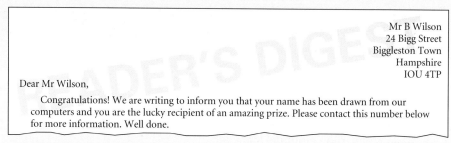

Mr B Wilson
24 Bigg Street
Biggleston Town
Hampshire
IOU 4TP

Dear Mr Wilson,

    Congratulations! We are writing to inform you that your name has been drawn from our computers and you are the lucky recipient of an amazing prize. Please contact this number below for more information. Well done.

Fig 6.6 *A standard mail merge letter*

Before you start on a mail merge you will learn how to create a template in Microsoft Word.

Creating a letterhead template

You should first of all create a letterhead. This is a document with the logo and address of the company. You want to use it over and over again, every time you create a letter for them, so you will save it as a template.

In Word, select **File/New**. Do not click on the New Blank Document button on the Standard toolbar. When you select **File/New** you are given many more options.

In the New dialogue box, click on the icon for the Blank Document (see Fig 6.7). Then in the Create New section, select **Template**.

Template

A template is a special type of document that you can use again and again as the basis for letters and other standard business documents.

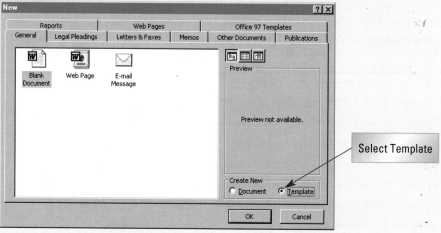

Select Template

Fig 6.7 *The New Document dialogue window*

Fig 6.8 *The letterhead*

A new document appears in the usual way. But if you look at the very top of the window you will see that it is called Template1 instead of Document1.

Create a simple letter heading, with the name and address of the business and its logo (Fig 6.8).

Click on the Save button.

In the Save As dialogue box (Fig 6.9), you will see that you are in a folder called Templates. All Word templates have the filename extension .dot. Call this template letterhead.dot.

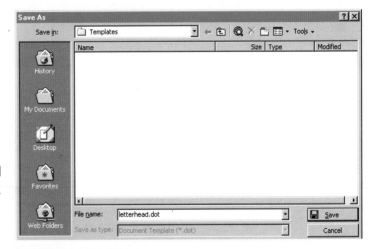

Fig 6.9 *Saving a template*

Using a template

Whenever you want to use this template for a letter, select **File/New** and click on the letterhead template.

Select **File/New**. You will see the letterhead template in the list of templates (Fig 6.10). Select this.

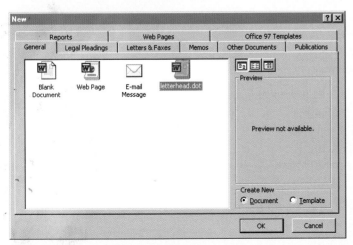

Fig 6.10 *Selecting the letterhead template*

You can now add anything to the document and save it as a new document. The template itself will not be changed, so you can go back and use it again for another letter.

Using mail merge in Microsoft Word

The mail merge function in Microsoft Word allows you to create a simple database of records that can be used in conjunction with a main word-processed document.

You need:

- a *main document*, which is the actual letter; and
- a *data source*, which is another Word document that contains a simple flat-file database.

The main document and the data source are linked to each other.

The steps are:

Step 1: create a main document.

Step 2: create or identify a data source.

Step 3: merge the data with the main document to produce a set of printed documents.

Case study

Kingsmond Garden Centre sometimes sends out letters to its customers telling them about a new product.

In this example you will be setting up a mail merge letter for the company.

Step 1: Create the main document

Select **File/New** and click on the letterhead template. The new document that opens contains the logo and address. This is your main document for the mail merge. You are going to add more to it in a moment.

Save the document as Letter. Select **Mail Merge** in the Tools menu to bring up the Mail Merge Helper (Fig 6.11).

In Step 1, click on **Create**, select **Form Letters** and then click on Active Window (Fig 6.12).

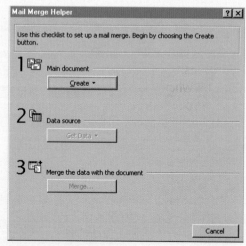

Fig 6.11 The Mail Merge Helper

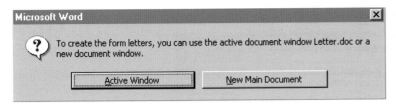

Fig 6.12 *Selecting the letter as the main document*

Step 2: Create the data source

In the Mail Merge Helper, click on Step 2, Get Data (Fig 6.13).

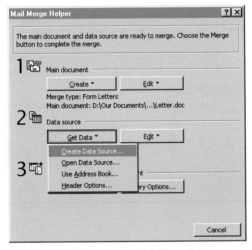

Fig 6.13 *Select Get Data in the Mail Merge Helper*

Select **Create Data Source**.
The Mail Merge Helper provides you with a standard set of fields for the Data Source (Fig 6.14). You can remove or add to these to meet your requirements.
You will need the following fields: Title, FirstName, LastName, Address1, Address2, City, PostalCode. In the list, click on the first field that you don't need, then click on Remove Field Name. Repeat this until you are just left with the fields you want. Note that Address1 and Address2 are for the separate lines in one address, not for two separate addresses.
Click **OK** when you have finished. You will be prompted to save your data source. Call it Customer data.
You have not yet entered any data. Click on Edit Data Source (Fig 6.15).

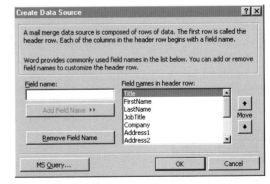

Fig 6.14 *Creating the data source*

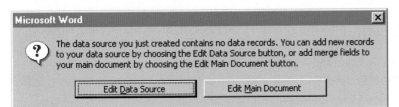

Fig 6.15 *Once the data source has been saved you are prompted to enter records*

The Data Form will appear (Fig 6.16).

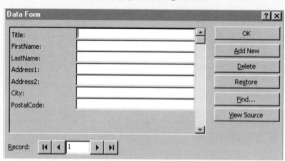

Fig 6.16 *The Data Form*

You can enter data into the fields in the Data Form. Click on Add New to create the next record. Create three records in all.
Scan between the records with the Browse buttons (Fig 6.17).

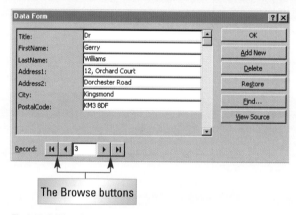

The Browse buttons

Fig 6.17 *Adding data and browsing between records*

Click on OK when finished.
You should now be viewing the main document (called 'Letter'). If you have already closed this document you should open it in the usual way. Word will automatically find the data source ('Customer data') that is associated with it. The Mail Merge toolbar has appeared either immediately above the document or as a floating toolbar (Fig 6.18). Some of the buttons will be 'greyed out' at this stage.

Fig 6.18 *The Mail Merge toolbar*

Check what each button does by placing the pointer over each for a few seconds. Check the greyed-out buttons as well. You will be using Insert Merge Field, View Merged Data, and the Mail Merge Helper button. You will also be using the Browse buttons – First Record, Previous Record, Next Record and Last Record.
You want to position the name and address of each customer on the left side of the letter. First make sure the cursor is at the position on the page where you want the name and address to appear. Select **Insert Merge Field** from the Mail Merge toolbar and then select **Title** (Fig 6.19).

Fig 6.19 *Select Title from the Insert Merge Field list*

The fieldname <<Title>> appears on the page (Fig 6.20). This is where the actual title (Mr, Mrs, etc.) will appear when the data and main document are merged to produce the final letters.

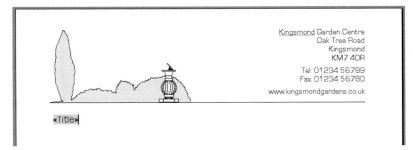

Fig 6.20 *The fieldname Title is placed on the page*

Select **Insert Merge Field** again to add all the other fieldnames to the page. You can insert spaces, punctuation and line returns wherever they are needed (Fig 6.21).

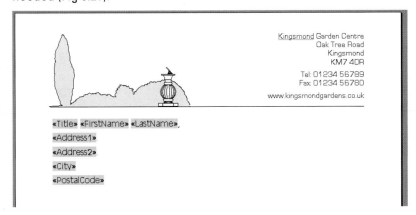

Fig 6.21 *The fieldnames added for the address*

Next add the salutation ('Dear …') followed by the relevant fieldnames. Write the rest of the letter telling customers about your new product (Fig 6.22). Save it.

Figure 6.22 *Merge fields inserted into the main document*

Click on the View Merged Data button to see what your merged documents will look like (Fig 6.23).

Fig 6.23 One of the merged documents viewed on screen

The merged data, such as 'Mrs Jane Williams', will not appear grey in the eventual printed letter.
Use the Browse buttons to check all the records. Click the View Merged Data button again to return to the main document.

Step 3: Merge the data with the main document

The final step is to merge all the data with the main documents and to print out the letters.
Click on the Mail Merge Helper button, then click on Step 3, Merge (Fig 6.24).

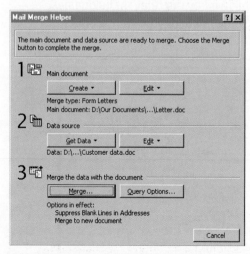

Fig 6.24 Select Merge in the Mail Merge Helper

You must make some selections in the Merge dialogue box (Fig 6.25). Under Merge to: select **Printer**. Under When merging records select **Don't print blank lines when data fields are empty**. Click **Merge**.

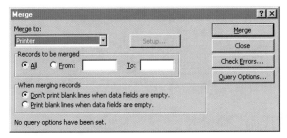

Fig 6.25 *The Merge dialogue box with the correct options selected*

The usual printer dialogue will appear.
Warning! It is very easy to make yourself unpopular by printing many mail merge letters at the same time. You only need to print off one of the letters at this stage, so make sure that you select which page you want to print (Fig 6.26).

Kingsmond Garden Centre
Oak Tree Road
Kingsmond
KM7 4DR

Tel: 01234 56789
Fax: 01234 56780

www.kingsmondgardens.co.uk

Mrs Jane Williams,
37, Windy Heights,
Kingsmond
KM6 3RT

Dear Mrs Williams,

Amazing new offer for keen gardeners!

As a valued customer we wanted you to be the first to hear about our new range of garden ponds.

Fig 6.26 *One of the mail merge letters*

Give it a go

Start from scratch again, and create a mail merge letter for the members of a club, telling them about an event they might like to attend.

Case study

Kingsmond Garden Centre have now set up a database in Access. This database contains a table called Mailing List which holds the names and addresses of customers. They want to use this as the data source for a mail merge letter.

Creating a mail merge using data held in Access

Start in Word by preparing the mail merge main document:

As before, select **File/New**, then select the letterhead template.
Save the document as Letter2.

Setting up the database in Access

Launch Microsoft Access and create a new database, called Kingsmond Garden Centre.mdb
Create a table with these fields: Customer ID (which should be of AutoNumber type), Title, FirstName, LastName, Address1, Address2, City, PostalCode.
Save the table with the name Mailing List.
Enter data for about ten people.

You are now ready to use this table as the data source for a mail merge document in Word.

Using a database table as a data source for a mail merge

Make sure you have closed and saved the table.
In the Tables window, select the Mailing List table.
Find the OfficeLinks button and drop-down menu on the toolbar (Fig 6.27).
Select **Merge it with MS Word**.

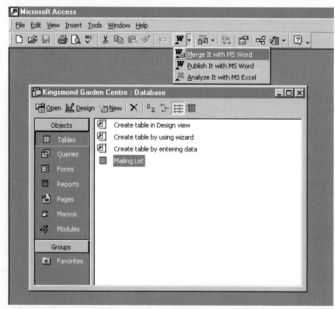

Fig 6.27 *Preparing to merge the data with Word*

The Mail Merge Wizard appears. Select the first option: **Link your data to an existing Microsoft Word document** (Fig 6.28)

You will then be asked to open the document that you will use as the main document for the mail merge. Select **Letter2.doc**.
The document is opened, and the Mail Merge toolbar is in place. Click on the Mail Merge Helper button.

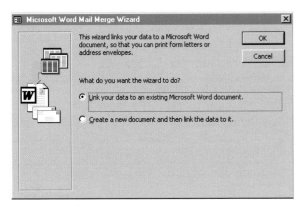

Fig 6.28 *The Mail Merge Wizard in Access*

In Fig 6.29 you can see that Letter2 is the main document. The Mailing List table in the Kingsmond Garden Centre database is the data source.

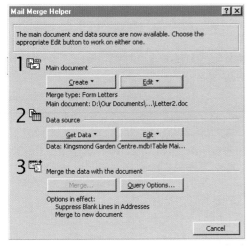

Fig 6.29 *The Mail Merge Helper*

You can now carry on as before, adding merge fields and extra text to the letter.

Practice questions

Foundation

1 Give two reasons why personal data stored on a computer system may be easier to misuse than data stored only on documents.

2 Which one of the following statements is true?
- **A** Anything that is available on the Internet is free of copyright.
- **B** A software licence allows the owner to make as many copies as they like of a program.
- **C** Copyright laws apply to all software as well as to books.
- **D** Software piracy is not actually illegal in the UK.

3 Hacking is another name for:
- **A** unauthorised access to a computer system
- **B** making changes to a computer program
- **C** breaking the lock on the door to a computer room
- **D** reading someone else's e-mails.

4 Computer disks should be protected from:
- **A** water **B** dust **C** daylight
- **D** heat **E** sounds

5 When a user logs on to a network they need to enter their:
- **A** username only
- **B** password only
- **C** username and password
- **D** username, password and their real name.

6 If a computer disk is stolen, the data stored on it is useless to the thief if it is:
- **A** encrypted
- **B** password protected
- **C** mail merged
- **D** written in a programming language.

7 Give two reasons why you might create a template for a document.

8 Which of the following could be produced using mail merge techniques?
- **A** An electricity bill.
- **B** A business card.
- **C** A letter from a mobile phone company to all its customers, telling them about new tariffs.
- **D** A letter thanking someone for a birthday present.
- **E** A party invitation.

Higher

9 Storage media can be damaged deliberately or by accident.
- **a** Describe three ways in which storage media can be protected from vandalism.
- **b** Describe three ways in which storage media can be protected from accidental damage.

10 Discuss the advantages and disadvantages of storing data on a computer system instead of on documents.

Developing applications

Case study: Kings United

Kings United is the local football club in Kingsmond. It plays in one of the smaller leagues, but it attracts a regular attendance of around 2,000 local supporters whenever it plays at home.

The football club would like to increase attendance and has decided to set up a Supporters Club. Members of the Supporters Club will receive a monthly newsletter and the chance to book tickets before the general public. They will also have their own website where they can post news and views.

Kings United hopes they will be able to sell more of their merchandise, such as scarves and hats, through the Supporters Club.

Matthew Short has volunteered to set up the Supporters Club. Kings United have provided him with a desk and networked computer at the club.

Matthew was a professional football player himself in the past. He was seriously injured in a road accident one day, and his sight was damaged. He can still read but he does need large print. He is a keen computer user and has adapted his home computer to meet his needs.

In spite of his visual impairment, Matthew is a keen fan and attends every match, home and away, during the season.

Developing applications software

You have used a number of pieces of applications software, such as Microsoft Word, FrontPage, Publisher, etc. You will also have played computer games. We sometimes refer to these as software 'packages', which reminds you that each is made up of very many files. Some of these files are programs, others contain data that the programs use.

Each program is a set of instructions to the central processing unit of a computer system.

Programming languages

Computer programs are written in computer programming languages. You may have heard of some of these languages, such as Visual Basic, C++ and Java. The actual instructions that make up a particular program are called the program code.

Application programmers

The people who design and create applications software are called application programmers.

As an ordinary computer user, you usually cannot see the programs that make up the software you are using. The application programmers will have made sure that you cannot change it in any way, otherwise things could go badly wrong.

Programming environments

Applications programmers themselves use specialist software to enable them to design and write the applications that you use. The software is known as a programming environment. A programming environment lets the programmer do three things – edit, compile and run a program:

◎ To *edit* a program, the programmer uses the code editor, which is a bit like a word processor. The programmer can use the code editor to write and edit a program in the programming language.
◎ To *compile* a program, the programmer uses the compiler. This converts the program code into the instructions that the CPU uses.
◎ To *run* (or execute) a program, the programmer simply clicks on a button and the instructions in the program are carried out.

Using a programming environment

You have, in fact, already used software that has a programming environment built into it. Microsoft Word, Excel and Access all include a programming environment which lets you become an application programmer yourself if you want to (Fig 7.1). The programming language used is Visual Basic, but you would have to learn quite a bit more about how programs are constructed before you could create anything useful.

The instructions in the program could be to:

◎ find some data stored on a disk and to load it into internal memory;
◎ carry out a calculation with some data and save the result;
◎ ask the person using the computer to enter some data;
◎ put a message on the screen;
◎ wait for someone to move the mouse, then move the pointer on the screen to match it;
◎ print out some data.

Give it a go

1 Launch Access, and select **Blank Database**, then click on OK. You will be asked to save the database immediately, so call it testdatabase.mbd and save it.

2 In the Objects list, click on Modules, then click on New. The Visual Basic programming environment appears.

3 The Code Editor window is waiting for you to enter some program code. Key in anything you like – it will not be program code!

4 Then select **Debug/Compile testdatabase**.

5 An error message appears because the compiler doesn't understand what you have written (Fig 7.2).

6 Try again. This time write this exactly as it is written:
Private Sub Message( )
    MsgBox "Hello everyone"
End Sub

7 The code editor will help you by writing the last line for you. It will also draw a line above this bit of code (Fig 7.3).

8 Now select **Debug/Compile testdatabase**. If you have made a mistake you will get another Compile Error message. If you have keyed the code in correctly, nothing happens. This is because the compiler has managed to convert the code successfully into the instructions that the CPU works with. You cannot see these instructions, but you can now see what they do.

9 You can now run the program, so click on the Run button in the main toolbar:
    ▶ the Run button.

10 You are now switched back to the main Access screen and your message appears in a message box (Fig 7.4). Click on OK to return to the programming environment.
You have now written your first (very simple!) computer program.

Application generators

An application generator is software that allows you to create a simple application of your own. You can usually do this without knowing any programming code at all. But if you want to, you can look at the code that has been written and change it to make it just right. This is referred to as 'customising' the application.

When you create a database, Microsoft Access generates the Visual Basic code for you in the background. Once you have set up a database, you can then go into the Visual Basic editor and customise it, by adding extra programming instructions.

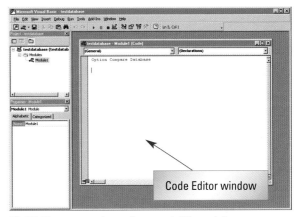

Fig 7.1 *The programming environment in Microsoft Access*

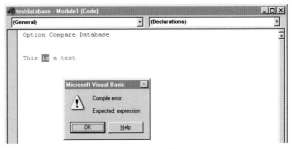

Fig 7.2 *An error message from the compiler*

Fig 7.3 *Some code in Visual Basic*

Fig 7.4 *A message box created by the program code*

Suiting the needs of users

The well-known applications software packages, like those produced by Microsoft and Corel, have been designed to suit all kinds of people. Sometimes the software isn't quite good enough for a user. It may be unsatisfactory because the user:

◎ wants it to do something that it cannot do;

◎ finds it too complicated;

◎ has some special needs, such as visual impairment.

There are two solutions to this problem. You can:

◎ configure the software so that it suits the user; or

◎ create software specially for the user (bespoke software).

Configuring applications software

On page 16 you saw that, in Word, you could drag a toolbar on to the page. It then became a floating toolbar (or tool box). You can do this in most Microsoft applications. This is one way in which you can configure the applications software to suit your needs, others include:

◎ Adding extra toolbars. If you right-click anywhere on one of the toolbars, you will be given a list of toolbars to choose from. Do not choose too many or there will be little space left for the document (Fig 7.5). Just choose the toolbars that will help you with your work.

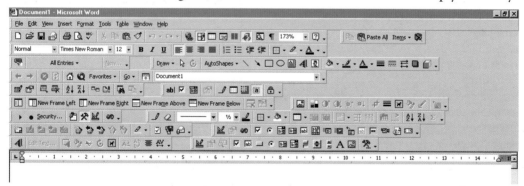

Fig 7.5 *Too many toolbars!*

◎ Changing the appearance of the buttons on the toolbars. Right-click on a toolbar and select **Customize**. In the Customize dialogue box (Fig 7.6), click on the Options tab. Click on Large icons (Fig 7.7).

◎ Configuring the home page in your browser. This is the page that is opened when the browser is launched. You may not realise that you can change

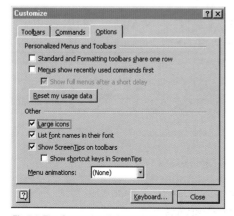

Fig 7.6 *The Customize dialogue box*

Fig 7.7 *Large icons*

this. The Home page can be any page on the Internet, or a web page that you have created and stored on the hard disk.

In Internet Explorer, first go to the page that you want to set as your home page. Select **Tools/Internet Options** (Fig 7.8). Click on Use Current, then on OK.

◎ In most applications you can configure the software to suit you. Check through the menus, and look out for Options or Preferences.

For example, the Options dialogue box in Excel can be found in the Tools menu. Try changing some of the options to see what they do (Fig 7.9).

Bespoke software

Bespoke software is very expensive. This is because it is created just once, so the programmers will not be able to sell it to other people as well.

A large business like a bank will be able to afford to employ its own applications programmers. They will then spend all their time creating bespoke software that exactly matches the needs of the business. They might devote thousands of hours to produce software that is just right for handling cash machines or customer accounts.

A smaller organisation may use consultants to develop bespoke software for them. A consultant is a self-employed person who works for a fixed time on a project for an organisation.

You can buy standard applications software just when you want it, but it does take time to develop bespoke software.

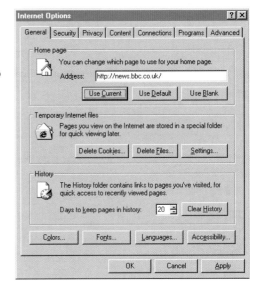

Fig 7.8 Configuring the Home page in Internet Explorer

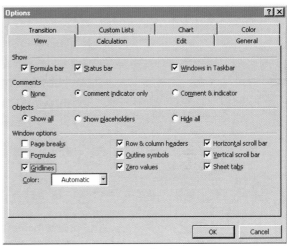

Fig 7.9 The Options dialogue box in Excel

Case study

Matthew Short, who has impaired vision, is now working as a volunteer at Kings United. He wants to configure his software to meet his needs, such as:

◎ Large text on the screen.

◎ Strong contrast between text and background.

◎ Easy access to the software that he uses most for word processing, database management and website design.

◎ Toolbars that just contain the buttons he needs.

Can you explain how he could do all this?

Can you suggest some other ways in which he could configure his system so that it is easier for him to use and so that it reflects his personality and interests?

ICT projects: finding a solution

The full course GCSE in ICT (Specification A), set by the examination board AQA, includes two pieces of coursework. You can read advice about your coursework on page 319.

Both pieces of coursework are examples of small ICT projects. ICT projects can vary in size from ones like these, right up to very extensive projects run by the government or large businesses. These can employ many people and cost millions of pounds.

In this section you will be looking at how ICT projects are developed in business. Whatever the size of the project, each one is developed in stages. The main stages are: analysis, design, implementation, testing, and evaluation.

At all stages, records have to be kept of what has been decided, what has been done and what will happen next. Also, manuals have to be provided so that users know what to do. All of this printed material is known as documentation.

Stages of development
ANALYSIS
DESIGN
IMPLEMENTATION
TESTING
EVALUATION

The problem

All ICT projects begin with a problem. For example:
◎ The staff in a school office want to create a number of templates so that they can produce letters, leaflets, newsletters and notices quickly.
◎ A company that sells clothes by mail order decides to use a website to sell its goods.
◎ The police in different counties need to be able to share information about suspected criminals.

Case study

The problem: Matthew Short is setting up a Supporters Club for Kings United. The supporters will get inside information about the teams and matches.

The solution

An ICT project produces a solution to a problem. It may not be the only solution, but it should be the best solution.

The result of any ICT project is a new system. The word 'system' can be used to mean any of these, or a combination of them:

◎ New computer hardware.   ◎ New applications software.
◎ New documents.   ◎ New ways of doing things.

Analysis

Much work has to be done by a systems analyst before anyone starts creating the solution to a problem.

Feasibility study

Does the organisation really need to do the project at all, and what will it cost? The systems analyst does a feasibility study, which includes these stages:

◎ It identifies the problem. People may have different ideas about what the problem is. It is important that the problem is stated clearly.
◎ It states how the organisation manages at present. Some projects are carried out to improve existing systems; others, such as the Supporters Club, start completely new activities.
◎ It calculates whether the organisation can afford a new system.

Investigation

The systems analyst next finds out what the organisation does at present and what its future needs are. Methods include the following:

◎ *Interview* An interview or discussion should be planned in advance.
◎ *Questionnaires* The systems analyst can send a questionnaire for someone to fill in before an interview. This will give the person time to think about the questions, and to do any research that may be needed. If there are too many people to interview, questionnaires can be sent instead.
◎ *Observation* If people in the organisation are already doing something about the problem, the systems analyst should observe what they do. Notes should be kept on what tasks are done, who does them and how long they take.

Identify possible solutions

Many problems have more than one solution. The systems analyst should identify a number of possible solutions, then discuss the advantages and disadvantages of each. Here are some things that should be considered:

◎ How long it will take to implement the solution.
◎ The cost of the solution.
◎ Whether the solution will meet all the needs.

Requirements

The systems analyst should identify the best solution. Then a document has to be prepared that lists exactly what is required.

In a large project, the list of requirements is highly important. It is used as part of a formal contract between the organisation and the professionals who are going to create the solution.

> **Case study**
>
> The problem of setting up a supporters club has several sub-problems – keeping a record of members, advertising the club, keeping members informed.

> **Case study**
>
> Here are some possible solutions that Matthew considers:
> ◎ Create a website for the Supporters Club, with lots of information about the team and about club activities. New members can join online. Link to it from the main football club website.
> ◎ Design a Supporters Club magazine, and mail it out to members. Create an application form so new members can join, and hand this out with match tickets.
>
> Which is the better solution?
>
> After investigation, Matthew decides to go for the second solution.

ICT projects: developing the solution

Design

The person who designs systems is often called a systems designer.

The task of the systems designer is to take the requirements document and to produce designs for any hardware and software that are needed for the solution. The problem is broken down into its sub-problems and the solutions for each are designed. This is called top-down design.

The system designer now has to:

◎ decide whether the organisation needs to purchase any new hardware or software, and what it should get;

◎ design any new software that has to be created;

◎ design a database, website or spreadsheet solution if needed; and

◎ create templates for all kinds of documents.

The designer has to make sure that all the parts of the solution work together. For example, if a letter is to be sent to a list of people in a database, it should be set up so that either mailing labels can be printed or mail merge used.

The design must meet the requirements, so the designer will plan how the solution will be tested eventually.

Case study

The overall problem can look like Fig 7.10.

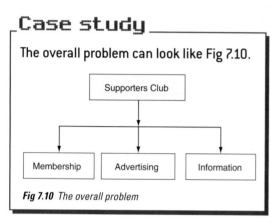

Fig 7.10 The overall problem

Case study

The Kings United Supporters Club already has all the hardware it needs. There are several possible ways in which Matthew can design the solution to the membership sub-problem:

◎ Use the mail merge facility in a word processor to store names and addresses of members.

◎ Set up a database of supporters using database management software.

◎ Design bespoke software to be specially written for the club.

Which would you choose?

Implementation

The design is implemented by a developer – this could be an applications programmer, a database developer, a website developer or an information systems engineer. The developer will create the solution and check that it works as it progresses.

Testing

A solution must be tested by the developer to see that it matches the requirements. The test plan drawn up by the system designer will be used for this.

The test plan includes data that can be input into the new system. For each set of data that is input the test plan lists the expected results.

The data in the test plan should include the following:

◎ *Typical data* – valid data that you would normally expect to input.
◎ *Extreme data* – data which is just about valid, such as long names.
◎ *Erroneous data* – this is invalid data, which may be entered by mistake.

The developer carries out each test in turn and then compares the result with the expected result. If there are any errors the developer goes back and works on the implementation a bit more.

Eventually all the mistakes should be sorted out. The final testing should prove that the system works as intended.

Evaluation

Once a solution has been tested it should be evaluated. Evaluation:

◎ checks whether the solution solves the original problem;
◎ checks whether the solution meets the requirements;
◎ identifies the good points about the solution;
◎ identifies any weaknesses in the solution; and
◎ suggests future improvements that could be made.

Documentation

When the solution is completed, documents have to be provided. There are two types of documentation:

◎ Technical documentation, which explains to another ICT professional (systems analyst, applications developer, etc.) how the system works.
◎ User documentation, which guides the ordinary user and shows him or her how to use the system. This can be in the form of a written manual or as online help.

The system life-cycle

The sequence of analysis, design, implementation, testing and evaluation is often referred to as the system life-cycle. The word 'cycle' suggests that things may happen again and again. That is because an ICT solution to a problem will not last for ever.

Over time the needs of the organisation may change and new technologies may come along. So every so often they should check that the ICT solution still meets their needs. If not, they have to start again with a new project.

Give it a go

You will have a chance to complete a full project as part of your coursework. There is more advice about this on page 319.

You will be acting as systems analyst, systems designer and developer all rolled into one.

You have to write a report on the analysis, design, implementation, testing and evaluation of your project – this is the technical documentation. For the user documentation you have to provide a printed user guide.

User interfaces

The user interface is how you, as a person, interact with the software. It includes whatever appears on the screen before you, any sounds you hear, the mouse and the keyboard.

A graphical user interface (GUI) uses images as well as text, as in the desktop calculator in Fig 7.11. The images and text are laid out on the screen so that it looks like a 'real' calculator. You use a pointer controlled by a mouse to click on the calculator 'keys'.

Some of the most creative interfaces are used on CD-ROM or DVD multimedia systems, such as encyclopedias and games (Fig 7.12).

Fig 7.12 A student resource user interface

Fig 7.11 Graphical user interface for an onscreen calculator

WIMP interfaces

GUIs are often referred to as WIMP interfaces (Fig 7.13). This stands for:

◎ **W**indow
◎ **I**con
◎ **M**enu
◎ **P**ointer

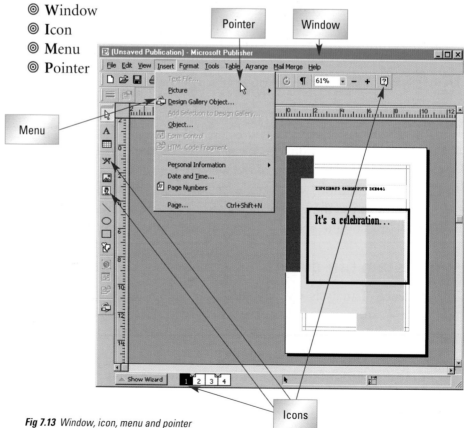

Fig 7.13 Window, icon, menu and pointer

Window

A window is a rectangular area which lets you work on a task – for example, to edit a picture, to save a document or to change preferences.

Several windows can be open at the same time and you can often switch between them. Only one window will be active – that is, ready for you to input. This will usually appear to be on top of the other windows (Fig 7.14).

A window is a feature that appears in many GUIs. Do not confuse it with Microsoft Windows, which is a specific piece of software.

Standard window

Standard windows can be scrolled if the data cannot be displayed fully, a scroll bar appears to the right and bottom of the window when needed. Standard windows can be resized, and they all have a close button.

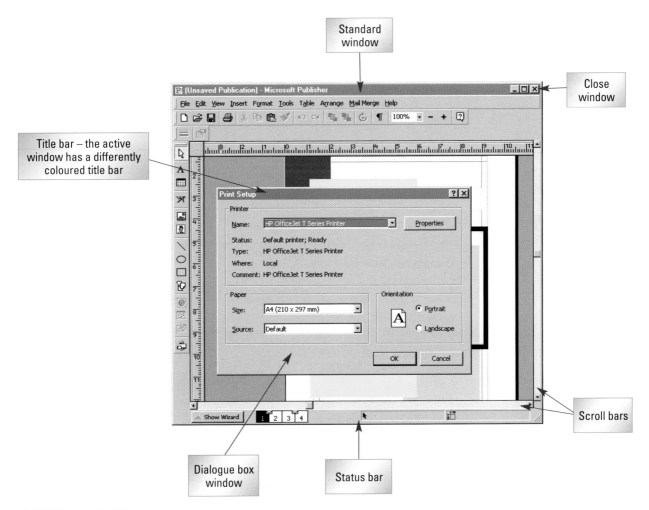

Fig 7.14 Windows in a GUI

Dialogue window

Dialogue box windows ask you to select options in order to carry out a specific action.

continued ▶

User interfaces (continued)

Icons and buttons

An icon is a small image that represents an action. A button has either an icon, or some words or both. Icons are used because:

◎ the size of the button can be reduced;
◎ often pictures are easier to understand than words; and
◎ they can be understood in many languages.

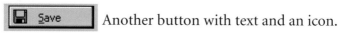 A button with text only.

 Another button with text and an icon.

A menu bar, or toolbar, is a set of buttons arranged as a menu, such as the one shown in Fig 7.15.

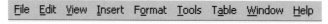

Figure 7.15 *Buttons arranged in a menu bar*

Menu

A menu is a list of options from which you can select one at a time.

Static menu

The menu bar along the top of many GUIs is a static menu and does not change (Fig 7.16). The main menus on websites are often referred to as navigation bars.

File Edit View Insert Format Tools Table Window Help

Fig 7.16 *A menu bar*

Pull-down menu

A pull-down menu (Fig 7.17) hides the choices until you are ready to make a decision. It drops down when one of the items in the main menu bar is selected and disappears again when not needed.

Figure 7.17 *A pull-down menu*

Pop-up menu

A pop-up menu (Fig 7.18) appears when you right-click on an object. It offers you choices that relate to the object on the screen.

Pointer

A pointer is an icon that can move around the screen under the control of the mouse, the arrow keys on the keyboard or some other input peripheral. It can be used to select objects on the screen.

Pointers can change in appearance depending on what you are doing.

Pointers are very important in a GUI as you feel as though you are directly carrying out the actions. For example, when you click on a button it feels like pressing a button in the real world. The action is made even more realistic if the button appears to depress when clicked and if a sound is heard.

Non-graphical user interfaces

Non-graphical (text-only) user interfaces are much simpler than GUIs. At a point-of-sale terminal (cash till) in a shop the screen just displays text in a simple display (Fig 7.19).

Non-graphical interfaces are useful for:

◎ fast data entry
◎ systems that cannot use a pointer
◎ expert use
◎ the visually impaired.

A GUI can be very slow, and it is often quicker to hit a key than to move a mouse and click.

There are two main types of non-graphical user interfaces, command driven and menu driven.

Command driven interface

The operating system, Microsoft Windows, is built on top of an older system called MS-DOS. Find the MS-DOS icon in the Start menu: **MS-DOS Prompt** the MS-DOS prompt.

This opens up a non-graphical window, with white text on a black background: `C:\>` . You are in the C drive and the > symbol is prompting you to enter a command: `C:\>del letter8.doc` . You enter this command, which is an instruction to delete the named file. `C:\>dir` . This command lists all the files in the directory.

Menu driven interface

The simplest menu system is that offered by Teletext (Fig 7.20). You key in the number you require on a remote control, which is simply a small keyboard.

The accommodation at the resort leaves much to be desired.

Figure 7.18 *A pop-up menu*

⬚ Normal pointer

⬚ What's this (Help)

⬚ Waiting

⬚ Move

⬚ Link

I Text cursor, known as an I-bar

Fig 7.19 *A point-of-sale terminal*

Fig 7.20 *Teletext*

Designing user interfaces

Colour

In any user interface colour can be used to draw attention, make an icon clearer or make it easier to read the text.

There are a number of problems:

Fig 7.21 *Red used for a virus alert*

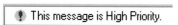

Fig 7.22 *Red used to mark an e-mail as high priority*

- Some bright colours are very tiring to look at.
- Some people cannot distinguish colours well. Colours must vary in contrast.
- Colours may mean different things. A virus program may use red to alert the user about a virus (Fig 7.21). But red is also used to mark an e-mail as high priority (Fig 7.22).

Light grey is used very widely in GUIs, for all these reasons.

Sound

Sound can be used to emphasise an action on the screen or to make it seem more real. For example, when you click on a button you may hear a clicking sound.

Position of objects

Which objects on the screen do you notice first? Most people start looking at the top left of the screen, so it is not a good idea to put important information down at the bottom.

Give it a go

Some buttons, such as OK, Cancel and Help, keep appearing in dialogue boxes. These should be in the same position every time so that you do not make any silly mistakes. Where are they usually placed?

Consistency

When you use any Microsoft software you find that certain things always appear the same

- The File, View and Help menus are always in the same position.
- The same icons (e.g. for Print) are used.
- Some dialogue boxes (e.g. for saving a file) are the same.
- Some formatting toolbars are very similar.

This helps you when you learn to use a new application.

Help

All applications software should provide some help. This can be through the following:

Fig 7.23 *A screen tip*

- *Screen tips* (Fig 7.23) – these pop up when you pass the mouse over an icon or some text.
- *Help screens* (Fig 7.24) – pages of information with hyperlinks and a search engine.
- *Interface agents* (Fig 7.25) – a screen character that checks what you are doing and gives you intelligent advice.

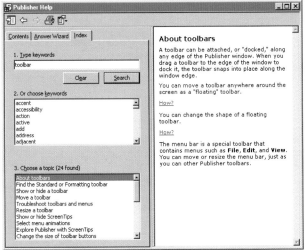

Fig 7.24 Help screens

Fig 7.25 An interface agent

Thinking about the user

Many user interfaces are designed with the needs of a particular type of user in mind. Users can be described by the work they do, how experienced they are at using ICT, their age, their interests, their cultural background, or any disabilities they might have.

◎ Command driven interfaces are often preferred by experienced technical users, such as network administrators. They know the commands off by heart and can work much more rapidly than by using a mouse. But it does take some time for a newcomer to learn the skills.

◎ Menu driven interfaces are still used today by employees, such as shop assistants who work on specialist business systems. These screens are often quite small, so it is not possible to use a full graphical interface. The employees need to be trained to use these systems.

◎ Graphical interfaces are designed for the general public, including children and the elderly. They do take up a great deal of computer memory and some users find them too slow. They can easily be adapted for users with disabilities.

Give it a go

How many methods are there for accessing Help in Word? Why are there so many alternatives? What type of user would prefer each method?

Practice questions

Foundation

1a Give one reason why an organisation might choose to have software specially written for it, rather than buying a ready-made software package.

b State one disadvantage of making this choice.

2 Describe two ways in which a software package can be configured to meet the needs of a user.

3 Put these stages in an ICT project in their correct order.

    A Design   **B** Evaluation

    C Testing   **D** Analysis

    E Implementation

4 Which one of these questions would **NOT** be answered at the Analysis stage of a project.

    A What is the problem that needs to be solved?

    B What is missing from the present system?

    C How much will a new system cost?

    D Does the new system work?

5 Give one example from everyday life of each of the following types of user interface.

    a Command driven.   **b** Menu driven.   **c** Graphical.

6 Give two examples of a helpful use of colour in a user interface.

Higher

7 The test plan for a project lists all the tests that will be carried out on a solution, together with the expected results. Explain the advantages in drawing up a test plan before the solution is implemented, rather than afterwards.

8 Jenna has just completed her GCSE project coursework. In the evaluation section she wrote the following.
'The project went quite well, but I didn't have enough time to finish it. I learnt a lot from doing the project, for example, I didn't know how to create a relational database before. I can now set up tables and design forms and reports.'
Explain why she was awarded no marks for this. Outline what she should have written in her evaluation.

9 Gerry Richards is 73 years old and has just bought his first computer. He wants to keep in contact by email with his grandchildren who live in Australia and Canada, and he wants to learn to use a word processor. Explain the advantages for Gerry of using a graphical user interface.

10 Explain why software packages often do not have a printed user manual.

Processing data

Case study: Overtons

Overtons is a large department store in the centre of Kingsmond. It has all the usual departments, including clothes, perfumery, sports, furniture, soft furnishings, toys and electrical.

Data about all the stock (items for sale) in Overtons is kept in the stock file. The fields in this file include the stock code (the primary key), stock description, price and number in stock.

Overtons has one specialist department, called ArtWorks, that exhibits and sells paintings by local artists. It is run as an independent franchise so the stock records for this department are kept separate from the main stock file.

Sheri Weekes

Sheri works as a sales assistant in the toy department. The point-of-sale (POS) that she uses has a bar-code scanner. The labels on all the toys carry bar code labels, so she uses the scanner to enter the stock code rapidly. In December the toy department is particularly busy, and the bar code scanner speeds up the processing considerably.

Protecting the staff

Sheri, like all staff, carries an ID card which has a magnetic stripe on the back. When it is time for her lunch break she goes across the shop floor to the door marked 'Staff Only'.

The general public only see the sales floors at Overtons. But behind the scenes are offices, stock rooms and the staff restaurant. There have been some problems with intruders in the past, so a door entry system has been installed to prevent unauthorised people getting in. There is a card reader beside each of the doors marked 'Staff Only'.

Sheri swipes her ID card and the door unlocks. She makes her way to the staff restaurant. On her way back after lunch she stops to read the notice about the Staff Christmas Party. She must remember to tell Jacob that she is planning to attend.

Getting paid

Some days Sheri is asked to do overtime. She fills in an overtime claim form and gives it to her supervisor to sign. She gets paid monthly and, if she hands her claim form in late, she knows that she won't get her overtime pay until the following month.

What do you think?

How many different types of information system did you spot at Overtons?

Processing Files

In this section we are concentrating on the large and complicated information systems used in business. These are often hidden away from members of the public, so you will not be so familiar with them.

Processing data in an information system

Data is input into an information system. After it is processed in some way, information is created and output to the outside world.

Data files can be processed in many ways. Processing is carried out by the CPU as it follows the instructions in a program.

We will be looking at five main types of processing:

◎ updating files
◎ searching files
◎ merging files.
◎ validating files
◎ sorting files

In Section 5 you learnt that some data is stored in a flat-file database, and other data is stored in a relational database. In this section we will be concentrating on data organised as a flat file. In Access we can store a flat file in a table. In other systems it is simply referred to as a file.

Updating a file

You update a file when you bring it up to date by:

◎ adding new data;
◎ amending (changing) data; or
◎ deleting data.

In order to do these you often have to merge, search or sort files.

What do you think?

How many times today has a data file been updated because of something that you have done? For example:

◎ Have you bought anything?
◎ Have you swiped a travel ticket through a card reader?
◎ Does your school use an electronic register?
◎ Has someone recorded the marks you got in a test?

Case study

The stock file at Overtons holds the data about each type of stock that it holds. For example, the record in the stock file for a particular computer game could look like Fig 8.1.

Stock code	Stock description	Price	Number in stock
SP145690	Dark Materials 3	£39.99	34

Fig 8.1 A record in the stock file

This record is updated from time to time:

◎ Every time a game is sold, the number in stock is reduced by one.
◎ Every time new games arrive at the store, the number in stock is increased by the correct number.
◎ When the game is no longer on sale, the item is deleted from the stock file.
◎ When the store holds a sale, the price is reduced.

Validating a file

You validate a file when all the data is checked to see that it is valid. The main types of validation check are:

◎ presence check
◎ range check
◎ data type check
◎ check digit.

You can read more about validation in Section 5.

Case study

Look again at Figure 8.1. When data is first entered into this record, or whenever the record is updated, the system carries out validation checks. Can you suggest the types of validation check that it should use?

Searching a file

If you want to update a file, you often need to search for a record first.

When you use a filter to search a database in Access, you need to enter the criteria for the search. A criterion is a rule that picks out some of the records. Here are some of the examples you looked at:

◎ Make = "Ford"
◎ Year > 1999
◎ Model like "C*"
◎ NOT "Ford"
◎ Year > 1998 AND Year < 2003
◎ Make = "Ford" AND Year < 2000
◎ Make = "Honda" OR Make = "Nissan"
◎ Make = "Ford" AND Model like "S*" AND Year < 2000

Can you remember what each one does?

In each case, one or more of the fields acts as a *search field*.

Using the primary key as the search field

When very large files are searched the primary key is often used as the search field. When you hire a video, you hand over your membership card. This has your membership number on it, which the assistant then uses as the search field to find the record on the system.

If you forget your card, they will use another field, such as the address field, as the search field. But it is always easier to use the primary key field as the search field.

What do you think?

What could be used as the search field in these situations?

◎ You phone your usual pizza delivery shop to place an order.
◎ You call in at a bank to check how much money is in your account.

More processing

What does it mean?

Sort key field

A sort key field is used to sort the data into alphabetical or numerical order.

Sorting a file

It is much easier to search a file if the data is sorted in the first place. Most files are sorted using the primary key as the sort key field, but any field can be used. Data can be sorted:

◎ alphabetically – in the same way as in a dictionary; or
◎ numerically.

If you have a field with the 'date' data type, you can sort in date order. This is just a kind of numerical sort. Data can also be sorted:

◎ in ascending order – e.g. from A to Z, from 1 to 100, from 01/01/2000 to 31/12/2003; or
◎ in descending order – e.g. from Z to A, from 100 to 1, from 31/12/2003 to 01/01/2000.

Case study

In the ArtWorks department at Overtons each painting is given an Item code, which acts as the primary key. Buyers negotiate a price and, when a painting is sold, the date and value of the sale are entered (Fig 8.2).

Item code	Title of artwork	Date sold	Value of sale
456321	Minima	20/03/2002	£600.00
456322	Polzeath beach	14/05/2002	£250.00
456323	Abstract 23	25/04/2002	£1,000.00
456324	Over the hill	21/04/2002	£150.00
456325	Landscape with cat	17/05/2002	£800.00
456326	Abstract 24	18/03/2002	£325.00
*			£0.00

Fig 8.2 The database sorted by its primary key, Item code

Item code	Title of artwork	Date sold	Value of sale
456326	Abstract 24	18/03/2002	£325.00
456321	Minima	20/03/2002	£600.00
456324	Over the hill	21/04/2002	£150.00
456323	Abstract 23	25/04/2002	£1,000.00
456322	Polzeath beach	14/05/2002	£250.00
456325	Landscape with cat	17/05/2002	£800.00
*			£0.00

Fig 8.3 The data sorted in ascending order using the Date sold field

The database can also be sorted using the Date sold field as the sort key field (Fig 8.3).

Multiple sort key fields

In a telephone directory, if you want to find someone called Alexander Robertson, you first of all search the surnames for Robertson. As there are several people with this surname, you next search through them all for the forename Alexander.

Phone number	Surname	Forename
8237 0001	Robertson	Matthew
8237 0034	Rogers	Sara
8237 0096	Ronald	Toby
8237 0126	Robertson	James
8237 0209	Reed	Charlotte
8237 0276	Robertson	Alexander
8237 0355	Ronald	Emma
8237 0461	Robertson	Oliver

Fig 8.4 The Telephone database sorted by phone number, its primary key field

The primary key for the telephone database is the telephone number. At first, the database is sorted using the primary key field as the sort key field. The database in Fig 8.4 is very small, of course, but is used as an example.

How can we sort this correctly by name? Fig 8.5 shows the database when it has been sorted using the surname as the sort key field.

That seems to be helpful, but if you look at the Robertsons, their forenames are not in alphabetical order.

Telephone : Table		
Phone number	Surname	Forename
8237 0209	Reed	Charlotte
8237 0461	Robertson	Oliver
8237 0276	Robertson	Alexander
8237 0126	Robertson	James
8237 0001	Robertson	Matthew
8237 0034	Rogers	Sara
8237 0355	Ronald	Emma
8237 0096	Ronald	Toby

Record: 9 of 9

Fig 8.5 *The Telephone database sorted with Surname as the sort key field*

Telephone : Table		
Phone number	Surname	Forename
8237 0209	Reed	Charlotte
8237 0461	Robertson	Oliver
8237 0276	Robertson	Alexander
8237 0126	Robertson	James
8237 0001	Robertson	Matthew
8237 0034	Rogers	Sara
8237 0355	Ronald	Emma
8237 0096	Ronald	Toby

Record: 1 of 8

Fig 8.6 *Selecting two fields together as the sort key fields*

Telephone : Table		
Phone number	Surname	Forename
8237 0209	Reed	Charlotte
8237 0276	Robertson	Alexander
8237 0126	Robertson	James
8237 0001	Robertson	Matthew
8237 0461	Robertson	Oliver
8237 0034	Rogers	Sara
8237 0355	Ronald	Emma
8237 0096	Ronald	Toby

Record: 9 of 9

Fig 8.7 *The sorted database*

You should sort the database by using Surname and Forename *together* as sort key fields. Click on the fieldname Surname at the top of the column, hold the button down and move across so that the Forename column is also highlighted (Fig 8.6). Then click on the Sort Ascending button.

The database is now sorted as intended (Fig 8.7). Access makes sure that the data is sorted using the selected field on the left as the main sort key, with the field on the right doing the more detailed sort within that.

Give it a go

Set up the telephone table in Access. The phone number field should be Text, not a Number. That is because we put spaces in phone numbers.

Merging files

You merge two files when you combine them to give just one file. The simplest way to do this is by adding one file to the end of another file – this is called appending You can only do this if both files have exactly the same fields. We will be looking at a more complicated way of merging files later in this section.

Case study

ArtWorks stores details of all the sales of paintings since the department opened in 2000 in a file called ArtWorks Archive. At the end of 2002 the data is copied from the Sales this Year table to the Archive table. The tables have exactly the same fields, so you can merge them.

In the Tables Window, click on Artworks – Sales this Year, then click on Copy. Click on Paste. In the Paste Table As dialogue box (Fig 8.8), key in Artworks Archive, which is the name of the table that you want to paste it to. Then click on Append Data to Existing Table.

The records from Artworks – Sales this Year are now merged with the records in Artworks Archive (Fig 8.9). The data in ArtWorks – Sales this Year can now be deleted and the table used to store all the new sales in 2003.

Paste Table As

Table Name:
Artworks Archive

Paste Options
- ○ Structure Only
- ○ Structure and Data
- ● Append Data to Existing Table

OK | Cancel

Fig 8.8 *Appending one table to another*

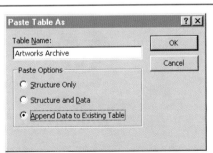

Artworks Archive : Table			
Item code	Title of artwork	Date sold	Value of sale
454727	Mary Jones	02/01/2000	£50.00
454728	Field	15/04/2000	£250.00
454729	The wealth of nations	17/06/2000	£1,250.00
454730	Marigolds	13/04/2000	£800.00
454731	Steaming	30/03/2000	£125.00
455976	Mrs Jones	04/01/2001	£1,500.00
455977	Through my window	12/06/2001	£550.00
455978	Red flowers	03/03/2001	£275.00
455979	Abstract 20	26/07/2001	£650.00
455980	Frameless painting	24/02/2001	£999.00
456321	Minima	20/03/2002	£600.00
456322	Polzeath beach	14/05/2002	£250.00
456323	Abstract 23	25/04/2002	£1,000.00
456324	Over the hill	21/04/2002	£150.00
456325	Landscape with cat	17/05/2002	£800.00
456326	Abstract 24	18/03/2002	£325.00
*			£0.00

Record: 1 of 16

Fig 8.9 *The merged tables*

Processing methods

We will look at four methods of processing data:

- ◎ interactive processing;
- ◎ real-time processing; and
- ◎ transaction processing;
- ◎ batch processing.

These processing methods all use different approaches to storing, updating, validating, searching, sorting and merging files.

Interactive processing

Interactive processing describes the kind of processing that you are most familiar with. If you have created a database in Access, you can:

- ◎ search for a record and then either amend it or delete it;
- ◎ add new records; or
- ◎ sort the records.

You do all this by yourself, by interacting directly with the software.

Interactive processing is mainly used for small databases, the data is only updated when someone gets round to doing it.

Case study

Jacob Cohen is organising the Staff Christmas Party, and has put up a notice on the staff noticeboard asking people to let him know if they are planning to attend. Jacob already has a database in Access with the names of all the staff, so he uses it to keep a record of all the people who say they are coming.

What do you think?

Is this a good way of storing the data about the party?

Will it be kept up to date?

Transaction processing

Transaction

A transaction is any activity which requires a single update in the data held on an information system.

Whenever you buy an item, book a ticket, make an appointment or withdraw cash you are carrying out a transaction. As each transaction is made, the record in the file or database is updated immediately.

Transaction processing is particularly important if there is a danger that the same item could be sold twice. For example, all the seats at a football match are individually numbered, so each seat can only be sold once. When a customer buys a ticket the transaction has to be carried out immediately, and the seat has to be marked as sold, so that no one else can buy it.

A transaction log file is kept alongside the main file or database. As each update takes place a copy of the transaction is put in the transaction log file. This is a useful backup in case things go wrong.

Case study

When Sheri sells a toy she scans the bar code, which holds the stock code. The point-of-sale (POS) terminal then sends the data about the transaction to the stock control system (Fig 8.10). Several things happen:

◎ The stock control system searches the file for that stock code.
◎ The number in the Number in stock field for that record is decreased by one.
◎ Information about the item and its price are sent to the POS.
◎ Data about the transaction is stored in the transaction log file.

This is repeated for each item that she sells.

Fig 8.10 A point-of-sale terminal

Real-time processing

A real-time processing system is one that reacts immediately to the input and generates some output straightaway. Real-time processing is mainly used in systems that work automatically and without a person involved. These are known as control systems and you will read more about them in Section 9. These systems have sensors which pick up data, and output devices such as motors or bells that are activated.

Real-time processing is used for:

◎ autopilots on aircraft;
◎ manufacturing processes;
◎ missile systems;
◎ alarm systems; and
◎ tracking systems, e.g. checking where all the trains are on a railway network.

In most of these systems a log file is created which records all the transactions. You will have heard of the 'black-box recorder' that is recovered from an aircraft after a crash. The black box contains the log file as well as audio recordings.

Case study

When someone like Sheri uses the door entry system (Fig 8.11):
◎ the ID is input from the magnetic stripe into the computer system;
◎ the system searches the files to check that the ID is genuine;
◎ if the ID is genuine, the system sends a signal to the door lock to open it;
◎ if the system recognises the ID as a fake, or as someone who no longer works at the shop, the system sends a signal to an alarm bell and also to the security guards; and
◎ if the ID is not recognised, the system sends a message to the door entry screen, which displays a message asking the person to try again.

Fig 8.11 A door entry system that uses a swipe card

System flowcharts

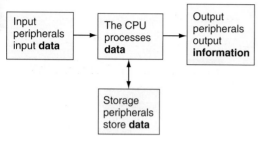

Fig 8.12 *Communication with the CPU*

Diagrams often explain things better than words. System flowcharts are used by system analysts and designers to give an overall picture of an information system.

Have another look at Fig 8.12. It shows how, in general, the input, output and storage peripherals communicate with the CPU. It is not a system flowchart, but it will help you to understand how they are constructed.

Suppose you wanted to draw a diagram about a particular system, like the door entry system shown in Fig 8.11. You would want to show more information than in Fig 8.12, such as the type of peripheral used and the sequence in which things happened. So you would use standard symbols to create a system flowchart.

Symbols used in a system flowchart

Input or output

Fig 8.13 *Input or output*

The top part of the symbol (Fig 8.13) shows the data that is input or the information that is output. The bottom part of the symbol shows the peripheral device used.

Storage

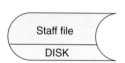

Fig 8.14 *Storage*

The top part of the symbol (Fig 8.14) shows the file. The bottom part of the symbol shows the storage medium used.

Process

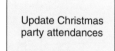

Fig 8.15 *Process*

This shows the process that is being carried out by the software. This will usually be one of:

◎ update (Fig 8.15)   ◎ validate   ◎ merge
◎ sort   ◎ search.

Interactive processing

The system flowchart for interactive processing is very simple (Fig 8.16). The double-ended arrow shows that when the staff file is updated, the data is read from the staff file, then new data is written back to it.

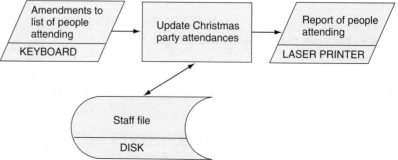

Fig 8.16 *A system flowchart for interactive processing (the Christmas party)*

Transaction processing

The system flowchart for transaction processing (Fig 8.17) is very similar to the one for interactive processing, except that the transaction log file stores data about each transaction, as a form of security.

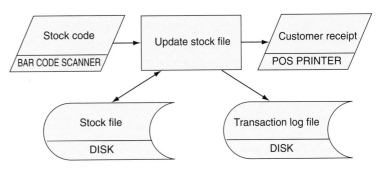

Fig 8.17 *A system flowchart for transaction processing (the POS terminal)*

Real-time processing

The system flowchart for real-time processing (Fig 8.18) is similar to that for transaction processing. The log file is often stored on tape.

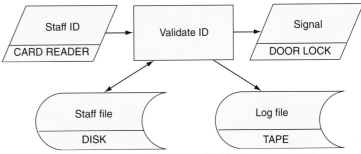

Fig 8.18 *A system flowchart for real-time processing (the door entry system)*

Alternative symbols

You may see system flowcharts that use differently shaped boxes (see Figs 8.19–8.21). The boxes used for input, output and storage are sometimes shaped to suggest the medium.

Fig 8.19 *Storage on hard disk*

Fig 8.20 *Storage on tape*

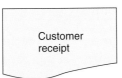

Fig 8.21 *Output to a printed document*

Give it a go

Here are some descriptions of data-processing activities. In each case:

◎ decide whether it is interactive, transaction or real-time processing; and
◎ draw the systems flowchart.

1 When customers buy things at Overtons they sometimes pay by credit card. Sheri swipes the card on a card reader and enters the amount. A signal is sent to the credit card company requesting authorisation for the transaction and, a few seconds later, the response is displayed on the small screen on the card reader.

2 Jacob uses a spreadsheet to keep the accounts for the staff party. He updates this whenever he has to spend any money.

Batch processing

Batch processing is the most complex type of processing, which is why we have left it until last. It is used when a large amount of data has to be processed all at the same time, and most of the processing is completely automatic. For example:

◎ Banks update their customers' accounts every night, processing all the transactions that have been carried out during the day.

◎ Organisations pay employees every week or every month using a payroll system.

Master file

The master file holds all the main records in the system. It has to be updated periodically – that means either once a day, once a week or once a month.

The master file is always sorted, using the primary key field as the sort key field. This could be an account number or, in the case of a payroll, the employee number.

Transaction file

A transaction is a single update to the data, so a transaction file holds all the transactions collected over a period of time. They are all stored in one file and then the master file is updated all at once. (Do not confuse this with a transaction log file.)

Batches

Batch processing is so called because the transactions are often entered and checked in batches of 50 or 100.

Case study

At Overtons it is very important that the details of people's pay are kept confidential. Like many organisations they use an outside company for this purpose. This means that no one inside Overtons can access any information on the payroll system.

All employees are paid once a month. The basic details about each employee and their rates of pay are stored on the master file held at Pay Services Ltd. Each month updates have to be made to the master file before employees can be paid. These updates include data about:

◎ new staff and their rates of pay;

◎ staff who have left during the month;

◎ the overtime hours that employees have worked; and

◎ pay rises.

The personnel staff at Overtons check the updates and enter all this data at a computer. The data is saved in a transaction file. The transaction file is then sent to Pay Services.

Batch processing step by step

Batch processing consists of four or five processes (see Fig 8.22). All apart from the first one are done automatically. A computer operator makes sure that the right tapes and disks are in place, then starts the next process.

The system flowchart in Fig 8.22 refers to the payroll case study. It looks very complicated, but follow it down as you read about the processes.

The processes are as follows:

1 *Create the transaction file* The data about all the updates is keyed in and then stored in a transaction file. The records in the transaction file will not be in any particular order.

2 *Validate the transaction file* All the records in the transaction file are checked to make sure that the data is valid. The valid records are saved to a new file. If any invalid data is found, then an error report is printed and the record with the invalid data is not saved to the new file. The invalid data is checked and corrected later.

3 *Sort the transaction file* The records in the transaction file are sorted using the primary key as the sort key. The next stage cannot be completed unless the transaction file is sorted in the same order as the master file.

4 *Merge the sorted transaction file with the master file* The records in the master file are read in one by one. If the next record in the transaction file has the same primary key as the record in the master file, then the transaction record is used to update the master file record. Each record in turn in the master file is copied across to the new master file – some of these will be updated by a transaction record, some will remain unchanged.

5 *Produce the required reports and files* Usually some kind of output has to be printed as a final stage. In the case of payroll this will be the payslips that are sent to employees. A file of instructions is also created which is then sent to the bank to arrange for the money to be paid into the employees' accounts.

Disks and tapes

The merge process is quite a long one as all the records in the master file have to be read in one after the other, and the new master file created. The fastest method is to store the master file on tape.

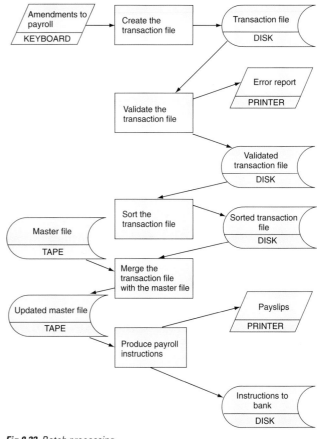

Fig 8.22 *Batch processing*

Backups

We all know that things go can go wrong with computers. For example:

◎ The hardware can malfunction, damaging the data held on disks.
◎ Errors in the software can mean that data is not saved properly.
◎ Viruses can invade the system and delete or corrupt data.
◎ Someone can delete a file or amend data by mistake.
◎ The hardware can be destroyed by fire or flood.
◎ Criminals can delete files or destroy hardware.

The data stored on computers is extremely valuable. If a large organisation lost all its data it would probably go out of business.

The need for backups

As we saw in Section 6, there are many ways in which computer systems can be protected from unauthorised access. But no organisation can rely 100% on these methods. They should always have a disaster recovery strategy which covers:

◎ replacing hardware as soon as possible; and
◎ recovering data from backups.

Backing up a complete system

You can create a backup of a single file, but it is often easier to back up everything on the hard disk at the same time. The two main types of system backup are as follows:

◎ *Full backup*   The system can be set up so that it automatically makes a backup of everything on a regular basis. Most organisations back up the data on their networks every night, when users will not be trying to access it.
◎ *Incremental backup*   An incremental backup copies only the files that have been changed since the last backup. Several of these may be done between one full backup and the next. Although incremental backups will be done during the working day, they will be much quicker than full backups so should not interrupt normal work.

Storing backups

Backup files should be stored on a medium that:

◎ makes fast copies; and
◎ can be stored in a secure place away from the original.

Digital tape (Fig 8.23) is commonly used to store full backups, as data can be copied to tape very rapidly.

All backup tapes and disks need to be labelled very carefully with the date and time.

All backups also need to be verified to ensure that all the data has been stored correctly. These backups are sometimes referred to as file dumps.

What does it mean? **Backup**

A backup is a copy of a file that is kept in a safe place in case the original is damaged.

What does it mean? **Disaster recovery**

Disaster recovery strategy is a means of getting back to normal as soon as possible if disaster does strike.

Fig 8.23 Digital tape

Recovery with backups

If disaster strikes, the last full backup will be used as a replacement for the files that are lost. If incremental backups have been used as well, they will be merged with the last full backup to give the most up-to-date version of the lost files.

Backups in interactive processing

The full backup of a complete system will include any interactive processing systems.

Backups in transaction processing

Many transactions can take place every day. Even if a full backup is taken regularly, with incremental backups in between, some data could still be lost. That is because transactions would still be going on between incremental backups.

As an extra precaution, a transaction log file is created. Every time a transaction is carried out a copy of the transaction is automatically added to the transaction log file. The log file can then be used, with the last full backup, if the original file is damaged.

Backups in real-time processing

When things go wrong in a real-time system, such as an aircraft autopilot system, there usually isn't time to load up a backup and start again. Instead, the whole system will be doubled up, with two complete computer systems. One can take over if the other one fails. In some cases a log file is kept (e.g. black-box recorder). This is only used after the event to try to work out what went wrong.

Backups in batch processing

When the master file is updated a new master file is created. The previous master file is stored safely away. If anything goes wrong with the new master file, it can all be done again from scratch using the old master file and the original transaction file.

The new master file now becomes the master file. The next time that transactions are processed this master file will be used, and yet another new master file will be produced.

All the master files should be kept, carefully labelled and dated, and stored safely. The transaction files should also be kept in case they are needed to reconstruct a master file.

This method of creating generations of master files is often referred to as the grandfather, father, son method.

Practice questions

Foundation

1 Sort the following dates in descending order:
   - 10th June 2003
   - 1st Jan 04
   - 30/09/04
   - 21/05/04
   - 5/5/05

2 You can merge two files together by simply adding the records in one file to the records in the other file. Which of these conditions must be true before that can happen?
   - **A** The number of records must be the same in each file.
   - **B** The data in one field must be the same in both files.
   - **C** The two files must each have the same set of fields.
   - **D** All the fields must have data in them.

3 Here are some examples of everyday data processing. In each case, state which of the following processing methods is being used.
   - Interactive processing.
   - Transaction processing.
   - Batch processing.
   - **a** Thomas buys a cinema ticket through a website.
   - **b** At a hospital, Sara checks all the claims for overtime pay made by staff, then sends them on to the company that handles payroll.
   - **c** Sasha has created a relational database using a standard software package. She changes the data in one of the tables by deleting the old data and entering new data in one record.

4 In batch processing:
   - **a** What is a transaction file?
   - **b** Why should the transaction file be sorted before it is merged with the master file?

5 Why is it important to create backups of files held on a computer?

Higher

6 An airline stores data about all the seats on all its flights. These are booked by travel agents and also directly by customers through the airline's website. Describe what steps the airline should take to make sure that it can recover from a disaster, such as a fire at its offices where all the data is stored.

7 Every day during the week, employees of a gas supplier go round to customers' homes. They record the readings from the gas meters on their hand-held computers. At the end of each day all these readings are uploaded to a transaction file. At the end of each three month period all the readings are merged with the master file of customer records and gas bills are printed for customers.

   Draw a system flowchart to illustrate this batch processing system.

Control and simulation

Case study: Adventureland

It's the school holidays. Karim and his friends are planning to spend the day at Adventureland, a theme park only a few miles from Kingsmond.

When Karim arrives he discovers that they will all have to pay for tickets at the adult rate of £15. He thinks this is a bit unfair as he doesn't have much money. No one in the group of friends is old enough to get a part-time job at the weekends. They wonder why children under 12 years of age only have to pay £10.

Once inside the park they try out all the white knuckle rides. They all go several times on The Darker Side, which is a rollercoaster that runs in pitch darkness with only occasional flashing lights.

Working at the theme park

Ellen has a job at Adventureland during the holidays. She usually works on the Ghost Boat, helping people on and off the boats, which run along a track just below the surface of the water.

Today Ellen has been moved to The Darker Side. The Ghost Boat is not running while some safety checks are being carried out. The engineers are worried because yesterday one of the boats came to a halt when it should not have done. Fortunately the computer controlled system immediately slowed down and stopped all the boats behind it, and prevented a collision.

Ticket prices

Although Karim does not know it, the managers of Adventureland are thinking about the ticket prices for next year. They are keen to attract more young people, so they are thinking of introducing a special rate for students in full-time education from the age of 12.

Adventureland has been getting, on average, 12,000 visitors a day throughout the summer season. They have already done a survey of their visitors and have found that on average each day they welcome 6,000 adults, 2,000 students and 4,000 children. This produces an income of £160,000 per day

They are planning to build some new rides at the theme park during the winter, and to pay for this they will have to increase the daily income from the sales of tickets by at least 10% to £176,000.

Creating a financial model

Creating a financial model

On the following pages you will learn what a financial model is. Work through this exercise.

Case study

What should Adventureland charge for tickets next year?

The managers at Adventureland think about several options, the first one is to simply increase the ticket prices by 10% to £16.50 and £11.

Set up a new spreadsheet as shown in Fig 9.1. Enter the values as shown.

	A	B	C	D	E
1		**Adventureland ticket pricing**			
2					
3					
4		**Average number of visitors per day**			**Target income**
5		Adults	6000		£176,000.00
6		Students	2000		
7		Children under 12	4000		
8					
9			**Option 1**		
10			**10% increase**		
11		Ticket price per adult	£16.50		
12		Ticket price per student	£16.50		
13		Ticket price per child	£11.00		
14					
15		**Income**			
16		Adult ticket sales			
17		Student ticket sales			
18		Child ticket sales			
19					
20		Total income per day			
21					
22					

Fig 9.1 *The start of a model*

The cells that contain money figures, C11, C12 and C13, should be formatted as currency, as well as E5. You are also going to have money sums in C16, C17, C18 and C20 so format these as well.

You now need to calculate the income from the sales of tickets to adults.

The formula in C16 is =$C$5*C11

You may remember that $C$5 is an absolute cell address. You will be copying this formula across to other columns later.

Using an absolute cell address means that it will remain as C5 and will not be changed in the usual way.

You now need to put in similar formulae for the sale of tickets to students and children.

The formula in C17 is =$C$6*C12

The formula in C18 is =$C$7*C13

The total income per day from ticket sales is found by adding these three together.

The formula in C20 is =C16+C17+C18

If you enter these formulae correctly you should see the values shown in the worksheet in Fig 9.2.

	A	B	C	D	E
1		**Adventureland ticket pricing**			
2					
3					
4		**Average number of visitors per day**			**Target income**
5		Adults	6000		£176,000.00
6		Students	2000		
7		Children under 12	4000		
8					
9			**Option 1**		
10			**10% increase**		
11		Ticket price per adult	£16.50		
12		Ticket price per student	£16.50		
13		Ticket price per child	£11.00		
14					
15		**Income**			
16		Adult ticket sales	£99,000.00		
17		Student ticket sales	£33,000.00		
18		Child ticket sales	£44,000.00		
19					
20		Total income per day	£176,000.00		
21					
22					

Fig 9.2 *The model develops*

Case study

Adventureland considers two other ticket pricing options.

◎ Option 2 increases the adult price by more than 10%, but offers the child price to students as well.

◎ Option 3 introduces three different prices, for adults, students and children.

Which option do you think might produce the greatest income?

Pricing options

You can add the other two ticket pricing options to the worksheet, as in Fig. 9.3 on page 290.

You now need to copy the formulae in C16, C17 and C18 across the other three columns. Highlight the three cells then drag the handle across the columns.

Excel has made an intelligent copy of the formulae, although the absolute cell addresses have not been changed. So, for example:

the formula in C16 is =$C$5*C11

the formula in D16 is =$C$5*D11

continued ▶

Creating a financial model (continued)

	A	B	C	D	E	
1		**Adventureland ticket pricing**				
2						
3						
4		**Average number of visitors per day**			**Target income**	
5		Adults	6000		£176,000.00	
6		Students	2000			
7		Children under 12	4000			
8						
9			**Option 1**	**Option 2**	**Option 3**	
10			**10% increase**	**Cheap student**	**Three prices**	
11		Ticket price per adult	£16.50	£18.00	£18.00	
12		Ticket price per student	£16.50	£11.00	£14.00	
13		Ticket price per child	£11.00	£11.00	£11.00	
14						
15		**Income**				
16		Adult ticket sales	£99,000.00			
17		Student ticket sales	£33,000.00			
18		Child ticket sales	£44,000.00			
19						
20		Total income per day	£176,000.00			
21						

Fig 9.3 *New pricing options added*

Finally, copy the formula in C20 across the other three columns as well. You now have the total income from ticket sales for each option.

The model should now look like Fig 9.4.

	A	B	C	D	E	
1		**Adventureland ticket pricing**				
2						
3						
4		**Average number of visitors per day**			**Target income**	
5		Adults	6000		£176,000.00	
6		Students	2000			
7		Children under 12	4000			
8						
9			**Option 1**	**Option 2**	**Option 3**	
10			**10% increase**	**Cheap student**	**Three prices**	
11		Ticket price per adult	£16.50	£18.00	£18.00	
12		Ticket price per student	£16.50	£11.00	£14.00	
13		Ticket price per child	£11.00	£11.00	£11.00	
14						
15		**Income**				
16		Adult ticket sales	£99,000.00	£108,000.00	£108,000.00	
17		Student ticket sales	£33,000.00	£22,000.00	£28,000.00	
18		Child ticket sales	£44,000.00	£44,000.00	£44,000.00	
19						
20		Total income per day	£176,000.00	£174,000.00	£180,000.00	
21						
22						

Fig 9.4 *Calculating the income*

Comparing income with target

You can now use row 21 to see whether the income from each option will meet the target, which is stored in cell E5.

To do this you need a formula for C21 that says:

'If C20 is less than $E$5, then write "Below target", otherwise C21 = C20 − $E$5'

Enter this formula in C21: =IF(C20<$E$5, "Below target", C20-$E$5)

Don't forget the = sign, and do not put a space after IF.

Although the formula has commas instead of words, it means exactly the same as the sentence above.

Highlight C21 and drag the formula across to the other two columns. You should see the result as in Fig 9.5.

	A	B	C	D	E
1		**Adventureland ticket pricing**			
2					
3					
4		Average number of visitors per day			Target income
5		Adults	6000		£176,000.00
6		Students	2000		
7		Children under 12	4000		
8					
9			Option 1	Option 2	Option 3
10			10% increase	Cheap student	Three prices
11		Ticket price per adult	£16.50	£18.00	£18.00
12		Ticket price per student	£16.50	£11.00	£14.00
13		Ticket price per child	£11.00	£11.00	£11.00
14					
15		Income			
16		Adult ticket sales	£99,000.00	£108,000.00	£108,000.00
17		Student ticket sales	£33,000.00	£22,000.00	£28,000.00
18		Child ticket sales	£44,000.00	£44,000.00	£44,000.00
19					
20		Total income per day	£176,000.00	£174,000.00	£180,000.00
21		Does income meet target?	£0.00	Below target	£4,000.00
22					
23					

Fig 9.5 The completed model

Changing the values

The model assumes that the number of visitors will remain the same. But the new prices and the new rides could encourage more students to attend, but reduce the number of families with small children.

Give it a go

Set up the spreadsheet as described above.

1 Now change the values in C5 to C7 to represent the following visitor numbers.
   a Adults and children each drop by 500, and students increase to 3,000.
   b The park attracts more adults and young people and even fewer small children. Try out different combinations, making sure that the total attendance stays at 12,000.
2 Which ticket pricing option would you expect Adventureland to choose?

Modelling

The ticket pricing spreadsheet that you have just created was an example of a computer model. A model is a set of rules. You try to work out rules that match real life. You can then use the model to help you make decisions in real life.

Financial models

You could create a model to do any one of the following:

◎ Work out how much money you will have in the future, depending on how much you earn and what your expenses are likely to be.
◎ Work out how much profit a small shop will make in a year, depending on the number of sales and the prices items are sold at.
◎ Compare the costs of a holiday using different flights, hotels and tour operators.

Design models

Many models do not deal with money at all. Models are commonly used by engineers when developing their designs.

A car designer will build a physical model of the car design, and test it in a wind tunnel. But we are thinking about a stage earlier than that, when the design is entirely on a computer. The engineers will test out some important aspects of their designs before they actually build anything at all. For example, a model could:

◎ calculate whether a bridge over a railway will remain firm, depending on the weight and speed of the traffic flowing over it, the speed of the wind and the vibration caused by the trains passing under it;
◎ compare the speeds that a new aircraft can reach at different heights and in different weather conditions; or
◎ check the expected fuel consumption in a new car under different driving conditions.

Predictive models

Some models are created to predict the future. They use current data, then make some guesses about how things might change in the future. The guesses are not just random, but are based on the experience of experts. A predictive model could:

◎ compare the food needs for a developing country, depending on how the population grows;
◎ forecast the weather; or
◎ predict how the populations of rare species of animals are likely to change.

Rules and formulae

The rules in a model are usually expressed as mathematical formulae. In the ticket pricing case study you used 15 different formulae, or rules.

Variables

All models allow you to change some of the values to get different results. You were able to change the values of the number of adults, students and children visiting the theme park.

Suppose you created a model to help you work out your living expenses. You could change some values to see what would happen if you had a low income, but lived in an expensive area; or if you had a high income but bought lots of designer clothes and a fast car. The model would give you the answer each time.

A variable is a value that can be changed in a model by inputting a new value. In the ticket pricing example, C5, C6 and C7 are variables.

Using a spreadsheet to create a model

A spreadsheet is ideal for creating and experimenting with models. It allows you to change values and see the effect this has on the result.

One problem with the ticket pricing model was that once you had changed the values in C5, C6 and C7 you then lost the previous results. The solution to this is to create some 'what if' scenarios, using C5, C6 and C7 as the changing values.

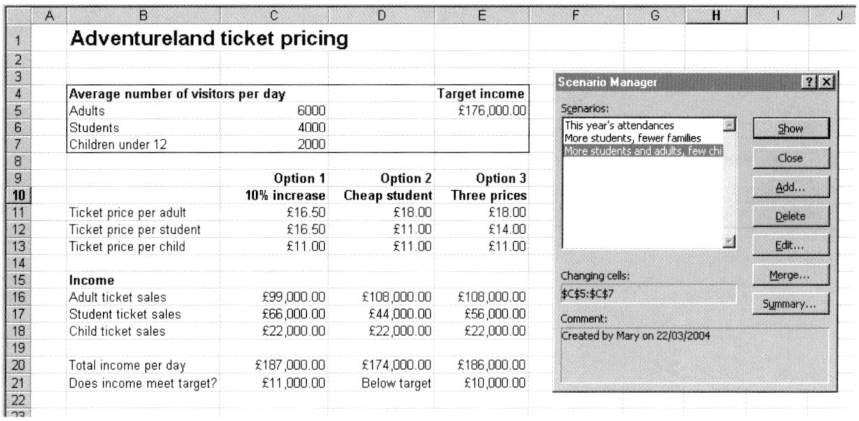

	B	C	D	E
1	**Adventureland ticket pricing**			
2				
3				
4	**Average number of visitors per day**			**Target income**
5	Adults	6000		£176,000.00
6	Students	4000		
7	Children under 12	2000		
8				
9		**Option 1**	**Option 2**	**Option 3**
10		**10% increase**	**Cheap student**	**Three prices**
11	Ticket price per adult	£16.50	£18.00	£18.00
12	Ticket price per student	£16.50	£11.00	£14.00
13	Ticket price per child	£11.00	£11.00	£11.00
14				
15	**Income**			
16	Adult ticket sales	£99,000.00	£108,000.00	£108,000.00
17	Student ticket sales	£66,000.00	£44,000.00	£56,000.00
18	Child ticket sales	£22,000.00	£22,000.00	£22,000.00
19				
20	Total income per day	£187,000.00	£174,000.00	£186,000.00
21	Does income meet target?	£11,000.00	Below target	£10,000.00
22				

Fig 9.6 *Using scenarios with a model*

You have already created a simple model on page 288, and, on that occasion, you set up scenarios for several pairs of possible changing values. You can do the same for the ticket pricing model (Fig 9.6).

Checking whether the rules are correct

A model is only any good if the rules, or formulae, that it uses are correct. The rules about the ticket pricing options were fairly straightforward. It is not difficult to see that the income from ticket sales to children is calculated by multiplying the price of the ticket by the number of tickets sold.

Some aspects of life and our environment are much more difficult to express mathematically. That is why the outcomes from some models, such as those used for weather forecasting, are not always accurate.

Simulations

A simulation shows the world how a model works. You can look at a model on a spreadsheet and just see numbers. When a model is used for a simulation you may see moving images, or hear sounds, or see charts in which the bars rise and fall, or even feel movement.

A simulation is a program that brings a model to life by allowing you to change the input values and to see the effect this has.

Playing simulation games

You may have come across a game called Sim City (Fig 9.7). It allows

Fig 9.7 Maxis Sim City

you to construct a landscape with hills, lakes and trees on screen. You then start building a town. Sometimes the town starts to crumble – houses fall down, riots break out, fires engulf areas. Sometimes your town thrives and you are able to add extravagant modern blocks and leisure facilities.

Other Sim series have been produced – in which you can run everything from a theme park, to a human family or even the whole earth.

The Sim (for simulation) games are not so very different from the software simulations that are used by town planners, environmentalists and engineers, although you will probably have more fun than they do.

Trying traffic simulators

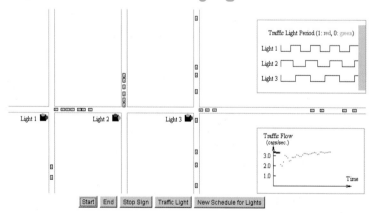

Fig 9.8 A traffic light simulation

A traffic simulation shows how traffic can build up at junctions and how the traffic lights affect the flow. You can change the values in the variables by making choices about the timing of the traffic lights. Large jams may develop, or you may help the traffic to move smoothly.

Using simulations for design

Designers and engineers create simulations, such as the one for the traffic lights, in order to experiment before they actually build something. They use a simulation to:

◎ experiment and find out the best combination of values;
◎ make quick changes and see immediately what the effect is;

- improve the design before actually spending money on building it;
- prove to other people that it will work; and
- test something which might be dangerous in real life.

Carrying out a virtual activity

A simulation can also be used to carry out a process that you might not enjoy doing in real life. For example, you can dissect a virtual frog in a simulation and find out all about its organs, without endangering any frogs or getting yourself messy (Fig 9.9).

You may have used simulation software, like the frog dissection, in science classes. You might use one to:

- do things that would not be safe in real life, e.g. exploring a nuclear reactor;
- do things that would be too expensive or difficult, e.g. landing on Mars;
- slow down a fast process, e.g. the beating of the wings of a bee;
- speed up a slow process, e.g. plants growing;
- enlarge objects, e.g. looking inside an atom;
- reduce the size of things, e.g. exploring a galaxy; or
- get a quick result, e.g. modelling an electronic circuit.

What does it mean? **Virtual**

In ICT 'virtual' means 'simulated'.

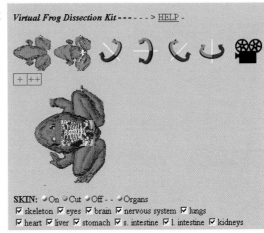

Fig 9.9 A virtual frog dissection

What do you think?

Have you used or viewed simulation software as part of your education? If so, write down the names of the software that you have used.
Why were simulations used?

Simulations and forecasting

Whenever you watch the weather forecast on television, you can see a simulation of the weather patterns for the next day or so (Fig 9.10).

Similar predictive simulations can be used to forecast the future. Planners use these simulations to:

- plan the provision of hospitals and schools in the future;
- decide whether they need to protect animal populations; and
- work out the effects of global warming and to prepare for it.

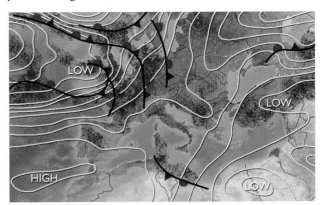

Fig 9.10 A weather map

Case study

The designers and planners at Adventureland use models and simulations to help them decide about the future development of the park. Can you suggest what they might use them for?

Data logging

All information systems need data input. In all your experience of using computers you have mainly been using interactive processing in which you, as the user, actively enter the data into the system.

It is also possible to input data into a computer system automatically, and without any humans being involved. This can be done when the data is collected by sensors.

Sensors are input devices that can work continuously, day and night, reading data and transferring it to the CPU. As we read in Section 1, they can measure things in the world such as temperature, humidity, light, sound, movement and pressure.

Data logging

When data is collected from sensors the process is known as data logging.

A variety of sensors can be used for data logging. These include the following:

◎ Temperature sensors, known as thermistors.
◎ Light sensors, which detect low light levels in lighting systems.
◎ Infrared sensors, which are used in burglar alarm systems to pick up unexpected movement (Fig 9.11).
◎ Humidity sensors, which measure the amount of moisture in the atmosphere and can be used for controlling the environment in greenhouses.
◎ Pressure sensors, which measure the pressure on an area.
◎ Movement sensors, which measure how far something has moved.

Fig 9.11 *An infrared sensor in a burglar alarm system*

Calibrating sensors

All sensors have to be calibrated before they can be used. A sensor is calibrated when the data it collects is expressed accurately in scientific units.

For example, a traffic engineer is thinking of installing traffic lights at a busy road junction. First, he or she will study the amount of traffic that flows along the roads. He or she can place mats, containing pressure sensors, on the roadways (Fig 9.12). He or she wants the pressure sensors to log each car that passes over the mat. But the engineer wants the sensors to ignore people, cats and dogs that may walk over the mats. The pressure sensor has to be calibrated so that it only logs a car when the pressure is above a certain level.

Fig 9.12 *Traffic sensors*

Collecting data over a period of time

Data can be logged over a short or long period of time.

In the case of the traffic flow measures, the data will probably be logged for a complete week, to allow for the variations on different days of the week.

Setting logging intervals

A sensor logs the data at fixed intervals. Even if a sensor appears to be working all the time, it does in fact take readings at regular intervals.

The logging interval is the time between one reading and the next.

When the logging interval is short, readings can be taken several times a minute. When the logging interval is long, readings can be taken once a day or once a week.

Collecting data over a distance

In many cases the sensor is attached directly to a computer. This often happens in scientific laboratories, where the results of an experiment are being logged over a period of time.

In other cases, the sensor is a long distance from the computer system. The data has to be transmitted, using radio or microwave signals. For example, data is transmitted from weather balloons high up in the earth's atmosphere (Fig 9.13).

Storing and processing logged data

The data collected through data logging can be:

◎ stored in the computer system and then analysed later – a form of batch processing; or
◎ acted on immediately – in real-time processing.

When a large amount of data is collected and analysed later, it is often stored in a spreadsheet.

Fig 9.13 A weather balloon

Case study

At Adventureland sensors are installed in all the rides. These detect where each car or boat is on a ride at any given moment.

◎ What kind of sensors would be used?
◎ How long would the logging interval be?
◎ How would the data be transferred to the computer system?

Control systems

We can use ICT to control machines automatically. That means the machines can work on their own without humans.

Here are some examples:

◎ Most electronic equipment in the home has some element of computer control, e.g. video recorders, digital televisions, digital cameras, washing machines, microwave ovens.

◎ Most of the more advanced transport vehicles are controlled to some extent by computer systems, e.g. autopilots on aircraft, driverless trains (Fig 9.14), fuel injection systems for car engines.

◎ Signalling systems on the railways, and traffic lights on roads, are usually under computer control.

◎ Factories are often largely automated, e.g. manufacturing chemicals, processing foods, building cars.

Fig 9.14 *The Docklands Light Railway – look, no driver!*

Control systems

Fig 9.15 shows a diagram of a control system. The inputs are provided automatically by the sensors, so the output data is triggered automatically by the processor. In control systems the processor is often referred to as the controller.

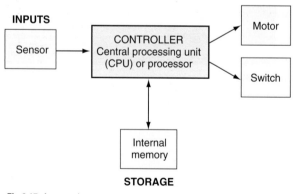

Fig 9.15 *A control system*

The motors and switches are part of the device that is being controlled, such as a railway signal.

The sensors may be part of the device that is being controlled, or may be completely separate from it.

For example, in a food-processing factory, a computer could control the paddles that rotate in a large container to mix the ingredients as they are being heated. The outputs from the controller switch the paddles on and off, and regulate their speed. A temperature sensor can be placed inside the container and will be constantly sending back data to the controller. When the temperature reaches a certain level the controller sends signals to the motors to slow the paddles down and stop them.

Remote control

Some machines are controlled by a controller that is at a distance. The controller sends data to the motors or switches by radio or infrared signals. The controller may also receive the data from the sensors in the same way.

The most extreme example of remote control are the signals sent from the Earth to control vehicles landed on the Moon or Mars. Sensors on the vehicles send signals back to the Earth.

Robots

Robots are sophisticated computer-controlled machines that can move around and carry out physical tasks. They are extremely expensive so are used in situations where it would be too dangerous to use a human, such as for bomb disposal. They are also used for manufacturing expensive products such as cars.

Fig 9.16 A robot arm

Checking the outputs

In many control systems the outputs are directly checked by the sensors. Think of an oven which has a dial that can be set to the desired temperature. This is connected to the controller of the oven heating system. Inside the oven there is a sensor that measures the temperature. The data from the sensor is input into the controller for the oven, which checks whether the temperature matches the required value. If the temperature is too high the controller sends a signal to switch off the heater; if the temperature is too low the controller sends a signal to switch the heater back on. The sensor is continually checking and feeding back data to the controller.

Feedback

This process of constantly checking the effect of the outputs is known as feedback.

You use feedback all the time in your daily life. You can think of your brain as a controller, your five senses as sensors and your muscles as motors. When you walk, your brain sends commands to your muscles. Your senses check where your legs are and send data back through the nerves. Without this constant feedback, whilst you are walking you would simply lose your balance and fall over.

Fig 9.17 A computerised oven

Robots have very similar feedback systems. They use sensors continually to monitor their position, which they then send as input data to the controller. Robots tend to move in a series of tiny movements one after another. After each movement the feedback input is checked before the next tiny movement is made. This happens very quickly so the overall movement appears smooth.

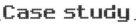
Case study

How can control systems be used in a theme park like Adventureland?

Virtual reality

The most sophisticated simulations are often referred to as virtual reality (VR) systems. They create an environment which is convincingly like the real world. The most complex VR systems combine simulation with control systems.

Using a flight simulator

Fig 9.18 A flight simulator

Flight simulators (Fig 9.18) are used to train pilots, especially in the early days of their training when it would be too risky to let them fly planes on their own. The trainee pilot sits in a mocked-up cockpit surrounded by all the dials, levers, buttons and screens that would be found in a real aircraft.

Outside the 'window' images of real locations will be shown. The cockpit itself is mounted on a chassis which can move as the 'aircraft' turns and banks. These effects give the pilot a very realistic impression of flying a real plane, but without any danger or expense if things go wrong.

Experienced pilots also use flight simulators to learn about the layout and approach to airports they have not visited before. They can familiarise themselves with the landscape and practise difficult landings.

Playing action games

Fig 9.19 A racing game

There are some computer games based on flight simulators. The ones designed for desktop computers do not, of course, give you the sense of motion, but they do represent the cockpit controls and the landscape.

Many computer games today simulate real action – from car racing to surfing. They all depend on complicated computer models. The models determine how a person or machine will move and how they will appear on the screen. You are able to control the action in some way. When you hit a key or move the mouse you are actually changing the values of variables in the model (Fig 9.19).

Simulation software similar to games can be used for serious training.

Using simulations for training

Flight simulators and other training simulations are used to:
- train people in safe conditions;
- build up the trainees' skills and confidence;
- reduce the cost of training on location; and
- speed up training.

Using virtual reality systems

When you get a chance to use a VR system you will probably wear some of these:

Figure 9.20 *A VR headset and data glove*

◎ *Data gloves* – you wear these like ordinary gloves (Fig 9.20). They have optical fibres built in to the fabric which detect the movement of the finger joints when, for example, you try to grasp something. Additional sensors measure the position of your hand and the way in which your wrist rotates.

◎ A *helmet* which can track the position and movement of your head. Sometimes these are combined with eye-gaze systems.

◎ An *eye-gaze* system, which can be fitted inside a helmet (Fig 9.20). It places a small (safe) laser unit in front of your eye. This records the movement of the eye and can be used as a hands-free method of moving an on-screen pointer.

◎ A *whole-body tracking* system, which has movement sensors either directly on your body or on your chair.

A VR system collects the data from the sensors. It uses real-time processing to send outputs back to you immediately. The outputs may be through:

◎ *screens* fitted inside the helmet just in front of the eyes. These give stereo vision;

◎ *speakers* placed inside the helmet by the ears; and

◎ *pressure* applied to your hands so that you feel as though you are touching things.

If you use a VR system you become completely immersed in the virtual world that you inhabit.

Case study

Karim and his friends try out the Flight Fright ride at Adventureland. They sit inside a capsule and are moved around as the scenery flashes past. Strictly speaking this is not a simulation, as it is pre-programmed to give a specific ride and the riders cannot control it in any way.

Elsewhere in the park Karim finds a genuine virtual reality game. He puts on a data glove and helmet and finds himself immersed in an adventure game, picking up virtual objects and moving around a virtual landscape.

Have you tried rides like these? How realistic was the experience?

Practice questions

Foundation

1 In ICT, what is a model? Is it ...
   A a scaled-down version of a product made in a cheap material.
   B a set of rules that match real-life conditions.
   C a person who acts as an example to everyone else.
   D a special sort of database.

2 Give two reasons why someone might set up a financial model.

3 Give two examples of models that are not financial.

4 Which of these statements are true?
   A All simulations are games.
   B A simulation is a model that uses images, sound or movement.
   C Simulations can be used to train people to do their work.
   D Simulations cannot be used to predict the future.

5 Could a sensor be used to log data in each of these examples?
   A Counting the number of cars that travel along a road.
   B Recording the number of people who catch flu during one season.
   C Measuring the rainfall at a remote place.
   D Recording the movement of the earth in an earthquake zone.

Higher

6 Today, large amounts of data are gathered automatically by sensors and then input into computer systems.
   a Explain the advantages and disadvantages of this method of collecting data.
   b Give examples of situations where data logging is of benefit to society.

7 In a factory that produces chocolate products, items are packaged using computer-controlled machines. Unwrapped chocolate bars are placed on a conveyor belt. Each bar is wrapped and the machine seals the wrapper. The wrapped bars are then moved to the next machine, which counts them and places them in the cardboard boxes that will be sent to supermarkets.
   a Identify two points in this process where sensors are needed.
   b Why is feedback important in this system? What could go wrong if there was no feedback?

10 The operating environment

Case study: Kingsmond District Hospital

Kingsmond District Hospital serves Kingsmond and the villages nearby. ICT is used widely throughout the hospital.

Patient administration

The patient administration system is used by many employees, for a number of purposes:

◎ *Patient records*   The details of all the patients who have visited the hospital are kept in a database. This holds personal data, such as name and address, the name of the patient's family doctor, and full details of all health problems and treatments.

◎ *Appointments*   The appointments system for outpatients is part of the patient administration system.

◎ *Waiting list*   The names of everyone who is waiting to be admitted to the hospital for treatment are kept on a waiting list.

◎ *Bed allocation*   When a patient is admitted to the hospital he or she is allocated a bed on a ward and this data has to be stored.

◎ *Communications* The hospital has to communicate with family doctors and other healthcare professionals.

Diagnosis and treatment

Many of the treatments that are given in the hospital are controlled by computers:

◎ *Monitors*   Patients can be wired up to monitors which check their temperature, breathing, heart rate, blood pressure, etc.

◎ *Scanners*   The complex scanners that take many pictures of the brain, or of the whole body, are carefully controlled by computer systems. Ultrasound scans are taken of babies in the womb.

◎ *Expert systems*   These are software packages that support the doctor by analysing symptoms and suggesting possible diagnoses.

◎ *Incubators*   A premature baby is placed in a special cot where the temperature is carefully controlled and the baby is monitored.

◎ *Laser surgery*   Lasers are used to treat a number of conditions. They have to be carefully positioned and controlled to avoid damaging cells.

Using an operating system

You are probably familiar with the operating system Microsoft Windows. It is the most widely used operating system on standalone, single-user computers, but it is by no means the only one. Alternative operating systems include the following:

◉ MacOS (Macintosh Operating System), which is used on computers manufactured by Apple.

◉ Linux, which can be run on Apple and other computers.

System software

All the software that is installed on a computer can be divided into two types – applications software and system software.

System software includes:

◉ all the many programs that make up an operating system, e.g. Microsoft Windows; and

◉ utilities, which are additional programs that add extra features to the operating system, e.g. a virus checker.

The graphical user interface

Table 10.1 Terms used to describe features in a GUI

Microsoft Windows	ICT term
Document	File
Folder	Directory
Desktop	File system
Recycle bin	Deleted files directory

Microsoft Windows has a GUI which allows the non-technical user to communicate with it. It uses words that relate to a desk in an office, such as desktop, document, folders and the recycle bin. These are not the terms that an ICT professional would normally use but they are clear to an ordinary user (see Table 10.1).

The desktop

Shortcut

In Microsoft Windows, a shortcut is a button that links directly with an application or file.

The Windows desktop (Fig 10.1) has:

◉ *icons* that give access to important parts of the system, such as My Computer;

◉ *shortcuts* to a number of applications, such as Internet Explorer; and

◉ a *taskbar* along the bottom of the screen, from the Start button on the left to the clock on the right.

On a standalone computer you can configure the desktop in very many ways, so no two will look the same. On a network, you may be more restricted in your configuration options.

The taskbar

The taskbar has buttons for each of the documents and applications that are open. The taskbar can also hold several extra toolbars, such as the Quick Launch one shown in Fig 10.1. To add a toolbar to the

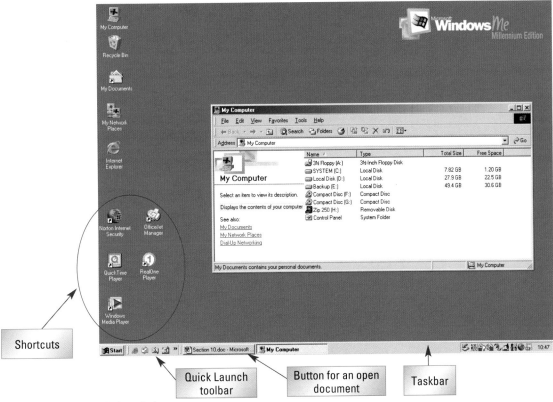

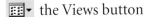

Shortcuts

Quick Launch toolbar

Button for an open document

Taskbar

Fig 10.1 *The Microsoft Windows desktop*

taskbar, right-click on a blank space anywhere along the taskbar, then select **toolbars** (Fig 10.2).

When you click the Start button a menu pops up. This contains shortcuts to:

◎ all the applications software on the system; and
◎ some utilities that you can use.

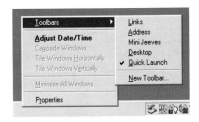

Fig 10.2 *Adding toolbars to the taskbar*

Drives, directories and files

Files are stored on the storage media – hard disks, floppy disks, CDs, DVDs, etc. Each disk drive is given a letter to identify it.

Double-click on the My Computer icon on the desktop to view a list of all the drives on your system (see Fig 10.3 on page 306). You can now double-click on one of the drives to see what it contains. You will see a list of directories and files. Directories are known as folders in Microsoft Windows.

There are several ways of displaying the contents of a directory. Click on the arrow beside the Views button:

the Views button

Then select **Details** to see it as shown in Fig 10.3.

continued ▶

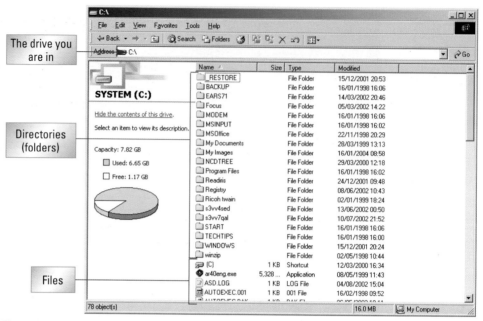

Fig 10.3 *Viewing the contents of a drive*

You are now looking at the root directory – it is the top-level directory when you look in a drive. You can double-click on each of the directories within the root directory to see what is in them – more directories and files (Fig 10.4).

Each file has a filename extension, such as .doc, .exe, .htm. Microsoft Windows uses icons to represent each type of file.

You can see the data that the operating system holds about each file.

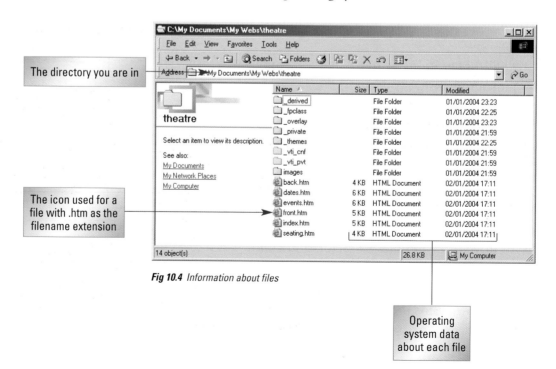

Fig 10.4 *Information about files*

Using Windows Explorer

You can carry out a number of file operations, such as deleting, copying or moving a file.

But be very careful and only try this with documents that you have created yourself. You can easily delete a file that is part of a software package by mistake, and then you may find the software does not work.

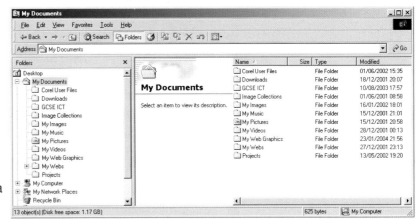

Fig 10.5 *Windows Explorer*

The easiest way to do this is to use a utility called Windows Explorer. Close any windows that are open. On the desktop, right-click on My Documents and then click on Explore. The window in Windows Explorer (Fig 10.5) is divided into two sections (known as panes). You can open directories in either pane, but you will only see the files in the pane on the right.

◎ You can then delete a file, by clicking on the file and clicking on the Delete button:

✕ the Delete button

◎ You can copy a file, by clicking on the file then using the Copy button.

◎ You can paste a file by clicking on the directory where you want it to go, then using the Paste button.

◎ You can move a file by dragging it to a new directory.

Control Panel

The Control Panel lists a number of system utilities that you can use to configure the operating system.

Click on the Start button, select **Settings**, then **Control Panel** (Fig 10.6). You can try out any of these. But, again, be careful not to make changes that you might regret.

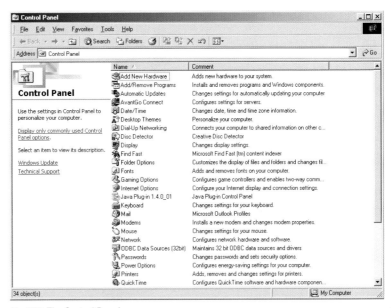

Fig 10.6 *The Control Panel*

Understanding an operating system

Some parts of an operating system can be managed directly by the user through a GUI. But this is only the tip of the iceberg – most of the work of the operating system is going on in the background without you being aware of it.

Applications software calls on the operating system all the time. Even though you may be working in a word processing software package, the software makes a request to the operating system every time it needs to:

◎ open a file;

◎ save a file; or

◎ send a document to the printer.

Less obviously, the applications software uses the operating system whenever it:

◎ receives data from the keyboard or mouse;

◎ sends data to the screen;

◎ sends sound data to a speaker;

◎ creates a new document; or

◎ edits a document.

All these processes, and many more, can be handed over to the operating system. Without an operating system each applications software package would have to include its own instructions for handling all this. Over the next pages you will read about some of the hidden tasks carried out by an operating system.

Receiving data from an input peripheral

When you click on a mouse or press a key on the keyboard, a signal is sent to the computer system. What happens if you do both at the same time?

In fact, the operating system checks the inputs that are arriving from peripherals one after another. The operating system decides which one to accept next, then runs the part of the operating system that deals with input from that source.

Sending data to an output peripheral

When you send a document to the printer, the data is copied from internal memory and transferred to the printer. The operating system actually has a brief (electronic) conversation with the printer, asking if it is ready to receive data. When the printer responds, the operating systems organises the transfer.

Something similar happens, but much faster, as data is being sent from the internal memory to the screen.

Organising files on storage media

The storage space on a hard disk is divided into blocks, each of which holds a fixed amount of data. Each block has an address, which is a set of numbers that show where the block is on the disk.

When a file is stored on a disk, it will take up one or more blocks of space. The operating system needs to know three pieces of information about each file:

◎ Its filename.
◎ The address of the first block that it uses.
◎ The size of the file, in kilobytes.

This information is stored on a file allocation table on the disk.

The file allocation table also stores other information, such as the date and time that the file was last saved and the directory that the file is in (as shown in Table 10.2). You can see some of this information when you use Windows Explorer.

Table 10.2 Information stored on the file allocation table

Filename	Filename extension	Date	Time	Address of first block	File size
myletter	.doc	21/05/04	15:35	6742	31
index	.htm	30/05/04	11:27	9213	25

Loading a file from the hard disk

When you open an existing file, the operating system first of all looks at the file allocation table on the hard disk. It finds the filename, then notes the address of the first block and the size of the file.

The operating system is then able to find the first block and transfer the data into internal memory. It carries on transferring blocks of data until the whole file has been transferred. This is often referred to as loading a file.

Saving a file to the hard disk

When you save a file for the first time, the operating system has to search the hard disk to find enough spare blocks to save the whole file.

In fact, it does not actually look through the whole disk itself. Instead it looks at the information in the file allocation table. This helps it to find unused blocks.

A new record is then created in the file allocation table for this new file. The first block is filled with data, and then the remaining blocks, until the whole file has been transferred.

More about operating systems

Main tasks of an operating system

The main tasks of an operating system on a standalone system are to:

◎ receive data from input peripherals;
◎ send data to output peripherals;
◎ organise the files held on storage media, such as hard disks;
◎ allocate space in internal memory;
◎ manage several activities, which appear to be happening at the same time (multi-tasking); and
◎ allow the user to configure certain options.

We will now explore more of these.

Allocating space in internal memory

Internal memory (RAM) is made up of millions of memory cells. Each of these cells is numbered. When a file is loaded from the hard disk to internal memory, the operating system has to decide exactly where the data will be placed, and it keeps a note of where it is.

Internal memory can hold many files at the same time (Fig 10.7). You can only use a file when it is in internal memory. If you are working on a document in a word processor it will hold all these files:

◎ Operating system files.
◎ Word processing software files.
◎ The document you are editing.

You will probably have noticed that you can open several documents at the same time. Each one needs space in internal memory.

You can also run more than one piece of applications software at the same time. Whilst you are working on a word-processed document you can also open a spreadsheet. You can then switch between them.

If you open too many documents and too many applications, you start noticing that the system is slowing down. That is because the operating system is having difficulty in finding any spare space in internal memory to store new data. Eventually you may get a message saying that the 'System is out of resources'. The internal memory is one of the resources of the system, so it is telling you that it is full up.

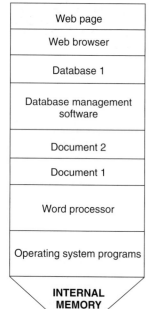

| Web page |
| Web browser |
| Database 1 |
| Database management software |
| Document 2 |
| Document 1 |
| Word processor |
| Operating system programs |

INTERNAL MEMORY

Fig 10.7 *Internal memory*

Multi-tasking

It often seems as though your computer is doing many tasks at the same time. For example, all these programs could be running simultaneously:

◎ A document is being printed.
◎ The clock is keeping time.
◎ E-mails are being downloaded.
◎ The virus checker is checking an email.
◎ You are editing a record in a database.

Multi-tasking is the ability of a computer system to work on several tasks or programs at the same time.

In fact, the CPU itself can only carry out one program instruction at a time. But it does these incredibly fast, with millions of instructions per second. Whilst it is working it switches rapidly from one program to another. It carries out some of the instructions from the first program, then some from the second program and so on. Because it is working in fractions of a second, it comes back to the first program very quickly.

This is known as time sharing. The operating system controls the time sharing by giving time to each program in turn.

As far as you are concerned you have no idea that the CPU is flicking between the programs, as they all seem to be working smoothly and continuously. It is rather like watching a film – you know that you are seeing lots of frames one after another, but they give the impression of continuous movement.

Choosing an operating system

When you buy a new desktop computer system the manufacturer will have set it up to run a particular operating system. In fact, you can change to a later version of the operating system, or to a completely different one if you wish.

Applications software is designed to run on a particular operating system. For example, you can use many popular software packages on both Microsoft Windows and MacOS. But you do have to make sure that you have bought the version of the package that was specifically written for the operating system you have. The version written for Windows will not work on the version written for MacOS.

Dealing with versions of an operating system

Applications software is also written to work on a particular version of the operating system. Table 10.3 shows some of the versions of Microsoft Windows and the year each first appeared.

Software written for one version may not run properly on an earlier version.

Table 10.3 Versions of Microsoft Windows

Version	Year
Windows 95	1995
Windows 98	1998
Windows 2000	2000
Windows XP	2001

Network operating systems

The servers that control networks need more complex operating systems, such as:

◎ Unix

◎ Windows NT.

When you are using a desktop computer you can communicate with the operating system through the graphical user interface. In the same way, a network administrator can communicate with a network operating system. Most of these systems have GUIs as well, but some of them still use a command line interface (see page 269)

You may like to read Section 4 again on networks before reading this topic.

Multi-user system

The network operating system is stored on the network server. A network can have many users at the same time, so is called a multi-user system.

A user at a workstation may want to load software or a document that is stored on the shared network hard disks. The workstation sends a request to the network operating system. The user may want to print out a document; once again a request is sent to the network operating system. And the same thing happens every time a file is saved.

The network operating system is having to deal with requests from all the workstations at the same time.

Main tasks of a network operating system

A network operating system does all the same tasks as an operating system for a standalone computer. In addition it manages:

◎ a multi-user system; and

◎ network security.

Managing a multi-user system

A multi-user network operating system has to handle many tasks, from many users, at the same time. So it uses the same technique as a standalone operating system uses with multi-tasking.

The network operating system uses time sharing to give each of the users a very short period of time – a time slice – one after the other. During each time slice the user has the undivided attention of the CPU in the network server, so is able to request any loading, saving, printing, etc., that needs to be done on the network system. The network operating system then goes to the users one after another, returning to the first user after a short interval.

All this happens so quickly that, normally, the user does not notice the gaps at all.

Managing network security

If a standalone computer is used by several people, you can set up a username and password for each user. This is particularly useful at home where parents may want to ensure that young children do not delete their work.

One person sets up the usernames, passwords and permissions for each user, which are then stored by the operating system. All users, including the children, have to log on with their own usernames and passwords. The operating system checks each log in and then arranges things so that each person can then only get at the files he or she has permission to use.

This is a simplified version of the security that can be created in a network operating system.

The network administrator can set up usernames and passwords for all the users on a network. Each user will be given a set of access privileges which will specify:

◎ files he or she can use but not change, such as applications software;
◎ files he or she cannot look at or use, such as some operating system programs;
◎ directories where he or she can save files (he or she will only be able to save in these directories);
◎ directories he or she cannot view at all; and
◎ the way in which the GUI is configured for him or her.

Give it a go

Find out which network operating system is used at your school. If possible, ask the network administrator to demonstrate how he or she adds a new username and password to the system and how he or she sorts out the permissions.

Case study

Go back and read the information about Kingsmond District Hospital on page 303.

◎ Can you suggest some contexts in which a standalone, single-user operating system would be used?
◎ Where would a network operating system be used?
◎ Why is network security important for the patient administration system?

The impact of ICT on our lives

We have all been affected by ICT in our lives, whether we use a computer directly or not.

Environmental issues: transport

Most forms of transport now rely on computer-controlled systems. When the computer systems go wrong they can cause a great deal of inconvenience to travellers:

Fig 10.8 *A system for controlling trains*

- Air-traffic controllers monitor all the planes flying over the country and allocate each a flying path. They guide the planes as they take off or land. If one of the air-traffic control systems is faulty, flights have to be cancelled or planes are diverted to other parts of the country.
- Railway signalling systems are controlled by computers (Fig 10.8). They log the positions of trains on the network, then use the signals to communicate with the drivers. If the signalling system fails the trains have to be halted.

Environmental issues: recycling

Old computers have to be disposed of in some way. They contain poisonous heavy metals and also forms of PVC that are not bio-degradable. These are perfectly safe whilst the computer is in use, but they can contaminate the landfill sites where rubbish is dumped.

It is thought that over 300 million computers were discarded by 2004.

Social issues: types of employment

Back in the 1970s many people were worried that they would lose their jobs because computers would be able to do things automatically.

In fact, far more jobs have been created because of ICT. Think of all these careers, none of which existed before computers were invented:

- network administrator
- database manager
- computer sales
- technology journalist
- computer engineer
- software developer
- web designer
- ICT teacher or trainer.

Social issues: working patterns

The use of ICT has changed the way in which people work and the skills they need:

- *ICT skills* Today you will be expected to have ICT skills for almost any job.
- *Training* Training will be very important throughout your life, because you will need to keep your skills up to date.

- *Growth of offices* Offices have grown in the UK, whilst manufacturing industry has declined. You are much more likely to work in an office than in a factory, so the nature of work has changed.
- *Teleworking* Many employees do not always have to be present in the office, for fixed hours from 9 am to 5 pm. You could work at home, using a portable computer with communications links into your company's network. This is known as homeworking or teleworking.
- *Flexitime* The use of email means that you can leave messages for colleagues who can deal with them when convenient. So you could work flexible hours (flexitime) to fit in with other commitments.
- *Time-displaced communications* Communications around the world can be made simple through email. In the past if you were in the UK and wanted to speak to a colleague in Japan you would have to call in the middle of the night. Today an email can be sent one afternoon and the reply read the next morning.
- *Virtual conferencing* People do not always have to be in the same room in order to hold a meeting. You can use telephone or Internet conferencing instead.

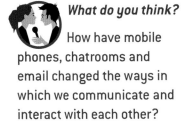

What do you think?

How have mobile phones, chatrooms and email changed the ways in which we communicate and interact with each other?

Social issues: communications

Communication systems have also changed:
- *Mobile phones* Mobile phones use computer technology both in the phones themselves and also in the systems that enable them to communicate with each other.
- *Internet* Chatrooms and email make it possible for you to communicate quickly and cheaply with people anywhere in the world.

Social issues: leisure

Many of the ways you spend your leisure are dependent on ICT, such as the following:
- *Computer games* You probably play them on computers and on games machines.
- *Music and video* All music is recorded digitally these days and stored on digital media such as CDs. Video is commonly recorded on DVD.
- *Light and sound* These are controlled by ICT systems at performance venues and nightclubs.
- *Computer-generated images* Most films use some computer graphics, if only to fill in the background of a scene. The most ambitious productions create complete characters that interact with live actors (Fig 10.9).

Fig 10.9 *Gollum from Lord of the Rings – a computer-generated image*

Ethical and moral issues

New technologies often raise very difficult moral questions, such as the following:

◎ Should we allow human cloning?
◎ Is it a good thing to grow genetically modified food?
◎ Should we spend billions of pounds to send a person to Mars?
◎ Who should be offered a new, but extremely expensive, life-saving medical treatment?

Advances in ICT

Some of the new information and communication technologies do make people think about moral issues:

◎ *The capacity of storage data.* It is now possible to create very large databases, which could, for example, hold data about every person in the country.
◎ *The speed at which data can be processed.* Computer control systems can be highly accurate and complicated.
◎ *The speed at which data can be accessed.* People demand, and can get, immediate access to information.
◎ *Global data communications and the Internet.* Information can be shared with anyone, anywhere in the world.

What do you think?

For each of these advances in ICT can you think of one good thing that could come out of it? Can you then think of one bad or unwelcome thing that could happen as a result of each advance?

Privacy and confidentiality

Everybody is entitled to privacy. That means no one should take photos of you or try to find out private information about you without your knowledge and consent.

The Data Protection Act helps to maintain your privacy. It ensures that no information is stored about you unless you agree.

When you visit a professional, such as a doctor, you do have to give that person some private information. But you do expect that any information will be kept confidential. That means the professional may not pass it on to anyone else at all, unless you have given him or her permission.

The Data Protection Act helps to maintain confidentiality. It ensures that any information that is held about you is never given to someone else without your knowledge.

Case study

At present, Kingsmond District Hospital has to pass data between the various professionals who are looking after a patient – family doctors, district nurses, etc.

Eventually every person in the UK will have a healthcare record which will be held centrally by the National Health Service. Each person will be allocated a health number which will stay with him or her throughout his or her life.

- ◎ Some people are worried about having a single healthcare record. Why?
- ◎ Can the hospital guarantee that a patient's privacy will not be abused and that confidentiality will be maintained?
- ◎ How can the system prevent abuse?

Offensive material and censorship

Computer users can, if they wish, get hold of a large amount of unpleasant material, in both text and graphical formats. Most of this is accessible through the Internet.

Some of this material is pornographic, excessively violent or racially offensive, and most people would be very upset by it.

Some of this offensive material is illegal in some countries. But it is very difficult to control the Internet, as any user can download pages from any country in the world. If something is banned in one country you can be sure that a criminal will move it to a server to another country where it is not illegal.

One important concern is to protect young children from offensive images. This can be done by installing 'nanny' software on a computer. The software checks the words on websites and does not allow the user to download any suspect sites or images.

Most people would want to protect children, but there is quite a lot of disagreement about whether adults should be protected in the same way. Some people argue that there should be no censorship, and that any adult should be able to view whatever he or she likes, provided it is not actually illegal. Others are concerned that people may be corrupted by looking at violent, pornographic or racist pages.

What do you think?

What are your views on censorship and the Internet?

Practice questions

Foundation

1 Which of the following actions are carried out by an operating system?
  A Saving a file to the hard disk.
  B Sorting records in a database.
  C Checking the username and password when someone logs on.
  D Keeping a record of directories and files.
  E Changing ink cartridges in a printer.
  F Sending data to a printer.

2 Which one of the following statements is true?
  A You can only run one program at a time on a computer system.
  B The operating system allocates internal memory to files.
  C Internal memory expands to hold all the files in it.
  D Program files are stored on backing storage and do not need to be copied to internal memory.

3 Multi-user operating systems are used on networks. Explain how the operating system uses time sharing so that many users can use it at the same time.

4 Give two reasons why operating systems on popular desktop computer systems usually use a graphical user interface.

5 Describe three tasks that a network administrator could carry out using a network operating system.

6 Describe a method that could be used to prevent young children from accessing unsuitable material on the Internet.

Higher

7 Describe the criteria you should consider when choosing a new operating system.

8 Discuss the impact that ICT has had on patterns of employment.

9 Many people are concerned that privacy and confidentiality may be undermined by growth of the Internet. Explain how this might occur, and suggest some steps that could be taken to reassure people.

Coursework

Introduction

This section is designed to help you understand what is required when you produce your GCSE ICT coursework, and to give you help and advice so you can gain the highest marks possible.

Coursework dominates the GCSE ICT course and it is therefore important that you produce good work and plan your time carefully to ensure that you complete the tasks on time. The best way to undertake coursework is to make sure that before you start, you fully understand what the examiner is looking for and that you are clear about how your are going to lay your coursework out. You need, therefore, to break your coursework down into small manageable tasks and to set yourself a timetable with target dates so that you can spread the load.

So why do you do coursework?

Coursework tests your ability to apply the knowledge you have gained through your theory work in practical terms. It lets you learn skills and techniques that cannot be taught in theory lessons alone. Because of this, coursework is a very important part of your GCSE ICT course, and it therefore takes up a great deal of time.

Breakdown of marks for the coursework

The coursework you must undertake accounts for 60% of the marks for the exam and, therefore, should take up at least 60% of the course.

The AQA-set Assignment consists of a booklet that will be given to you by your teacher. You should work through this booklet and produce a solution to the problem that it sets. This accounts for 30% of the marks.

The project is similar, but this time, you decide on the problem and its solution. You should apply the experience you gained from undertaking the set assignment to finding a solution to this problem. This, too, accounts for 30% of the final marks.

The AQA-set Assignment

The set assignment is based on the system life-cycle you read about in Section 7 of this book.

Analysis (10 marks)

When your teacher gives you the set assignment booklet you should read it through thoroughly, and then read it through again. Your first read through will help you to put the assignment into context and will give you an idea of the tasks that you have to undertake. In the second read-through you will pick up on all those things you missed the first time round. During this second read-through you should make notes about how you might complete the task. It is best to write these notes, in pencil, on the booklet itself, although you could write them on a piece of paper and make a note of the relevant pages.

Having completed this read-through, and having familiarised yourself with the problem and made a note of possible solutions, you should try to identify and list all the problems that you are going to solve. Some of these will be easy, whilst others will not, but a careful reading of the booklet will give you general ideas on which to build.

You should now take each task in turn and carry out the following procedures.

Inputs, processes and outputs

For each problem you need to list the *inputs* – i.e. the data that you are going to type in – and the *processing* that must be done in order to obtain the *outputs*.

You should make notes about what form the input and output will take, what information will be output and what data will generate this output – i.e. what you have to key in to the system in order to produce this output. The form the output must take will be written somewhere in your booklet, and so this is why it is important that you read the booklet carefully.

For example, you may might find the following sentence in an interview with a Mr Smith on page 3, paragraph 6:

Mr Smith wants you to produce an easy-to-read A4 poster to advertise the Wharmton Horse Show being held at Clayton Fields on Saturday 11th June 2004.

We can break this sentence down into the following procedures:

Inputs (all the inputs can be found in paragraph 6 of the interview with Mr Smith)

◎ A drawing of a horse – to be imported from Clip Art.
◎ Details of the Wharmton Horse Show – to be keyed in.
◎ The date of the event – to be keyed in.
◎ The location of the event – to be keyed in.

Processing

Create the poster.

Outputs (all the outputs can be found in paragraph 6 of the interview with Mr Smith)

The finished poster must be A4 size and must include:

◎ a drawing of a horse;
◎ a banner stating that it is the Wharmton Horse Show;
◎ the date of the event;
◎ the location of the event.

Doing this will give you a clear idea of what has to be designed and what has to be produced.

Desired outcomes and performance criteria

Now write down what you would like the desired outcomes for this task to be and also some notes about how you think you will be able to show that you have achieved these (these are called performance criteria). If we use the example given above then we can list the desired outcomes and the performance criteria.

The performance criteria are the outcomes that can be measured. These will all be listed in the booklet and, therefore, it is important that you look for them and make a note where you found them. They can usually be found in the interview section.

In our example the performance criteria are listed in the booklet in the interview with Mr Smith:

Mr Smith wants an A4 Poster
On the poster he wants:

◎ A drawing of a horse
◎ A banner stating that it is the Wharmton Horse Show
◎ The date of the event
◎ The location of the event

After you have listed these performance criteria, you need to list your desired outcomes. These are not as easy to list as the performance criteria, but for our example, one is that the poster must be easy to read. Again write down where you found this in the booklet.

Testing

The booklet says that, for *each* problem, you must *state* if testing is needed or not. To use our example of the poster for the horse show:

What is the problem? Answer:
To produce an A4 poster advertising the horse show.

Do we need to test this? Answer:

Testing does not need to be carried out on this task.

You have now completed the analysis for this task. You now need to go back and analyse all the other tasks that you have identified.

Once you have completed all the analyses, you need to hand in your work for checking. Your teacher will mark your work and tell you if you have missed anything. If you have missed anything, you must do it before you continue with the rest of the assignment.

Design (25 marks)

You must split this part of the assignment into two distinct sections:

◎ The first section must include evidence of how you intend to solve the problem. You must include here notes about all the decisions. This must include all the decisions you have made.

◎ The second section must include an explanation of the software that you will be using to solve each of the tasks and of why you think this choice of software is appropriate. For example, a spreadsheet would be a good solution for a small business that wants to keep track of all its income and expenses.

Hint: A good design can be given to someone who, until now, knows nothing about the design, but who, without any help, can produce the solution that was originally intended. If you can do this with your designs, you will have achieved what you set out to do.

Your design should include layouts, drawings and sketches that clearly show what you are going to achieve with the software. Everything that you produce must be explained fully, and you must explain why you produced the design you did. (This is called justification.)

What are designs?

A design is a plan of how you are going to go about solving a problem. Designs can be changed if you find that your design does not work; you can go back and make changes, as long as you explain what you have done and why.

To return to our example of the horse show, the design we might produce could look like Fig 1.

Pencil drawings are acceptable for your designs, as are computer-generated designs like the one in Fig 1. It is important, however, that you make sure that your designs are neat and well produced.

The things to remember when you are producing your designs are the performance criteria and the desired outcomes. In the analysis section we saw that the poster must be an A4 size. Mr Smith wants us to put a drawing of a horse on the poster, a banner stating that it is the

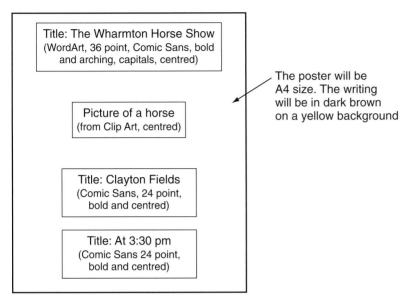

Fig 1 *The design for the poster*

Wharmton Horse Show, and the date and location of the event. The design we have produced contains all these.

Our desired outcomes state that the poster must be easy to read. Dark brown on a yellow background would be easy to read. Therefore the design has achieved what it was meant to achieve. You may need to put a few sentences on your design to explain how your design fulfils these desired outcomes.

It may be, however, that when you create the poster the colours do not make it easy to read, or the lettering is too large, etc. If so, you should go back to your design and change it. You must also make notes by making notes about the new or changed design, explaining why you have changed it.

Having completed your design you need to explain how the features of your chosen software will help you to implement (create) it:

◎ The layout of the poster is very important and you need to be able to change the font size and style. A feature of word processing packages, is that we can change the font style and size by highlighting the word and selecting a different style of font and a different size.

◎ Changing the position of the picture and the text will change the layout of the poster. We must also be able to import WordArt. A feature of word processing packages is that each element can be repositioned easily by dragging it to a new position, and WordArt can be imported from the Insert menu.

We will now look at another task to see how we can create a design for that:

Mr Smith wants to be able to produce a list of all the riders in the show-jumping event. The list will contain the names of the horse and the rider. When the riders enter the show they state whether they will be entering for show jumping.

In the analysis for this task it was decided to produce a database. The design for the database will be as shown in Table 1.

Table 1 The database design

Field name	Type	Length	Comments
Rider number	Autonumber		Range of 1–9999 Key field
Rider First Name	Text	20	First name of the rider
Rider Last Name	Text	20	Last name of the rider
Horse Name	Text	30	The name of the horse
Horse Type	Text	30	The breed of horse
Size	Number		The height of the horse in hands, 2 decimal places
Show jumping	Text	1	Y or N

To find all the riders who are entered for the show jumping we will need to search the database, and that means that we have to produce a design for the search.
To search for all the riders entered for the show jumping:
Show jumping = "Y"

To produce a list of all the riders entered for the show jumping we will need to design a report. This can either be produced on a computer or written out by hand (Fig 2).

Rider Number   Rider Last Name   Horse Name ← List Arial, 10 point

Fig 2 The design for the report

We now need to describe the features of the software that will help us to create the database:

We need to be able to search for all the riders entered for the show jumping.

The part of the software that will help us to do this is the search feature. This will allow us to search on the field Show jumping.

We need to be able to print out a list of all the riders and horses entered for the show jumping. The part of the software that will help us to do this is the report feature. This allows us to take the results of the search and present them as a report so that they can be printed out on to paper.

Designing the test plan

Having completed your designs, you now need to explain how you are going to go about testing your solution – that is, if testing is needed. This takes the form of a strategy. A strategy is a plan that explains what testing you are going to do and why.

Your test plan will therefore describe the test you are going to undertake, the test data you will use and the expected result from the test. A test plan ensures you can achieve the results listed in the booklet, so, before designing your test plan, you need to reread your booklet and check what has to be produced.

You should aim to test all parts of your solution and to use different types of test data – for example, data that you know will work and data that you know will not work.

The A4 poster did not need testing and therefore we simply made a note of this. But the search for riders entered in the show jumping can be tested, so we could create a table to help us with this (see Table 2).

Table 2 Testing the database search

Test data	Expected result	Comment
Y	A list of riders will be displayed	This is a normal piece of data within the range
YES	No riders will be displayed	This is the wrong data as only Y is accepted

Implementation (45 marks)

This is by far the largest section of your assignment. However it tends to be the most enjoyable as this is the part of your project where you create solutions to the tasks. You should make sure that you set aside enough time to complete this section and that you do not rush your work as this could result in lost marks.

Having designed your solution, you must now take these designs and implement (create) them. No one can implement a piece of work and produce perfect solutions every time, so you must be prepared to make changes as you go along in order to improve your work. Some of these changes will affect your designs and therefore you must make amendments to them, but make sure you make a note of any changes you have made.

To help you with your implementation, you should produce a project, log as programmers do in real life. A project log is a diary of all the changes that you have made to the design and the implementation. It will also help you to remember the problems you had and how you overcame them. A simple project log is shown in Fig 3.

Date	Problem encountered	How it was solved	Changes noted
04/02/2004	Had problems with the layout of the report. The writing was chopped off.	Realigning the text and changing the orientation to landscape.	Changes made to the design section to show this.
05/02/2004			

Fig 3 *A project log*

In order to complete this part of the assignment you must prove that you have implemented your designs. You can do this by noting the changes you made to your documentation in your project log, and by producing annotated printouts/screen shots.

If we return to the second of our designs, the search for riders who entered the show jumping, as you can see from Fig 4, you can demonstrate that you have implemented the database and created the search.

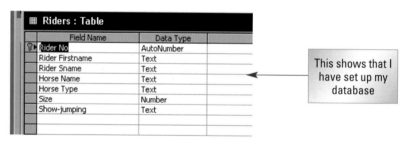

Riders : Table

Field Name	Data Type	
Rider No	AutoNumber	
Rider Firstname	Text	
Rider Sname	Text	
Horse Name	Text	
Horse Type	Text	
Size	Number	
Show-jumping	Text	

This shows that I have set up my database

Riders : Table

Rider No	Rider Firstname	Rider Sname	Horse Name	Horse Type	Size	Show-jumping
1	Harvey	Smith	Bullet	Thoroughbred	8.2	Y
2	Pat	Whittaker	The Clown	Thoroughbred	8.4	N
3	Phil	Archer	Red Rum	Shetland	6.3	N
4	Michael	Wogan	Funky Angel	Arab	8.4	Y
5	Sarah	Blading	Cockney	Arab	8.3	Y
(AutoNumber)					0	

This shows the data that I typed in to my database

This shows the results of the search for riders entered for the show jumping

Riders taking part in the Show-jumping

Rider No	Rider Firstname	Rider Sname	Horse Name
1	Harvey	Smith	Bullet
4	Michael	Wogan	Funky Angel
5	Sarah	Blading	Cockney

Fig 4 *Sample annotated screen shots and printout*

Date	Problem encountered	How it was solved	Changes noted
11/02/2004	Every time I added a new rider I had to key in the rider number and check that it was unique.	I changed the field type to AutoNumber so that it created a new number automatically.	See AutoNumber heading on screen shot.
12/02/2004	Misspelling of the horse types.	By creating a drop-down list so that the user can select a name from the list.	See screen shot of table design.

Fig 5 *Sample log: design improvements*

As you begin to create your solution you will find that you can make improvements to your designs. These can be listed in your log (see Fig 5).

You need to annotate everything that you produce, either on the printouts or as separate sets of notes. You must explain clearly what you did and how you did it; you must describe any changes you made and how you achieved these. You could use a step-by-step approach to explain to your teacher how you set up the database, for example.

Fig 6 shows an early stage in the design of the poster.

All the faults have been identified and annotated. You would now need to explain what changes you would make and produce another printout to show these changes (Fig 7). As with the database you could produce a step-by-step guide to show how your solution was developed.

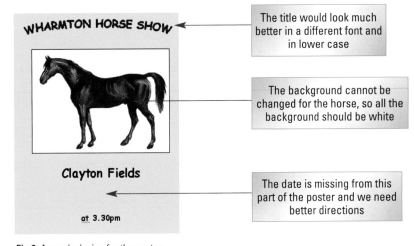

The title would look much better in a different font and in lower case

The background cannot be changed for the horse, so all the background should be white

The date is missing from this part of the poster and we need better directions

Fig 6 *An early design for the poster*

Fig 7 *The revised poster design*

Testing (10 marks)

As we saw earlier you test your design to see if your solution will achieve the results outlined in the booklet. When you carry out the test, you need to prove that you have actually input the data and produced a result. You can do this by producing an annotated printout or screen shot. You must then comment on the results and explain any changes that you need to make if the expected output does not match the actual output. After you have made the changes, you must run the test again to show that you have made the changes and that the design now does what it is supposed to do.

We can redesign the table we created earlier to test the database search (Table 2) to show that we have tested the solution (Table 3). No changes were necessary so the final column is left blank.

Table 3 The redesigned database table

Test data	Expected result	Actual result	Changes made
Y	A list of riders will be displayed	See Test 1 screen shot	
YES	No riders will be displayed	See Test 2 screen shot	

The Test 1 screen shot is shown in Fig 8 and Test 2 in Fig 9.

Riders taking part in the Show-jumping

Rider No	Rider Firstname	Rider Sname	Horse Name
1	Harvey	Smith	Bullet
4	Michael	Wogan	Funky Angel
5	Sarah	Blading	Cockney

I keyed Y in to the search field and I expected that a list of riders would be produced

Fig 8 Test 1

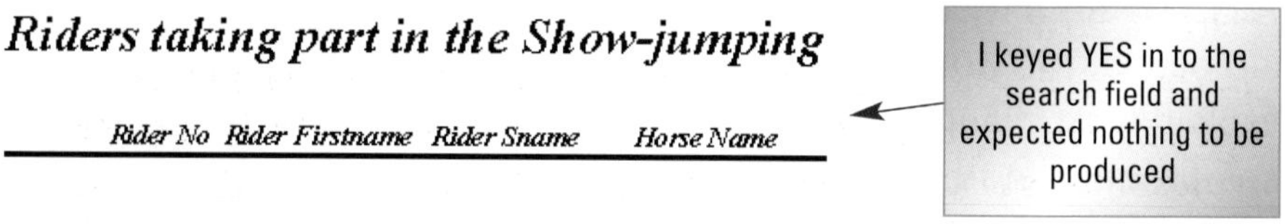

Riders taking part in the Show-jumping

Rider No	Rider Firstname	Rider Sname	Horse Name

I keyed YES in to the search field and expected nothing to be produced

Fig 9 Test 2

The first two columns in Table 3 are taken from your test plan. You can put notes in the 'Actual results' column that refer to a printout or screen shot, as here. Do not, however, try to reduce the size of a screen shot so it will fit into a cell of the table, as it will be difficult to read.

If any changes are needed as a result of your test, you will need to make these and then re-test to make sure the changes work.

Evaluation (10 marks)

The evaluation part of the assignment consists of a review of your work. This should take the form of a short paragraph about each of the problems that you solved. You should review each problem and state how successful they were in achieving your desired result. You will need to copy the performance criteria and the desired outcomes from your analysis section before starting on the evaluation.

For the poster, the *performance criteria* are again listed below:

> Mr Smith wants an A4 Poster
> On the poster he wants:
> > A drawing of a horse
> > A banner stating that it is the Wharmton Horse Show
> > The date of the event
> > The location of the event

> The *desired outcome* is an A4 poster that will be pleasing to look at and that shows all the information about the horse show.

You must now take each of the above points in turn and discuss how well your solution fulfilled the performance criteria and desired outcomes. For example, for the performance criteria:

> Mr Smith wants an A4 poster that matches his criteria:

> I produced an A4 poster using a word processor. I encountered a few problems in my initial attempt but, after careful consideration, I was able to produce a revised version which showed a picture of a horse, a banner stating what the horse show was, the date of the event and where it was. Therefore these criteria were met.

Now for the desired outcome:

> The poster must look pleasing and show all the information about the horse show.

> The poster showed all the information about the show and was pleasing to look at. However, having spoken to other people, I decided it did not look professional, so I looked at it again and changed some of the colours to make them more striking.

> Therefore the solution I produced for the poster was effective as it showed all the information that was required in a pleasing way.

When you have completed your assignment, all that you now need to do is go through the documentation carefully to check for obvious errors, making sure that you correct everything that is wrong, and also making sure all your printouts are in place.

Your work then needs to be handed in for marking.

Summary

Analysis

◎ Read through the booklet (do not make any notes).
◎ Read through the booklet again, making notes as you go along.
◎ Identify all the problems that you are required to solve.
◎ For each task list the inputs, processing and outputs that are needed.
◎ Write down the form the output will take, the information that will be output, and the input that is needed to produce this output.
◎ For each task produce a list of criteria which you can use to prove that you have completed the task.
◎ For each task, state the testing that you will have to carry out.
◎ Hand your analysis in for marking by your teacher.

Design

◎ Design the way of solving each of the tasks by producing pictures, sketches, etc. describing how you are going to solve the tasks.
◎ Justify each of your decisions and link back to the analysis section.
◎ Describe the features of the software that you are going to use.
◎ Hand your analysis in for marking by your teacher.

Implementation

◎ For each of your tasks you must provide evidence that you have implemented your designs.
◎ Show any corrections, improvements, etc. that you have made.
◎ Annotate all your work clearly.

Testing

◎ Take the test plan that you produced as part of the design section and work through it systematically and logically.
◎ Show all the outcomes of the testing as a printout or screenshot.
◎ Make comments where the actual result does not match the required output.
◎ Make and test the changes that you have had to make as a result of the testing.
◎ Annotate all printouts/screenshots that you have produced.

Evaluation

◎ For each of the problems write a review of how well you completed the task and how successful the solution was.
◎ Re-read the performance criteria and desired outcomes from your analysis and explain how well your solution meets these criteria.

The project

This coursework is based on the system life-cycle you read about in Section 7 of this book.

Introduction

There are some differences between the project and the set assignment. The project is far more comprehensive than the assignment and therefore you need to describe everything you do as fully as possible. In the assignment the work you produce is a one-off piece but, in the project, the work is part of an ongoing task. You must, therefore, take this into account. For example, if you produce a poster for an event, it must be reusable in the future. Therefore it must be saved, and you must be able to change the date and other information easily.

Choosing the correct project

The hardest part of the project is deciding on something that will give you the maximum marks possible. Below are a few points that you may wish to consider when choosing your project:

◎ First of all, try not to be too ambitious. Choose a project that you will be able to do well within the allotted time. If the project is too big, you will not complete it in time. If it is too small, you will struggle to find enough tasks to complete.

◎ You should aim to have between three and five sub-tasks in your project (see later in this section). Look back at the set assignment to see what kind of tasks you should be doing.

◎ Look at examples of projects. You can find these in textbooks, perhaps in a list supplied by your teacher, from past and current set assignments and from the Internet.

◎ Try to choose a project that interests you. This will make it much more enjoyable and will keep you motivated.

◎ Try to choose a real-life topic – one where you can talk to other people about what is involved. This will make the task more interesting as you will be able to share it with others.

Good examples of projects are:

◎ the school tuckshop
◎ the Scout camp
◎ a school field trip
◎ running a hairdressing business that makes home visits
◎ an estate agent's
◎ booking rooms in a hotel.

Analysis (15 marks)

Before you start on your project, you should discuss your ideas with your teacher, as he or she may be able to help you expand on them.

Getting started: research

You must do some research to prepare the ground for your project. It is always best to collect as much information as you can before you start to plan out what you are going to do. You could do this by talking to people who know about the topic, by using a questionnaire, or by observing the problem you wish to find a solution to. For example, if your proposed project was about organising a school field trip, you could do the following to obtain your background information:

◎ Talk to teachers to find out how field trips are currently organised and what the problems are.

◎ Produce a questionnaire and hand this to the organising teacher for him or her to fill in.

◎ Look at the current process of organising a field trip to see how it is done.

This would give you a good starting point. You might find it easier to produce a diagram of your thoughts – a spider diagram or a mind map. Diagrams make it easier to see where the sub-tasks link together.

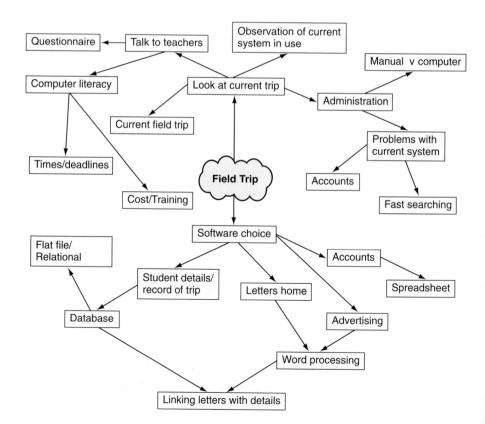

Setting the scene

The examiner knows nothing about the problem you are going to solve, so you must tell him or her all about it. This will be in the form of an introduction, or scene setter. This will give the examiner some background information about the problem and about what you are trying to do.

For example:

> Kingsmond Scouts are organising a Scout camp in the Forest of Treen. There are 36 Scouts in the troop, organised into six groups. Every year the Scouts book to go on their annual camp, where they take part in a number of activities, some of which are free and some of which have to be paid for in advance. Each Scout is allowed to take pocket money with him but, for safety, the Scout Master looks after this. There has always been a problem in keeping track of the flow of money into and out of the Scout Camp Account. Therefore the Scout Master wants a simple, efficient way of managing the booking and accounts for this camp.

> To obtain information for this project, I visited the Scout Leader and asked him a few questions about how the account was managed and what the problems were with running it. He showed me the accounts book he kept. I then saw the problem. A page was set aside for each Scout and, when money was taken out of the account, the old amount was crossed out and a new one put in. This made the book look a mess and it was difficult to read.

> There were no booking forms in the book. These were written on a piece of paper, as were the receipts for the money received. This also created problems, as there was no record of the money that went into the account.

It is very important that you set the scene well and research the task properly, as this will identify many of the sub-tasks that you are going to solve. It may even identify more than are required, in which case you must choose which ones you are going to solve and which ones you are not going to solve. Once you have done this, look carefully at the sub-tasks to identify which ones are going to be re-usable. These are an important part of the project. For example, in the above description the accounts are re-usable, as they are written in a book, but the booking forms are not necessarily re-usable as they are simply written on bits of paper. In the solution to the problem, the accounts will not be re-usable, but the booking form can be written out as a template and therefore re-used.

You should make sure you have between three and five sub-tasks. Some of these must produce re-usable solutions. You should also make sure that the sub-tasks are linked in some way.

For example:

Kingsmond Theatre is planning a Christmas pantomime. They are having problems planning this event. The sub-tasks I need to undertake to help them plan this event are as follows:

- Create a poster to publicise the pantomime.
- Create the programme for the show.
- Produce a layout of the stage for the scene designers.
- Improve the way the accounts are recorded so that the producer can see exactly how much money has been made by the production.
- Produce a booking plan.

You need to say why each sub-task is important and how they will all link together to help the organisers plan the pantomime. You need to write a short paragraph about this. For example, for the pantomime, one of the links could be that the poster and the programme will have similar data, so the same data could be imported into both. There is also a link between the poster, the programme, the accounts and the booking plan, as the same logo or title will appear on all these. The layout of the stage and the booking plan could also be linked as both could show the stage.

How do you go about completing these sub-tasks?

You must now decide how you are going to tackle each sub-task. There might be several ways of doing each sub-task, such as using different types of software, or even using a piece of software as one way and doing it manually as the other.

For example:

Create a poster to publicise the pantomime

One way of producing the solution would be simply to produce the poster on A3 paper using pens and paint:

- *The advantages* of using this method are that it is an easy way of producing a smart piece of artwork and it is cheap.
- *The disadvantages* are that it is a one-off poster that will take a long time to produce. The designer must also be an artist. If a mistake is made the whole poster would be ruined.

The second way is to design the poster on paper and then use a desktop publishing package to create it.

- *The advantages* of this method are that the poster can be saved and used for other productions with the minimum of changes. Special effects can be used, and the size can be changed easily, so it can be used for fliers, etc.

◎ *The disadvantages* of this method are that the user has to be computer literate and a computer artist. Using the software could also be more expensive than the manual method.

I have decided to choose the second way of producing the poster, using a DTP package.

Create the programme for the show

This can be achieved by designing the programme on paper and then using a word processing package to produce it.

It could also be produced on a desktop publishing package, as this would be easy to do and would look more professional.

Improve the way the accounts recorded

This could be achieved by the use of an accounting book and a calculator.

It could also be achieved by using a spreadsheet to record all the finances of the production.

You would then need to describe all the advantages and disadvantages of the other sub-tasks. You must be careful that you use different advantages and disadvantages for each sub-task, and that you explain why you have chosen the solutions you have.

Desired outcomes and performance criteria

What is each sub-task going to produce in terms of output? You need to be clear about exactly what you will be able to produce to demonstrate that each sub-task has solved the problem you set out to solve.

For example, the solution for the pantomime poster would need to be an A3 printout, in colour, showing the name of the theatre and the name of the production company, etc. This poster could be saved and used for future shows. You would simply need to change the picture, and the details of the production, etc.

You need to work out the output for the other sub-tasks in the project but remember: you need to show linkages between the sub-tasks. You can do this by explaining how data from one sub-task can be used in other sub-tasks.

Having decided on all the sub-tasks and on the output for each one, you must now produce criteria to evaluate your solution.

For example, we could take the spreadsheet for the accounts. The desired outcomes and the performance criteria could be as follows:

> The spreadsheet will have a sheet showing expenditure, income and the total profit and loss figures. The losses will be highlighted in red whilst the profits will be in black. There will be one of these sheets for each week of the show. There will be a final balance sheet showing the total profit and loss figures for the entire run of the show. The profits and losses will be calculated automatically and each weekly total will be transferred automatically to the final balance sheet.

Design (20 marks)

We saw earlier that a good design produces the intended solution, even if someone other than the designer implements it.

The best way to produce a good design for your project is to plan, test and evaluate each sub-task separately, rather than trying to do everything at once.

You will be using several different types of software to solve your sub-tasks but, essentially, your plans will be similar for each type of software. What follows, therefore, is a general plan that can be used for all types of software.

Planning your designs

Your designs should be well laid out. All your work should be clear and legible, and it should contain sufficient detail. This will ensure that someone else reading your work can see clearly what is required to produce your designs.

Gathering the right information

You need to know what to include in your designs, and whether the data that you are going to use is re-usable or not.

For example, The Royal is a hotel and conference centre in the heart of London. The hotel management has asked you to produce a leaflet to publicise their conference facilities. Table 4 summarises the information you will need to know in order to create this.

Table 4 Royal Hotel information

Information needed	Re-usable
Hotel logo	✓
Location information (including a map, directions, etc.)	✓
Address	✓
Tel. number, fax number, email address	✓
Personnel names	✓
Car parking details	✓
Facilities	✓
Special deals	

Re-usable data can also be classified as *fixed* data. This means such data stays the same every time the leaflet is changed for some reason. Data like this can therefore be used in templates.

Planning it out

The Royal Hotel has also asked you to suggest a way of producing the accounts for each conference, and to design a spreadsheet for this.

Table 5 suggests a way that you might do this. You will see from this table that you need to plan everything out – from the size of the font you intend to use to the formulae needed to do the calculations. You can create your plans on a word processor (as here), or you could do them by hand. Either way, you should include an explanation of why you have included the features you have. In Table 5, these explanations are given in the final column.

Table 5 The design for the spreadsheet

Cell	Type	Format	Formula	Explanation
B2	Text	10 point Arial		This is the name of each conference and is imported from the conference database (see below)
H2	Date	10 point Arial		This is the date of each conference and is imported from the conference database
H4	Number	10 point Arial		This is the number of people attending each conference and is imported from the conference database
I6	Currency	10 point Arial	=B6*G6	This is calculated by multiplying the number of hours for each conference by the rate per hour.

Why am I using the chosen software?

Having completed your designs, you must justify your choice of software. This is quite simple: look at your designs and look at the features the software offers you, then write about how you are going to use those features to solve each sub-task.

For example, The Royal Hotel wants you to set up a database in order to store the names of the people who have booked conferences at the hotel, and the conferences they have booked.

When you have produced the designs for this database, you need to justify why you are going to use a database to solve this particular sub-task.

A database will allow me to set up a number of tables that I can then link together. These tables, which will store the details of the customers, the details of the conferences, and the details of the bookings, will be able to store the hotel's data as text, numbers, dates or currency.

To enable data to be entered correctly, the database will have validation rules so, if data is entered incorrectly, error messages will appear. Data can be added to the database using a form, which can be created, and the information can be displayed/printed out using a report. All the data can be sorted into any order, and specific pieces of data can be searched for.

The person booking the conference suite will need to be contacted by mail, and this can be achieved by using the database with a mail merge.

All the features noted above will be used to create my database and to produce a solution to this sub-task.

The data used in the database can be exported to other software to solve other sub-tasks. For example, the customer details, the details of the conference room bookings and the booking dates can all be used in the spreadsheet. The person's data and the booking details can be used with the mail merge to send a confirmation of the booking.

Devising a test plan

You should design a test plan at this point so that when you come to testing the system, all you need to do is to work through your test plan and note the results.

For example, let's produce a test plan for the spreadsheet we designed earlier for the hotel. First of all we need to produce a template to show our tests. Table 6 is an example of a completed test plan template.

Table 6 Completed test plan template

Test number	What is to be tested?	Reasons for the test	Test data	Expected result
1.1	To test the calculation for the total cost (hours)	To test that the calculation works	B7 = 8 G6 = £12.00	
1.2			B7 = 0 G7 = £12.00	£0.00
1.3			B7 = −8 G7 = £12.00	Error message as there cannot be a negative number of hours
2.1	To test the calculation for the total cost (meals)	To test the calculation works	B8 = 20 G8 = £15.00	£300.00
2.2			B8 = 0 G8 = £15.00	£0.00
2.3			B8 = −20 G8 = £15.00	Error message as there cannot be a negative number of people

This should give you an idea of the type of testing that you need to carry out. It is better to devise three tests: one correct, one giving zero and one incorrect.

Implementation (35 marks)

Having completed the design, you need to start creating the solution to each of the sub-tasks. In order to get high marks in this section, you must follow the designs you produced closely and you must justify all the features of the software that you have used in the solution.

The best way to do this is to work through the designs systematically and then produce printouts or screen shots of every major stage in their production. These printouts/screen shots should then be fully annotated in order to explain how you reached this point in the process. For the best results, your annotations should show the examiner exactly what you did and how you did it.

As you work through your designs you will find that some of the things could have been solved much better, or perhaps the designs didn't quite work when you implemented them. This is not a problem and happens in real life. All you need to do is to explain all the changes you made to your original design and include this with your project.

User guide (10 marks)

Your user guide should help the user to understand and operate the system you have solved and it must be produced as a separate booklet. As with all booklets there must be a contents page. Your guide must set out clearly how to operate your new system. You can achieve this by producing a step-by-step guide using screen shots for each process. As with the main documentation, it would be easier for the user if you placed each sub-task in a separate section and then noted this on the contents page.

The guide should explain how to *use* the system; it should not contain any information about how you implemented it.

For example:

You have been asked to help improve the running of your school's revision system for A-level ICT students. One of the sub-tasks that you have identified is the setting up of a database of past papers.

Your guide needs to explain that, when a user loads the database, he or she will automatically be connected to a menu screen like the one shown in Fig 10. Notice how this screen shot has labels (annotations) to explain what each feature does.

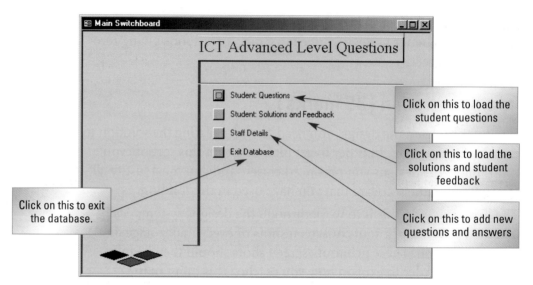

Fig 10 Database opening window

The next screen shot explains how students can search for a particular set of questions (Fig 11).

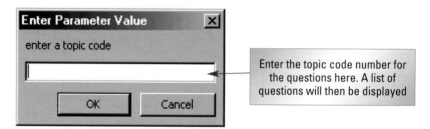

Fig 11 Searching for particular topics

The more menus and buttons you have in your solution (as in the examples above) the easier it will be to write your user guide.

Testing (15 marks)

To gain the maximum marks for this section, you must work systematically through your test plan and produce annotated screen shots/printouts of your results. If any changes need to be made as a result of this testing, you should note these and make the necessary changes.

One test that you may not have considered is to test your user guide. You will have spent a great deal of time producing the user guide, but does it do what it should do? To test this you should give your user guide to someone else and ask him or her to work through your solution, using the software you have specified. If he or she encounters any problems you should change the guide accordingly, but you must keep the original guide in your project to show that it has been tested and improved.

Let's go back to the test plan that we produced for the spreadsheet. As you can see from the revised plan shown in Table 7 we have added an extra column, **Actual result**. This should contain explanations of what happened when you ran the tests or references to any annotated screen shots/printouts you have produced. (NB Do not put these in the test plan itself; they will be too small to see.)

Table 7 Revised test plan

Test number	What is to be tested?	Reasons for the test	Test data	Expected result	Actual result
1.1	To test the calculation for the total cost (hours)	To test that the calculation works	B7 = 8 G7 = £12.00	£96.00	Result produced as expected
1.2			B7 = 0 G7 = £12.00	£0.00	Result produced as expected
1.3			B7 = −8 G7 = £12.00	Error message as there cannot be a negative number of hours	See screenshot 1.3 (labelled here as Fig 12)
2.1	To test the calculation for the total cost (meals)	To test that the calculation works	B8 = 20 G8 = £15.00	£300.00	Result produced as expected
2.2			B8 = 0 G8 = £15.00	£0.00	Result produced as expected
2.3			B8 = −20 G* = £15.00	Error message as there cannot be a negative number of people	

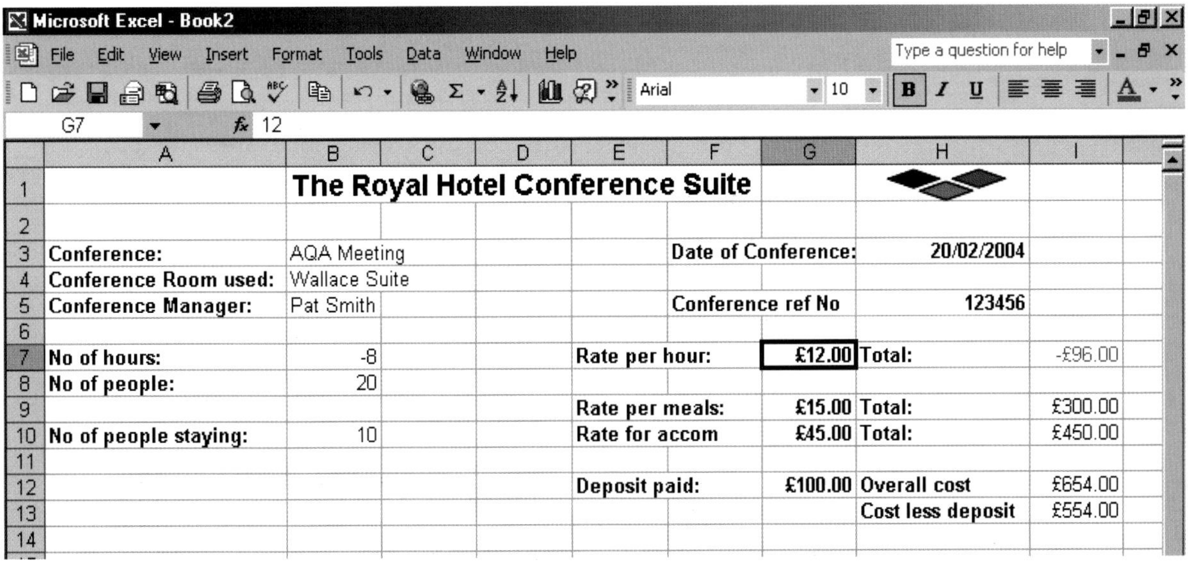

Fig 12 Screen shot 1.3

Test 1.3 produced a result of -£96.00 in cell I7. This answer, although correct, could not exist in a system like this – you cannot have a negative number of people! Therefore corrective action needs to be taken. We need a validation check for the total in I7:

=if(B7*G7)<0,"Error",(B7*G7)

This means that if the result in I7 is less than zero, an error message will be displayed (see Fig 13).

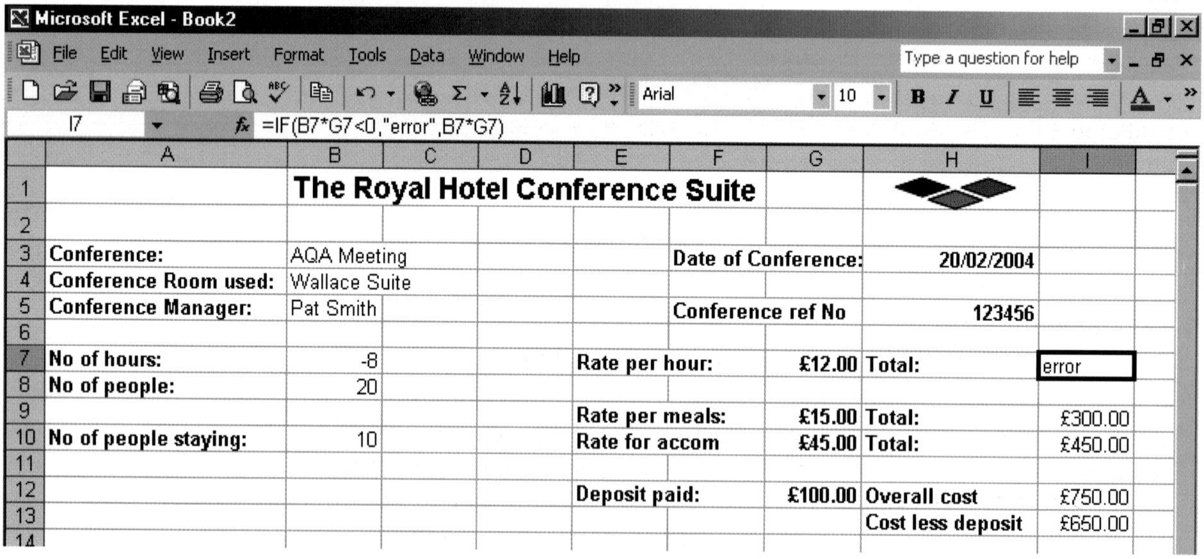

I7			fx	=IF(B7*G7<0,"error",B7*G7)					

Microsoft Excel - Book2

The Royal Hotel Conference Suite

	A	B	C	D	E	F	G	H	I
3	Conference:	AQA Meeting				Date of Conference:		20/02/2004	
4	Conference Room used:	Wallace Suite							
5	Conference Manager:	Pat Smith				Conference ref No		123456	
7	No of hours:	-8				Rate per hour:	£12.00	Total:	error
8	No of people:	20							
9						Rate per meals:	£15.00	Total:	£300.00
10	No of people staying:	10				Rate for accom	£45.00	Total:	£450.00
12						Deposit paid:	£100.00	Overall cost	£750.00
13								Cost less deposit	£650.00

Fig 13 *Error message displayed in cell I7*

Evaluation (5 marks)

Whilst the evaluation part of your project comes last, you do not have to leave it to the end. The best way is to evaluate each sub-task in turn, after you have implemented and tested it. Then when you have completed your project, you need to produce an evaluation as a separate piece of work.

Points not to note in your evaluation

Your evaluation is about how well or not you solved the problem. It must not, therefore, include references to the amount of time that you were given, or to equipment that you had to use in school. For example, you should not include comments such as these:

◉ If I had more time then I could have completed this project.

◉ If the printer had not broken down in the last two weeks of the project then I could have completed it.

To complete the evaluation, you need to copy and paste the desired outcomes and performance criteria from your analysis section in to your evaluation section. You then use these to explain whether or not you achieved what you set out to achieve. Remember to note any changes you made to your designs and implementations, and to justify everything you did.

As an example of this, the performance criteria for the spreadsheet for the pantomime is pasted below:

> The spreadsheet will have a sheet showing expenditure, income and the total profit and loss figures. The losses will be highlighted in red whilst the profits will be in black. There will be one of these sheets for each day of the show. There will be a final balance sheet showing the total profit and loss figures for the entire run of the show. The profits and losses will be calculated automatically and each daily total will be transferred automatically to the final balance sheet.

To complete the evaluation, you must state whether the spreadsheet worked as you intended. Below is part of this evaluation. As you can see, it explains changes made to the spreadsheet during the implementation stage and gives reasons why these were made:

> I created a spreadsheet as required by the user. The separate sections of the spreadsheet easily showed the user where the pantomime had made a loss on each of the days and where it had made a profit. The user could easily check the overall profit and loss of the performances, and from this data could analyse the figures to help plan future shows.
>
> The final balance sheet gave a quick, easy-to-read summary of the profit and loss over the duration of the show, and was very useful to the user.
>
> If I were to improve the spreadsheet then I would add a chart to the final balance sheet to make it easier to read the total profit and loss of each performance, as it is easier to read the figures in a graphical form.

Index